Christmas 1975

Daddy –

In preparation for your
next trip over.

Much love
Peggy & Tony

LONDON *The Biography of a City*

By the same author

CHRISTOPHER HIBBERT

LONDON

The Biography of a City

Longmans

LONGMANS, GREEN AND CO. LTD.
London and Harlow
Associated companies, branches and representatives throughout the world

© Christopher Hibbert 1969
First published 1969

SBN: 582 10796 2

Photoset in Great Britain by Photoprint Plates Ltd.
and printed in Hong Kong by
Dai Nippon Printing Co. (International) Ltd.

For Stewart and Rachel

Author's note

Although this book is mainly intended as an introduction to the history of the development of London and of the social life of its people, I have at the same time tried to make it, in some sense, a guide-book. It cannot pretend to be a comprehensive one; but at the back I have included some information about all the buildings, sights, treasures and delights of London which are mentioned or illustrated in the text and which are still to be enjoyed here. The book will, therefore, I hope, be of some practical use to the stranger who visits London, and, indeed, to those who know it well, yet, like myself, can never know it well enough, nor ever tire of the unique and multifarious pleasures it has to offer.

I would like to thank my friend, Dr F. H. W. Sheppard, General Editor of *The Survey of London,* for his great kindness in having read the manuscript and for having given me much useful advice; I am most grateful also to Mr Hamish Francis for having read the proofs, to my wife for having prepared the index, and to Illustration Research Service for collecting together all the pictures many of which are here reproduced for the first time.

Contents

Illustrations

COLOUR PLATES

1. *Facing page* **2**. Bacchus riding a tiger: the centre of a Roman mosaic pavement excavated in Leadenhall Street. *British Museum, Dept of Prehistory and Roman Britain. Photo: John Freeman.*

2. *Facing page* **3**. Edward the Confessor discussing the building of Westminster Abbey with architect and workmen: mid-thirteenth century. *University Library, Cambridge, MS Ee. 3.59.*

3. *Facing page* **3**. St Peter consecrating Westminster Abbey: mid-thirteenth century. *University Library, Cambridge, MS Ee. 3.59.*

4. *Facing page* **18**. The rich clothes of the fifteenth century: a miniature of the legendary King Uther Pendragon's court in London. *British Museum, Dept of MSS, Royal MS 15 E iv f.134.*

5. *Facing page* **19**. Detail from the Fishmongers' Company's funeral pall; late fifteenth century with arms and supporters added later. *The Fishmongers' Company. Photo: Edwin Smith.*

6. *Facing page* **42**. Lord Mayor, Alderman and Liveryman by Lucas de Heere, *c.* 1570. *British Museum Dept. of MSS, Add. MS 28330 f.2.*

7. *Between pages* **42** *and* **43**. A marriage fete in rural Bermondsey by Jons Hoefnagel, *c.* 1590. *The Marquess of Salisbury, KG. Photo: A. C. Cooper.*

8. *Facing page* **43**. London Bridge with the Tower and Southwark Cathedral by Richard Garth, 1575. *Bodleian Library, Oxford, Dept of Western MSS, MS Douce 68, f.47.*

9. *Facing page* **58**. 'The Benefits of the Government of James I': detail of Rubens's ceiling for Inigo Jones's Banqueting House, 1634. *Photo: Crown Copyright, Ministry of Public Building and Works.*

10. *Between pages* **58** *and* **59**. The Earl of Bedford's development at Covent Garden: detail from a painting by Samuel Scott of the 1740s. *The Earl of Pembroke and Montgomery. Photo: A. C. Cooper.*

11. *Facing page* **59**. Inigo Jones's design for the costume of a torchbearer in Ben Jonson's *Masque of Blackness* performed on 6 January 1605. *Devonshire Collection, Chatsworth. Reproduced by permission of the Trustees of the Chatsworth Settlement.*

12. *Facing page* **82**. Sir Christopher Wren by J. B. Closterman. *The Royal Society.*

13. *Facing page* **83**. The Saddlers' Company's ballot box originally made for the Court of the East India Company in 1619. *The Saddlers' Company. Photo: Edwin Smith.*

14. *Facing page* **98**. Charles II on Horseguards Parade *c.* 1680: detail from a painting, British school. *The Duke of Roxburgh. Photo: Douglas Scott.*

15. *Facing page* **99**. Titus Oates in the pillory, 1687: detail from a painting by an imitator of Jan Wyck. *London Museum. Photo: R. Todd-White.*

16. *Facing page* **106**. The courtyard of the Royal Exchange *c.* 1725: detail from a painting by an unknown artist. *The Mercers' Company. Photo: R. Todd-White.*

17. *Between pages* **106** *and* **107**. A frost fair on the Thames, 1683–84: painting attributed to Abraham Hondius. *London Museum. Photo: R. B. Fleming.*

18. *Facing page* **107**. A London coffee-house *c.* 1700 (detail). *British Museum, Dept of Prints and Drawings.*

19. *Facing page* **122**. James Wyatt's Pantheon in Oxford Street, by William Hodges; the figures are perhaps by Johann Zoffany. *City of Leeds Art Gallery, Temple Newsam House. Photo: G.L.C.*

20. *Between pages* **122** *and* **123**. The City, south London and Westminster Bridge, seen from Montagu House, Whitehall: by Robert Griffier, 1748. *The Duke of Buccleuch and Queensberry, KT, GCVO. Photo: R. Todd-White.*

21. *Facing page* **123**. Robert Adam's design for a section of the drawing-room of Northumberland House, Charing Cross. *The Trustees of Sir John Soane's Museum. Photo: R. Todd-White.*

22. *Facing page* **138**. John Nash by Sir Thomas Lawrence. *Mrs Allan Cameron. Photo: Douglas Scott.*

23. *Between pages* **138** *and* **139**. George IV going in state down Whitehall to the House of Lords, 23 January 1821 (detail). *London Museum. Photo: R. Todd-White.*

24. *Facing page* **139**. The National Gallery still hung in Mr Angerstein's house in Pall Mall: watercolour by Frederick McKenzie. *Victoria and Albert Museum. Photo: R. Todd-White.*

25. *Facing page* **139**. Laying the foundations of the British Museum's Lycian Room, 1845: watercolour by George Scharf. *British Museum, Dept of Prints and Drawings. Photo: John Freeman.*

26. *Facing page* **146**. James Boswell by Sir Joshua Reynolds. *National Portrait Gallery.*

27. *Facing page* **147**. The House of Commons in 1730, by Sir James Thornhill and William Hogarth. *The National Trust, Clandon Park, Surrey. Photo: Weycolour.*

28. *Facing page* **162**. London street scene: *The Cherry Barrow* by H. Walton, 1779. *The Trustees of the Sitwell Estate. Photo: R. Todd-White.*

29. *Facing page* **163**. The Bow Street Office, 1808: engraved by Rowlandson and Pugin. *Mansell Collection.*

30. *Facing page* **170**. Ranelagh Grove by Francis Hayman (detail). *The Trustees of the Ilchester Estate. Photo: R. Todd-White.*

31. *Between pages* **170** *and* **171**. An orgy at the Rose Tavern, Covent Garden: from Hogarth's *Rake's Progress* series. *The Trustees of Sir John Soane's Museum. Photo: R. B. Fleming.*

32. *Facing page* **171**. Lord's Cricket Ground: lithograph by C. Atkinson, *c.* 1830. *Marylebone Cricket Club. Photo: R. Todd-White.*

33. *Facing page* **171**. Skating in Regent's Park: aquatint by B. Read, 1838–39. *Westminster City Libraries, Archives Dept, Marylebone Road. Photo: R. Todd-White.*

34. *Facing page* **186**. Mlle Rachel's farewell benefit at Her Majesty's Theatre, June 1841: watercolour

by Eugène Lami. *Victoria and Albert Museum, Print Room. Photo: R. Todd-White.*

35. *Facing page* **186**. Evening prayers in an upper-class home: lithograph after Eugéne Lami, 1829. *British Museum, Dept of Prints and Drawings. Photo: John Freeman.*

36. *Between pages* **186** *and* **187**. Contrasts in transport—the driver of 1832 and the driver of 1852: aquatints from Fore's *Contrasts. Guildhall Library. Photo: R. B. Fleming.*

37. *Facing page* **187**. The opening of the Great Exhibition of 1851 by Queen Victoria: detail from a colour lithograph. *Victoria and Albert Museum. Photo: R. Todd-White.*

38. *Facing page* **210**. Cremorne Gardens in 1864, by Phoebus Levin. *London Museum. Photo: R. Todd-White.*

39. *Facing page* **210**. The Zoo, Regent's Park, in 1835: colour lithograph after George Scharf. *Westminster City Libraries, Archives Dept, Marylebone Road. Photo: John Freeman.*

40. *Facing page* **211**. A detail from W. P. Frith's *Paddington Station*, 1862. *Royal Holloway College. Photo: R. Todd-White.*

41. *Facing page* **218**. Holborn in 1861, by Arthur Boyd Houghton (detail). *The Trustees of Sir Colin and Lady Anderson.*

42. *Between pages* **218** *and* **219**. London street scene with posters, by John Parry, 1835. *Alfred Dunhill Ltd. Photo: R. Todd-White.*

43. *Facing page* **219**. Joe Haynes and Little Dot Hetherington at the Old Bedford Music Hall, by Walter Sickert, 1889 (detail). *Private Collection. Photo: Ayer.*

44. *Facing page* **226**. The rush hour by the Royal Exchange in 1898, by Fritz Werner. *The Mercers' Company. Photo: R. Todd-White.*

45. *Facing page* **227**. St. Paul's and the modern City: a detail from *London 1967* by David Thomas. *Guildhall Art Gallery. Photo: R. Todd-White.*

MONOCHROME ILLUSTRATIONS

Page **xiv**. Surviving section of the Roman city wall in Cooper's Row, *c.* 200 A.D. *Photo: Edwin Smith.*

Page **2**. The impression of a child's feet on a tile found in the flue channel of the bath in Cheapside; early second century. *The Sun Life Assurance Society Ltd.*

Page **4**. Bronze steelyard found at Walbrook; first or second century. *British Museum, Dept of Prehistory and Roman Britain.*

Page **4**. Pierced leather shoe found in the streambed of the Walbrook; first or second century. *Guildhall Museum.*

Page **5**. Statuette of Bacchus accompanied by Silenus, a satyr, a maenad and a panther; from the Temple of Mithras, Walbrook. *Guildhall Museum.*

Page **6**. Tombs of Knights Templar in the Temple Church; thirteenth century. *Photo: Edwin Smith.*

Page **8**. Animal figures from the base of a Saxon cross *c.* 1040, found on the site of All Hallows, Barking. *Photo: Edwin Smith.*

Page **9**. Westminster Abbey: from a thirteenth-century manuscript of Matthew Paris, *Historia Anglorum. British Museum, Dept of MSS, Royal MS 14C vii f. 138.*

Page **11**. Baynard's Castle: a nineteenth-century engraving. *Guildhall Museum. Photo: R. B. Fleming.*

Page **13**. Hugh Herland's hammerbeam roof in Westminster Hall, *c.* 1400. *Photo: Edwin Smith.*

Page **15**. A hawking party, early fourteenth century. *British Museum, Dept of MSS, Royal MS 2B vii f. 151b.*

Page **17**. The central medallion from a silver dish of *c.* 1325 from St Mary Magdalene, Bermondsey. *Church of St Mary Magdalene, Bermondsey: on loan to Victoria and Albert Museum. Photo: Crown Copyright.*

Page **18**. A thirteenth-century medical school: from the MS of Bartholomew the Englishman. *British Museum, Dept of MSS, Royal MS 17E iii f.93.*

Page **20**. An apothecary's dispensary, twelfth century. *Library of Trinity College, Cambridge, MS 0.1.20 f. 239.*

Page **21**. The dagger which by tradition killed Wat Tyler. *The Fishmongers' Company. Photo: Edwin Smith.*

Page **22**. London Bridge: detail of a drawing by Anthonis van den Wyngaerde, 1543-44. *Ashmolean Museum, Oxford, Dept of Western Art.*

Page **24**. The punishment of a fraudulent baker: a drawing from the MS *Liber de Assisa Panis* (1293-1438). *Guildhall Record Office.*

Page **28**. Sir Richard Whittington with his legendary cat: engraving by R. Elstrack. *Photo: National Portrait Gallery.*

Page **29**. *The Triumph of Riches*, a fresco by Holbein, now destroyed, for the Hansa Merchants' Banqueting Hall: from a copy by Jan de Bisschop, *c.* 1670. *British Museum, Dept of Prints and Drawings.*

Page **31**. Lead badge of St Thomas à Becket found in the Thames; fourteenth or fifteenth century. *London Museum.*

Page **31**. Wax impression of the seal of St Paul's; thirteenth century. *The Dean and Chapter of St Paul's Cathedral. Photo: R. B. Fleming.*

Page **33**. The Barber-Surgeons' Guild's silver instrument case; before 1525. *Photo: the Goldsmiths' Company.*

Page **34**. 'Tittle-Tattle; Or, the several Branches of Gossipping': detail from a broadside of the end of Elizabeth's reign. *British Museum, Dept of Prints and Drawings.*

Page **35**. John Stow (d. 1605), author of the *Survey of London;* from his tomb by Nicholas Johnson in St Andrew Undershaft. *Photo: Edwin Smith.*

Page **37**. Westcheap: drawing by Ralph Treswell, 1585. *British Museum, Dept of Prints and Drawings.*

Page **38**. Bowling: from *Le Centre de l'Amour* published in Paris *c.* 1600. *British Museum, Library. Photo: R. B. Fleming.*

Page **40**. Sir Thomas Gresham, attributed to A. Key. *National Portrait Gallery.*

Page **40**. Wolsey in 1526; painting, English school. *The Bishop of Durham and the Church Commissioners. Photo: Courtauld Institute of Art.*

Page **42**. The Holbein Gate, Whitehall Palace: from *London Survey'd* by William Morgan, 1681-82. *British Museum, Map Room. Photo: John Freeman.*

Page **45**. The courtyard of Arundel House: etching by W. Hollar, 1646. *British Museum, Dept of Prints and Drawings. Photo: John Freeman.*

Page **46**. The Globe Theatre: detail from Visscher's view of London, 1616. *British Museum, Dept of Prints and Drawings. Photo: John Freeman.*

Page **49**. Sir Hugh Myddleton: engraving by Vertue after Cornelius Johnson's portrait of 1632. *British Museum, Dept of Prints and Drawings. Photo: John Freeman.*

Page **50**. The Waterhouse at the New River Head: etching by W. Hollar, 1665. *British Museum, Dept of Prints and Drawings. Photo: John Freeman.*

Page **54**. 'The English Gentleman and English Gentlewoman': engraved titlepage by W. Marshall to a book by R. Braithwait, 1641. *British Museum, Library. Photo: John Freeman.*

Page **57**. Inigo Jones: engraving by Vorst after Van Dyck's portrait of 1632. *Mansell Collection.*

Page **57**. Francis Russell, fourth Earl of Bedford: engraving by Vertue after Van Dyck's portrait of 1636. *Victoria and Albert Museum, Print Room. Photo: R. Todd-White.*

Page **59**. A drawing for a masque scene by Inigo Jones, executed for Ben Jonson's *Time Vindicated*, performed in the Banqueting House 19 January 1623. *Private Collection, London. Photo: Millar & Harris.*

Page **60**. 'Winter': etching by W. Hollar, 1643. *British Museum, Dept of Prints and Drawings. Photo: John Freeman.*

Page **64**. Charles II's triumphal entry into the City at his Restoration, 1660: a later engraving.

The maps were drawn by Sheila Waters. The drawings in the Guide on pp. 245ff. are by Andrew Dodds.

Roman London 61–457

In the seventh year of the reign of the Emperor Nero, a savage rebellion of Celtic tribesmen broke out in the newly conquered province of Britain. Already restlessly discontented under the arrogance of Roman rule, the Iceni of Norfolk were driven to fury when in A.D. 61 Roman soldiers forced their way into the palace of their Queen, Boadicea, flogged her for resisting the confiscation of Icenian property and raped her two daughters.

The Iceni, supported by the neighbouring tribe of Trinovantes, swarmed down towards the Roman town of Colchester, massacred its inhabitants, set fire to its buildings, and routed the 9th Legion which had arrived from Lincoln too late for its defence. Then, led by Boadicea, they turned south for the Thames and within a few days their rough and massive army was looking down upon the port of Londinium.

There was no fortress, no defending wall. For, although it must have contained large supplies of military stores, Londinium was a riverside trading centre, not a military stronghold. There were a few buildings of ragstone and tile, but the houses were mainly of wood and thatch, fragile and vulnerable. The timber quays piled high with bales and cases, jars and barrels; the jetties and wharfs supported on piles driven into the shingle beneath the clear tidal water; the jumble of warehouses, shops and taverns that lined the waterfront; the wattle huts of the swineherds and charcoal burners beyond the stalls of the market, all lay open to attack.

The Roman Governor, Suetonius Paulinus, most of whose troops had been far away in Wales when the uprising began, accepted the impossibility of defending the port from the fierce tribesmen from the north and abandoned it to its fate. Its destruction was swift and complete. Londinium was burned to the ground; its inhabitants were massacred; its streets and buildings and open places soon buried beneath a mass of rubble and soft red ash.

Boadicea had had her revenge; but there could be no final victory. Backed by the incalculable resources of Nero's Empire, Paulinus brought the British tribesmen to formal battle and overwhelmed them. Rather than fall into his hands, Boadicea took poison and joined the uncounted thousands of dead.

But although she had entirely destroyed the first Londinium, another

Surviving section of the Roman city wall in Cooper's Row, *c*. 200 A.D.

and finer town soon rose to take its place. For the Romans recognised that the site was the key to the British province.

Long before the Romans had come, the native people of the island and its previous invaders had established themselves in settlements along the banks of the wide river on which Londinium stood, using the river as a means of transport as well as a source of food, a link not only between settlement and settlement but between the island itself and the continental mainland to which Britain had once been joined, before the inrush of the northern seas. But along the course of this wide river, there was only one place which could serve the Romans as a site for the building of an important port and commercial centre. This was the ground upon which Londinium was built. The settlements further downstream, lacking Londinium's gravel beds, could supply neither bridge nor ford; upstream, the river, about a hundred feet wider and at least fifteen feet lower than it is today, could not accommodate the large ships of the Empire's merchant fleet. At Londinium there was both tidal water for the fleet and a safe crossing place to draw together the complex of roads on which Roman power and security depended.

As year succeeded year London grew and prospered. By the middle of the third century, when it had become the administrative and financial as well as the commercial capital of the province, it contained perhaps as many as 30,000 people; fifty years later there may even have been almost twice that number. These early fourth-century Romano-British Londoners lived in a semi-circular area of 326 acres enclosed by three miles of strong stone walls,

The impression of a child's feet on a tile found in the flue channel of the bath in Cheapside; early second century.

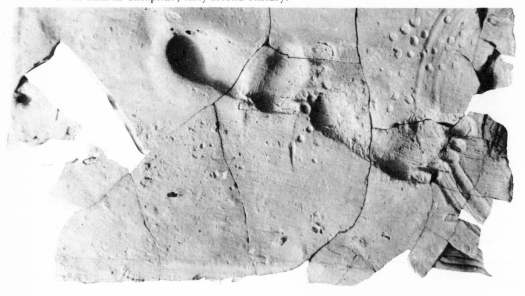

1. Bacchus riding a tiger: the centre of a Roman mosaic pavement excavated in Leadenhall Street.

Au pople preche meillat
ben cordenement lur dir
icele nuit passa tamise
s eint pere. e dedia sa iglise
p e le sacez garde en pleines
d cer termin nuit en seianes.

q ui cors i gravera e deinse
e sepulture en tele iglise
e pur ses duns ben afermer
a resme fair ia en never
v est dimmund li maire segre
ki ert enbulle privilege

roi aedward; cel seint lincsa
n ciel la porte. auanie eam
a al legliie ert neuz e de rut
m co issur veoir grant rute
e matinis e charpoises se
y ben seit. ne fair li anglers

O us hom ses crie. e ne se alasse
o e la tamise. ke en le passe:
o ut prie. e dit ke dura:
l uer. bi utre le merra:
v n peschur pi co ont enet:

l i peschur of seint pere a rine
l a tent. e ser ala riue
e eint pere du ciel clauer:
y a sa iglise dedier:
c er angeles nuit grant partie

l i angele chant ent du siule
a nuit quant dedient ligliie
c ant ia du ciel luur:
b uis est au peschur:
b e la solalz e la lune:

about eight feet thick at their base and up to twenty feet high. Pierced by gates where the main roads led into the city and strengthened later by a series of projecting bastions and towers and by a fort near Cripplegate, the walls stretched all round the town and along the river front from the hill where the Tower of London now stands to where the Fleet River, long since covered by the modern town, discharged its waters into the Thames over a mile away to the west.[1]

Across the Thames, a little further downstream than the present London Bridge, was a wooden bridge, wide enough to carry two streams of traffic, one leaving Londinium for the transriverine suburb, whose site now lies buried beneath the streets of Southwark, the other stream entering the city through the gate whose towers looked down upon the square-rigged ships moored at the long wharfs below.

Inside the walls the paved main streets of the city's centre were wide and straight and regular, the buildings that lined them solid and imposing. Although the labourers and the men who worked on the docks still lived in little huts like beehives or in wooden houses with thatched or shingle roofs, much of the Roman reconstruction that had followed the devastation of the city by Boadicea had been carried out in brick, stone and tile. Most buildings, their walls painted a dark red, their low-pitched roofs a lighter, salmon colour, were small and low; but there were others, it seems, four or even five storeys high with fountains playing in their courtyards and vines growing against their garden walls.

The Basilica, centre of commerce and government, which faced the traveller as he entered the city through the river gate, was a vast and impressive building on Cornhill, five hundred feet long, whose arcaded walls, lined inside with marble, were about seventy feet high; while the temple dedicated to the mysterious Mithras, the Persian god of light whose cult had been adopted by the Legions, was as graceful as any to be found in the western provinces of the Empire.[2]

The public baths by the various gates, the wide-arched fronts of the numerous shops and offices, the porticoed villas of the merchants, the mint producing its steady stream of gold and silvered copper coins, all confirmed the traveller in his belief that the city deserved the new name of Augusta which had been accorded to it in the reign of the Emperor Gratian.

Life in the city was highly civilised and agreeable for all but the very poor. The farms outside the walls and the gardens within them produced the finest meat and vegetables and fruit; fresh, clear water, piped in hollowed tree trunks, was plentiful; the rivers – not only the Thames and the Fleet that flowed past the south and west walls, but also the smaller Walbrook which, winding in twin streams through the marshy ground beside the road to Colchester, passed through culverts in the northern wall and then on,

2. Edward the Confessor discussing the building of Westminster Abbey with architect and workmen.
3. St Peter consecrating Westminster Abbey: mid-thirteenth century MS.

shored-up and bridged, close to the very heart of the city – all were full of fish, salmon and trout as well as shoals of coarse fish.

Along the eastern bank of the Walbrook, and north of the Basilica, the houses of the richer citizens – kept warm in winter by heated flues beneath the tessellated floors – were brightly painted, attractively furnished and lavishly decorated with porphyry and marble, bronze ornaments and terracotta figurines (plate 1). The numerous fragments of their contents which have survived show how well these houses were supplied with all manner of aids to a gracious, pleasant and cultured way of life – blue and amber glass dishes and bowls, silver plates, knives and spoons and kitchen forks, oil lamps and candlesticks, ink wells and pens, styli and wax tablets, bone flutes and whistles, dice and counters, bronze bells and mirrors, ear-picks, skin-scrapers, and the whole range of objects to be found on a Roman dressing-table, from boxwood combs, ointment jars, scent bottles and lip rouge pots, to beads, earrings, bracelets and manicure sets.

Sometimes an object is discovered which evokes a less pleasing picture of Londinium Augusta – a plaited bronze wire scourge used to flay the back of an unruly servant, the marble tombstone of a gladiator, or a wax writing tablet bearing the words: TAKE GOOD CARE YOU TURN THAT SLAVE-GIRL INTO CASH. At other times an object is unearthed which suddenly seems to close the gap left by the passing of sixteen centuries – a set of surgical instruments, a pair of delicate scales, the stamp used by an eye-specialist to mark his prescriptions, the Latin inscription on a bonding tile, scratched there by a bricklayer irritated by the behaviour of a lazy fellow-workman: AUSTALIS

Bronze steelyard found at Walbrook; first or second century.

Pierced leather shoe found in the streambed of the Walbrook; first or second century.

There can have been no shortage of work in Londinium. There were brick-fields inside the walls, potteries and glass-works, joiners' shops and mills, masons' yards and factories where tools and agricultural implements were made, as well as furniture and footwear. Most of the cloth was spun in the home, but the leather shoes and sandals (all specially made, for no two are alike) with their intricately decorated soles and their owners' initials worked into the leather are surely the work of expert cobblers.

Nor, for those who could afford it, was there any lack of luxury. Wine (better than the British fermentations) and olive oil were imported from Italy, carpets and fabrics from Egypt, ivory, silk, pepper and spices from the East. So that although an outpost of Rome, Londinium was not only the largest town in Britain, not only the fifth largest in the western Empire, but one of the most pleasant to be found anywhere north of the Alps.

During the course of the fourth century, however, the prosperity of Londinium began to decline. The Empire was crumbling and much of the city was crumbling with it. Even before the Emperor Honorius withdrew his Legions from the province, the shores around it were infested with pirates; and Saxon invaders had already established settlements along the south-east coast. In 457 the men of Londinium, a town then sadly fallen from its former greatness, received the British survivors of a battle fought in Kent against the fierce warriors of the Saxon chieftain, Hengist; and thereafter for a century and a half there is no further mention of the town in recorded history.

Statuette of Bacchus accompanied by Silenus, a satyr, a maenad and a panther; from the Temple of Mithras, Walbrook.

2 *London in the Early Middle Ages 604–1381*

Whether Londinium lay almost deserted and entirely desolate, with a few poor squatters scratching for a livelihood amidst the weeds and tumbled ruins, or whether – as seems more likely – by coming to terms with the invaders, its inhabitants ensured for themselves some form of independent survival, it is certain that in 604 the town had regained enough of its former importance for St Augustine to provide it with a bishop, a monk from Rome named Mellitus.

Mellitus, however, found the staunchly heathen Londoners far more intractable than St Augustine had found the people of Canterbury; and although a cathedral was founded in London and dedicated to St Paul, when Mellitus's patron, the Christian King Sebert of Kent, died, the men of London drove the bishop out of the city and returned to their old religion and their former priests.

This display of determined conservatism and proud independence was characteristic of the kind of individuality London had already created for herself in the first five hundred years of her history. As in Roman times, when Londinium had been neither a tribal capital (like Canterbury and Cirencester) nor a *colonia* (a place like Colchester or York, where ex-legionaries were settled as a reserve of veterans in time of trouble), so in early Saxon times, London stood outside and aloof from the organisation and legal system of the country as a whole.

When the Danes sacked London in 851, setting fire to the highly inflammable buildings and destroying most of what still remained of the Roman city, the devastation was appalling; yet the spirit and character of London survived; and King Alfred, England's champion against the Danish invaders, understood that while its jealously-held notions of independence might have one day to be checked, its restoration was essential to the survival of the kingdom.

Alfred knew that London must be secured, not only as a barrier on the Thames to the vikings' huge galleys, but also as a base for operations by land; and in 883 it *was* secured. The Danish occupying forces were driven out, the walls rebuilt to prevent their return, its citizens organised into a

Tombs of Knights Templar in the Temple Church; thirteenth century.

Animal figures from the base of a Saxon cross *c.* 1040, found on the site of All Hallows, Barking.

well-trained and powerful army; and Ethelred, King Alfred's capable son-in-law, was appointed its governor.

In order to encourage the town's redevelopment, Alfred granted blocks of land inside its walls to those capable of restoring it to its former importance, giving each of them, bishops, noblemen and members of his own family, an area which would allow easy access to the river and to one or other of the two markets that had by then been established – Eastcheap, the market of the citizens, on the site of the present Cheapside, and Westcheap, which served the household of the King whose palace, as Christian tradition then required, was close by the city's cathedral.

Under Alfred, Ethelred and their successors, Lunduntown – as its people then called it – expanded northwards from the river and outwards from St Paul's as further grants of land were made and as the new owners brought in settlers from their estates elsewhere and from abroad. It was probably in the reign of Alfred's great-grandson Edgar, between 957 and 975, that the wine merchants of Rouen were settled in the area of the present Vintners' Place and that some few years later a colony of German merchants became established nearby at Dowgate. Certainly, after the Londoners accepted the Danish leader Cnut as their king in 1016, many Danes settled in the city, many others outside it. Most of those who lived beyond the walls were to be found along the riverside to the east, but there were others beyond Ludgate to the west, in the area where the church of St Clement Danes now stands guard between Fleet Street and the Strand; while several more families established themselves at Clapham, which derives its name from their leader

Osgod Clapa, and on the river Lea at Hackney which was then known as Hakon's Ea, or Hakon's island.

During these years the settlement at the southern end of London Bridge grew in size and importance, becoming a royal borough, with the right to hold a fair and a market, and with a reputation, which it was not to lose for centuries, of being a wild, disorderly haunt of rakes, drunkards and whores.

The taverns and stalls and fishermen's hovels of Sudwerke, frequently flattened and ruined in viking raids, were also often destroyed by fire. Fire was one of the main hazards, too, within the walls of London, since most of the Saxon town was built of wood, except for some rich men's houses and a few churches such as All Hallows Barking.[1]

In 961 a fierce fire burned out the first Cathedral of St Paul's; and twenty-one years later another fire swept across the town from Bishopsgate to the river, destroying what little of Roman London had been left standing above ground after the Danish attack in 851. But although stone was scarce, having to be brought up river from Kent or by road from Merstham thirty miles to the south, timber was plentiful only a mile or so from the northern gates; so the town was soon rebuilt above the ashes.

In about 1060 a vast new area became available for redevelopment when Edward the Confessor forsook the Wardrobe palace by St Paul's as his principal residence in London and moved to a new palace, a mile and a half upstream to the west, where the minster of the monks of St Peter's was now being rebuilt at the Confessor's expense (plates 2 and 3).

Westminster was then on an island, Thornea or Thorney Island (the

Westminster Abbey after Henry III's rebuilding, and the five great bells he gave it: from a thirteenth-century manuscript.

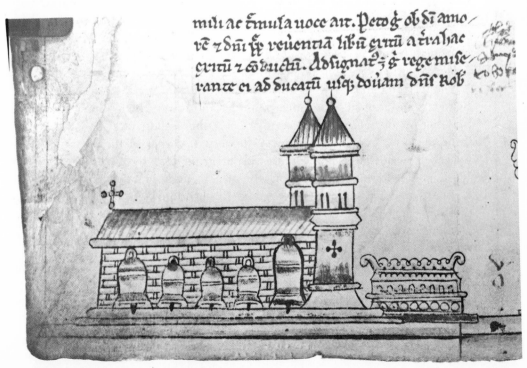

isle of Brambles), one of a number, such as Chelsea (the isle of shingle), Bermondsey (Bermond's isle), and Battersea (Peter's isle), standing above the level of the shallow lagoons which dotted the marshy ground upstream from the city's western wall.

The new palace which Edward began at Westminster, replacing a far meaner one which had once been used by Cnut, was soon a splendid edifice with noble stone walls, painted chambers, and rows of offices, kitchens and cellars along the waterfront. The abbey nearby, built of Caen stone on a cruciform plan in the Norman manner, with a central and two western towers, was even finer. It was consecrated at Christmas, 1065, a few weeks before the death of its frail and pious founder.

The next Christmas Day, 1066, Edward's successor, William, Duke of Normandy, came to Westminster to be anointed King of the country he had so recently conquered. Following the example of his dead rival, Harold Godwinson, whom William had defeated two months before at Hastings, the Conqueror had himself crowned in the abbey, which was thereafter to remain indissolubly associated with the monarchs of England for almost a thousand years.[2]

The Conqueror's distrust of the people of London was apparent from the first. Theirs was not only the richest town in his new kingdom, but its army, trained and tested in the fight against the vikings, had made the citizens more than ever conscious of their power, more than ever determined to insist upon the rights and privileges which no king from now on dared deny them. William gave them a charter which confirmed these rights without presuming to suggest that they were the subject of a royal grant; they in turn acknowledged him as their King. But the relationship was a wary one. As soon as the coronation ceremony was over William moved to Barking in Essex where St Eorcenwald, the most zealous of the early bishops of London, had founded an abbey ten miles from the town's northern gate. Here William remained 'while certain strongholds were made in the town against the fickleness of the vast and fierce populace'.

These strongholds, at first perhaps no more than earthworks surrounded by moats and topped by wooden palisades and towers, before long developed into highly distinctive and sternly forbidding landmarks of the London scene. Two of them were in the south-western corner of the town – Montfichet's Tower, somewhere on the rising ground to the right bank of the Fleet, and below it, Baynard's Castle which, under its first custodian Ralf Baignard and his successors, remained the headquarters of London's army until the reign of Edward I (1272–1307) when it was handed over to the Dominican Friars, the Blackfriars whose name is still commemorated along that part of the waterfront.

The third stronghold, the White Tower – finished in 1097 to the design of

Gundulf, the Benedictine monk who became Bishop of Rochester – was built on the mound where the old Roman wall ran down to the Thames in the east. And there it still stands – often attacked and often besieged, but never captured – its four grey turrets of Caen stone and Kentish rag looking down upon the river, a memorial to Norman power and a symbol of the city itself.

The White Tower, now the central feature of the Tower of London, was not only a fortress and a prison; it was also a palace, a jewel house and wardrobe. When at last William's descendants and, in particular, Henry III, had finished contributing their additions and embellishments to the design of its original architect, the white-washed Tower, ninety feet high from ground to battlements, contained, as well as dungeons and armouries and cages for the royal collection of wild and exotic beasts, as well as quarters for the garrison and the King's guard of yeomen, painted halls and courts, council rooms, sleeping chambers, and the sombrely beautiful chapel of St John.[3] Comfortable as it was, however, the White Tower was not the principal residence of the Norman Kings which remained at Westminster where William Rufus, the Conqueror's son, had greatly extended the palace begun by Edward the Confessor.

Westminster Hall, the only part of that palace to survive, was its main feature. When at last it was finished, William Rufus, arrogant, extravagant and ostentatious, professed himself disappointed with the size of the Hall. It was, he protested, a 'mere bedchamber' compared with what he had intended to have built. But for all its founder's disparagement, Westminster

Baynard's Castle: a nineteenth-century engraving.

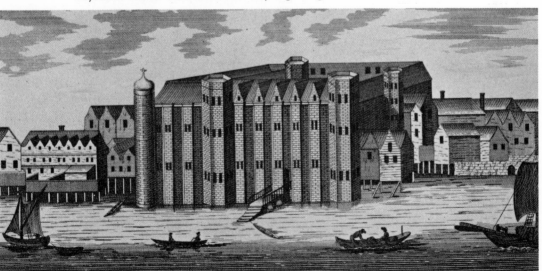

Hall was a magnificent structure. Nearly 240 feet long and almost forty feet high, its walls, six feet eight inches thick, were pierced by a row of round-headed Norman windows. Inside, these walls were plastered and painted, and running round them twenty feet from the floor was a wide, railed gallery. By the time Hugh Herland's splendid hammer-beam roof was installed in the reign of Richard II (1377–1400), Westminster Hall had become the centre of the Kingdom's administrative life, the home of the royal courts of law, and so had ensured that the government of the country was carried on outside the walls of the nearby city.[4]

Within those walls the life of the twelfth-century Londoner went on almost as though the Normans had never come. Many of the new grants of land, which included rights of private jurisdiction, were naturally made to those of Norman blood. Yet most of the city's land and nearly all of its trade remained in the hands of those who had controlled it before the Conquest. Norman styles in architecture – already, in fact, becoming fashionable in Edward the Confessor's time – began to change the physical aspect of some parts of the city. But all the parish churches of late twelfth-century London were Saxon foundations. Both the boundaries of the wards into which the city was divided and the type of man who represented these wards as aldermen, continued much as before. Imported wines continued to be landed on the wharfs at Dowgate, fish, corn and salt at Billingsgate, garlic at Garlickhythe; the big street markets at Cheapside and Eastcheap remained unchanged, as noisy, as busy and smelly as ever; travellers entering London still had to pass over the same wooden bridge or through the same gaps in the Roman wall at Ludgate or Newgate in the west, Aldersgate, Cripplegate or Bishopsgate in the north, and Aldgate in the east, and then had to traverse the rough and muddled Saxon streets that overlay the long-lost regularity of Roman paving. Fires were still a constant threat, large areas of the city being burned out in 1087 in a holocaust which once more reduced St Paul's to a heap of cinders, and in 1135, when the flames, sweeping west from Billingsgate, destroyed all the buildings between the bridge and the Fleet river.

St Paul's was again rebuilt, this time in stone; and in 1176 work began on a new stone bridge across the river, to take the place of the wooden structure which, repeatedly repaired and rebuilt, had done duty for a thousand years. Completed at last in 1209, four years after the death of its designer, a London parish priest, Peter of Colechurch, the new bridge was as familiar and distinctive a London landmark as the White Tower that loomed domineeringly above it (plate 8). A chapel dedicated to St Thomas à Becket was built above the central pier of its twenty-two irregular pointed arches, and Peter of Colechurch was buried in its undercroft. Later, when the bridge was broadened, houses and shops were crowded round the walls

Hugh Herland's hammerbeam roof in Westminster Hall, *c.* 1400.

of this chapel, eventually filling the span from end to end.

Old London Bridge, the only bridge London had until 1750, was pulled down in 1832; old St Paul's was destroyed in the Great Fire of 1666. But there are still to be found in London vivid evocations of the Norman city, none of them more powerful than the lines of sturdily rounded Romanesque columns and semi-circular arches in the fine monastic church of St Bartholomew-the-Great, Smithfield – the oldest church fabric in London after the Chapel of St John in the Tower – founded about 1123 by Rahere, the Augustinian prior who had once been a wild and wanton prodigal at the English Court.[5]

Here, in Rahere's church, it is possible to sense the atmosphere of the London of Henry II as described by Thomas à Becket's secretary, William FitzStephen, whose biography of his master was written in about 1180.

FitzStephen, like his hero, was born in London, and to him the city was a place of perfect delight and constant enchantment. Down by the river were sold the fish that teemed in the sparkling waters, wine not yet unloaded from the ships, hot dishes of tender meat cunningly roasted in the public cook-shops and covered with those hotly spiced sauces which had become so pleasing to the medieval palate. In the middle of the town the good-looking, healthy citizens worked hard and long and were happy to do so. The young students in the schools, the priests at their devotions, the virtuous ladies at their spinning-wheels lived together in peaceful harmony. Close to the northern wall and outside its gates were market gardens and orchards, while beyond them stretched pastures and meadows, intersected by streams turning the mill-wheels with 'merry din', and dotted with wells around whose sweet clear waters the people of the city came to sit and play on holidays.

The culverts made by the Romans in the northern wall, through which the tributary streams of the Walbrook used to flow, had now become blocked so that in winter the marshy land to the north of the town was flooded and frozen. There, on Moorfields, young men came out to skate with the shin bones of animals lashed to their feet. Watched by the less adventurous, who sat on huge seats of ice in the shape of millstones, the more daring and reckless charged at each other, propelling themselves with iron-shod poles, until they met head on, fell flat on their backs, and skidded apart like curling stones.

They played a version of this dangerous game on the river, too. Standing up in the bow of a rowing boat with lances in their hands, the protagonists were rowed towards each other, or at shields fixed to posts in mid-stream, as fast as the oarsmen could take them. Only the most skilful could keep their balance while breaking their lances, the others being plunged by the impact into the water. After dinner on Sundays the outlying fields were full of young men on horseback, practising their skill with lance and shield, the smaller of them removing the steel tip from their lances and wielding the staff alone.

Throughout the summer evenings Tothill Fields and Smithfield were full of energetic youths perfecting these warlike arts, fighting each other with sword and buckler, tilting at the target on the quintain, practising archery and wrestling, running and jumping, putting the stone and throwing the javelin. Further away in the woods beyond Hampstead and Islington their fathers went hunting with falcons and dogs and chased the wild deer through the clearings.

In Smithfield, a pleasant open area surrounded by trees and clear ponds, there was a horse-fair most Saturdays where ambling palfreys, colts with glistening coats, and costly destriers with quivering ears, high necks and plump buttocks, were rowdily offered for sale or exchange, while farmers' boys raced each other across the grass, three to a single horse's bare back. There were cattle for sale as well as horses, mares for the plough, cows with swollen udders or with bellies big with young; and sledges and carts, pitchforks and barrows, pails and pigs.

In the evenings inside the walls there were miracle plays to watch, cock-fights and dog-fights, fights between wild hogs and foaming bears. And on days of special celebration the houses were hung with banners and flags, escutcheons and shields; there were bonfires in the streets, dancing and singing round the maypole; the public water cisterns flowed with wine. On occasions such as these London suffered from the only two plagues which, so William FitzStephen thought, ever cursed it, the immoderate drinking of fools and the frequency of fires.

A hawking party, early fourteenth century.

Fires remained a constant threat, since London was still a packed con-glomeration of mostly wooden buildings confined within the Roman walls. There was the growing suburb of Southwark; there was a gradually extend-ing line of rich men's houses and bishops' palaces along the country road between Ludgate and Westminster; there were one or two small monasteries, hostelries, groups of huntsmen's kennels, riding and fencing schools outside the other gates. But it was not for another three hundred years that the city began to lose the general shape that the Roman walls had imposed upon it.

Inside the walls the population in FitzStephen's time was perhaps about 40,000, almost certainly less than the city had contained in its Roman heyday. And never, even at those times when the plague had been mercifully less virulent, can there have been more than 75,000 inhabitants at the most. There was, indeed, scarcely room for more, as the walled gardens and orchards of the noblemen and the monasteries covered acre upon acre of ground in all parts of the town.

The workmen were huddled together, trade by trade, for the most part living and working with their families in one small room. The tanners, the fullers, cordwainers and saddlers, the bell-founders and cloth-dressers, the tailors and dyers, all had their separate quarters, and their special places of sale grouped together in the market. As in other old towns in Britain, as indeed throughout the world, the names of London streets often indicate the former centre of a trade or craft or the place where its goods were sold in the market. So Fish Street Hill is where the fishmongers had their stalls, Sea Coal Lane where the coal merchants were established by their stores near the Fleet River from the time of Henry III, Lombard Street where the Italian bankers settled after the expulsion of the Jews from London in 1290, and Jewry Street and Old Jewry are where the Jewish ghettoes were before that time. The names of the streets leading off Cheapside – Wood Street, Milk Street, Ironmonger Lane, Poultry, Bread Street – all indicate where the stalls of the various trades were kept in the market before its open ground was covered with buildings.

Association, for some trades, was not so much a convenience as a necessity. It was a way of ensuring that the men practising any particular craft never grew too numerous, and that standards of quality and skill were maintained; also it facilitated the sharing of tools, the ready supply of raw materials, the maintenance of those who could no longer work – a goldsmith blinded by the fire and smoke of quicksilver, or an old loriner no longer able to grasp his hammer with sufficient strength. From such beginnings, as well as from organisations with a purely benevolent or religious basis, were developed the medieval guilds which were to play so important a part in the life of the city.

The guilds concerned themselves with the spiritual as well as the social welfare of their members, laying down rules for the celebration of Masses for the dead and for regular Church attendance. And no foreign merchant who came to London could fail to be struck by the number of churches that the city contained for the workers' devotions. In addition to St Paul's, whose dominating tower with its huge lantern windows and its timber spire, finished in 1221, now rose to a height of 245 feet; in addition to the chapels of the monasteries and convents, there were – by William FitzStephen's count – already no less than 126 parish churches at the end of the twelfth century; and during the thirteenth more and more were built by wealthy citizens as anxious, perhaps, to benefit their clerical friends or relations, to whom the livings were presented, as to glorify God. Most of them were small and dark, some still built of split tree trunks in the primitive Saxon way; but there were others that were imposing structures with fine stone towers, and stained glass windows like the windows of St Paul's, with interiors splendidly decorated in red and gold, with tombs of marble and alabaster, finely wrought gold candlesticks and jewelled crucifixes.

The coming of the friars from the Continent in the thirteenth century as missionaries to preach to and help the poor – the Black Friars in 1221, the Grey Friars in 1223, the White Friars in 1241, the Austin Friars in 1253 and the Crossed or Crutched Friars in 1298 – increased the number of religious houses throughout the city, particularly in the poorer and less desirable districts where the early friars first settled and where their selfless work amongst the sick and needy aroused the sympathy of the rich. Thus the

A lady places a helmet on the head of a kneeling knight: the central medallion from a silver dish of *c.* 1325 from St Mary Magdalene, Bermondsey.

A thirteenth-century medical school.

Greyfriars, whose first small house was built in Stinking Lane near Newgate amongst the butchers' shambles, earned the admiration of patrons with money to pay for the church, chapter house, priory, and other buildings which eventually sprawled across many acres of ground between Newgate Street and St Bartholomew's Hospital, a hospital already a hundred years old when the Greyfriars came and still a hospital today. So, too, the Austin Friars, settling at first just inside the wall between Bishopsgate and Moorgate, were soon able to build for themselves a church whose nave was even wider than that of Winchester Cathedral. At this time, also, the military order of monks, the Knights Templars, founded in 1118 for the defence of pilgrims to the Holy City – although resident in London since the twelfth century when their round church, modelled on the Holy Sepulchre in Jerusalem, was first built[6] – enlarged and extended their rambling quarters down by the river south-west of Ludgate.

The growth of fine and solid buildings in the poorer and less healthy parts of the city was nothing strange, however, to the thirteenth-century Londoner. For, although tradesmen tended to congregate in particular areas, the richer citizens, as a rule, did not. There were large and comfortable houses, including the mansion of the Neville family, amidst the jumble of workers' hovels and slaughter-houses inside Newgate; just as there were wretched sheds and tenements piled up against the garden walls of the Bishop of London's palace. And this pattern of development was slow to change. The earls of Arundel had a town house in Bishopsgate till the end of the sixteenth century; the Earls of Northumberland lived for many years in Crutched Friars; Humphrey,

18

4. The rich clothes of the fifteenth century: a miniature of the legendary King Uther Pendragon's court in London.

Duke of Gloucester, brother of Henry V, built himself a house on the water-front not far from Puddle Dock; William De La Pole, Duke of Suffolk, lived close to the fishmongers' stalls in Ducksfoot Lane, originally his foot-path to the river; the Black Prince, son of Edward III, lived on Fish Street Hill itself.

The noxious smells of the streets were kept at bay in these big houses by strong perfumes, bunches of herbs and smoking incense; but on a hot summer's day the gentlest breeze would waft up from the filthy streets so foul a stench that not even the most potent antidotes could deaden it. Year after year attempts were made to prevent the citizens from throwing rubbish and ordure into the streets, from building pigsties outside their front doors, from blocking the gutters with offal, oyster shells and fishheads, from tipping rubble into the public latrines which were to be found at the gates and on platforms overhanging the Walbrook, from throwing dead animals into the river and into the ditch that was dug all round the city outside the wall during the troubled reign of King John when London sided with the Barons against the royal power.

But the very frequency of the orders and proclamations, issued both by the king and the city corporation – the corporate unity of the citizens was recognised and the mayoralty established at the end of the twelfth century – indicate that they had as little effect as the repeated injunctions against lepers remaining inside the walls: one leprous baker, although 'oftentimes before' commanded to depart, seems to have stubbornly carried on his trade in the city for many years.

Nor does it seem that the regulations about methods of construction of new buildings were any more faithfully observed. In 1189, the year of Henry II's death, it was enacted that the lower part of all houses in the city must be of stone and the roofs of tiles; but a few years later an official condemnation of reeds, rushes, stubble and straw in the construction of roofs suggests that the previous order had not been enforced. Also, since the meaner sort of house was warmed by an open brazier and had no chimney, fires continued to be common throughout the Middle Ages, despite the precautionary orders which required each ward to provide the equipment – poles, hooks, chains and ropes – for the instant demolition of a burning house, and which ordered every well-to-do citizen to keep a ladder in his courtyard for the safety of his poorer neighbour and, in hot weather, a barrel full of water outside his door.

Fire was but one hazard to life in the city: disease was a greater danger. The filth in the streets and in the huddled houses, most of which had matted rushes or straw trampled into the vermin-covered clay floors; the impurity of the water which, although available in cisterns in Cheapside and else-where as early as 1236, was still for the most part brought up by carriers in buckets from the river; the rats which swarmed down the cables of the ships,

5. The wealth of the City: detail from the Fishmongers' Company's
funeral pall; late fifteenth century with arms and supporters added later.

across the wharfs and into the cellars and warehouses along Thames Street, all ensured that plague was a constant spectre and regular visitor. The most virulent outbreak, the Black Death of 1348–49, killed off almost, it has been estimated, two-thirds of the inhabitants of the city. Certainly as many as 50,000 corpses were tipped into vast pits in West Smithfield in ground bought and consecrated by the Bishop of London, who was concerned by the enormous number of bodies already buried in unhallowed ground within the walls.

As well as the danger of disease and fire, there was the ever-present threat of violence. Quarrels between apprentices and between competing trades-men frequently ended in ferocious fights at the call of 'Clubs! Clubs!' which would fill the streets with brawling men slashing at each other with knives and the tools of their craft. In 1327 there was a pitched battle between a band of saddlers and an alliance of joiners, painters and loriners, over some trade dispute; in 1339 several men were killed when the skinners fought the fishmongers; and two years later numerous apprentices and several in-cautious bystanders were clubbed to death after an argument in a tavern had developed into a wild riot. Scarcely a year passed when there was not a battle between the tailors and the drapers, the pepperers and the spicers, the fishmongers and the poulterers, the saddlers and the lorimers, between London workmen and country workmen prepared to work for lower rates, between Londoners and men from Westminster after what had begun as a friendly contest. In 1222, for example, when a London team beat Westminster at wrestling, the Westminster wrestlers armed themselves for the return match and gravely injured several of their opponents, who immediately revenged themselves by pulling down the house of the Steward of the Abbey, beating up the Abbot's servants, and throwing stones at the Abbot himself.

Although a cosmopolitan people, the Londoners were particularly resent-ful of any interference in their trades by newly-arrived foreigners, and any alien who set up a stall in the market did so at the risk of a broken head. In the summer of 1381 numerous peaceful Flemish traders were murdered

An apothecary's dispensary, twelfth century.

in Clerkenwell and St Martin's Vintry; and a century and a half later what became known as Evil May Day – which led to the execution of thirteen youths for taking part in a riot – was sparked off by an order forbidding the city's apprentices to go out of doors on the eve of May Day because of the violent antipathy they had displayed during Easter Week to foreign passers-by in the streets.

It was not the workers, though, who were the worst troublemakers. Gangs of young noblemen and squires, fighting each other, breaking into shops and houses, throwing dogs and cats they found in the streets through nearby windows, frequently marauded through the city at night. Often, also, the arrival in town of the blustering retinue of a rich and powerful nobleman would provoke a vicious fight; while the liveried retainers usually to be found hanging about outside the gatehouse of their master's mansion were always on the watch for a chance to shout an insult and start a brawl.

Nor could the curfew, a variable hour, which, announced by the clanging of the church bells, sometimes closed the taverns as early as eight o'clock, succeed in its purpose of clearing the streets at night; not yet could the early fourteenth-century prohibition against all but city officials, and royal and baronial servants carrying arms in the streets, limit the regular out-breaks of violence.

During the Peasants' Revolt of 1381, when the workers of the country rose against their cruel exploitation by the ruling class and marched on London, the apprentices opened their gates to them; and many a London tradesman and drunken young squire joined the angry rebels in blockading the young Richard II in the Tower, in murdering several of his ministers, and in parading the head of the Chancellor, Archbishop Sudbury, round the streets on a pike. It was not until 15 June after the rebel leader, Wat Tyler, had been pulled from his horse by the Mayor at a conference at Smithfield and stabbed to death that the revolt in London was brought to an end.

The dagger which by tradition killed Wat Tyler.

3 London Life in the Fifteenth Century 1381–1485

Although a city of such violence, squalor and disease, London – long since recognised as the undisputed capital of England – continued to increase in wealth, fame and importance as the Middle Ages drew to their close.

In the fifteenth century, while the nobility of the country exhausted themselves in the fury and smoke of the Wars of the Roses, battling with each other for the crown of England, the Londoner peacefully went about his daily business in a city which, for all its overt abominations and hidden misery, was as full of splendour as of vigorous life and wonderful variety.

The countryman who entered the town was astounded by the size of the place, its noise and bustle. On passing through Westminster he would have found – as the misused hero of *London Lickpenny,* the contemporary of the Suffolk-born poet, John Lydgate, found – the streets full of Flemish merchants selling hats and spectacles, and all kinds of other street vendors loudly advertising their wares, or encouraging any sort of indiscriminate purchase by shouting, 'Buy! Buy! Buy! What d'ye lack? What d'ye lack? What'll you buy? What'll you buy?'

Street thieves, keeping a close look out for the unwary, awaited an opportunity to snatch the bag from the hand of a passing clod-hopper or the hood from a foreign merchant's head, and to run away through Westminster Gate, past the cooks' shops where bread and wine, London ale spiced with pepper, hot meat pies, porpoise tongues and ribs of beef were laid out for sale on trestle tables.

Beyond the gate, the Strand, a country highway lined on both sides now with the houses and gardens of noblemen, stretched towards the bridge across the Fleet and to London's wall. Before Ludgate was reached, the noise of the city could be heard – the screech and rattle of carts across the cobbles and through the ruts of mud, the regular chiming of innumerable church bells, the raucous shouts of the apprentices bawling the virtues of their masters' wares in the stalls and the little shops which were all open to the street, the protests of passers-by seized by the hand and pulled inside, the cries of the chapmen and the hawkers selling cherries or peascods, hot sheep's feet or mackerel, pies and pasties and 'rushes, faire and grene'.

London Bridge: detail of a drawing by Anthonis van den Wyngaerde, 1543–44.

To enter the city the traveller had to walk across the drawbridge that spanned the ditch and under the raised portcullis of the gate, past the guards posted there to turn back lepers; and then he would come out to face the labyrinth of streets that led to the market. The main streets were wide and regular enough, but others were scarcely streets at all, the buildings in them holding to no particular line and facing any chosen angle, while some were alleys so narrow that a man could stretch out his arms and touch the buildings on either side.

All of them, whatever their size or shape, were as full of colour and movement as of noise. The vivid liveries of the noblemen's retainers and the bright French silks of the young squires were in sharp contrast to the sombre tunic of the Death Crier, to the plain cloth hoods, short jerkins and flat caps of the apprentices, the dirty leather aprons of the blacksmiths' casual-labourers, and to the mud-spattered garments of some wretched tradesman fixed in the pillory for selling adulterated goods, forced to stand in a barrel of his noxious wares, or dragged along on a hurdle with the offending article hanging round his neck.

More pleasing, and no less common, sights than these public punishments were the processions that so unfailingly delighted the medieval eye, from the modest parade of a few celebrating students marching through the streets with pipes, drums, flowers and banners, to the grand spectacle of a water pageant, the Mayor's Show, or some such triumphant cavalcade of scarlet-clad aldermen, citizens and craftsmen as that which attended Henry V from London Bridge to St Paul's after his return in 1415 from victory over the French chivalry at Agincourt.

The punishment of a fraudulent baker, with a loaf tied round his neck: a drawing from the MS *Liber de Assisa Panis* (1293–1438).

The King, bareheaded and in a purple robe, stood for a moment by the gatehouse on the bridge looking up at the statues 'of amazing magnitude' which had been erected at the top of its two towers. One was of a giant holding a battle-axe in his right hand and the keys of the city in his left; the other was of a woman dressed in a scarlet cloak and decorated with jewels and sparkling ornaments; around both of them, flags, banners and standards fluttered in the wind.

Henry raised his voice above the cheers and shouts of welcome, the trumpets, clarions and horns that 'sounded in various melody', and called out, 'Hail to the royal city!' Then, accompanied by a few knights and attendants, and followed by a forlorn group of awestruck French noblemen captured in the war, he continued on his way.

Beyond the bridge were other figures on both sides of the roadway, standing between columns draped with white and green cloth or in pavilions lined with tapestry – an antelope holding the royal sceptre between his paws, a lion displaying the royal standard, a statue of St George in armour, wearing a laurel wreath studded with pearls and precious stones. Beneath triumphal arches and inside velvet tents were 'innumerable boys, representing the angelic host, arrayed in white with their faces painted gold and with glittering wings and virgin locks set with precious sprigs of laurel' singing anthems to the sound of organs.

Farther along the route, which wound up Fish Street Hill through the cornmarket in Grass Church and down Leadenhall to St Paul's, were groups of old men 'of venerable hoariness' dressed in golden coats and mantles, as prophets, martyrs and kings, singing psalms of thanksgiving and letting fly 'great quantities of sparrows and little birds that alighted on the King's breast, some rested on his shoulders and some fluttered round about him'. Then there were raised pavilions filled with 'the most beautiful virgin girls, standing motionless like statues, decorated with very elegant ornaments, having in their hands cups of gold from which they blew, with gentle breath scarcely perceptible, round leaves of gold upon the King's head as he passed beneath them'; and choirs of girls 'singing with timbrel and dance'; and cherubs all dressed in white throwing down from the towers of the linen-covered castles that seemed 'to grow out of the buildings', gilt wafers and laurel leaves.

Beneath windows crowded with faces, beneath damask awnings, arches of halberds, velvet-covered poles, escutcheons, shields and standards, past banners and vast tapestries on which were worked scenes representing the deeds of English heroes, the King walked on towards St Paul's where he was met by eighteen bishops in their pontificals who conducted him to the High Altar.

On grand occasions like these the streets were swept and cleaned; but usually they were ankle-deep in mud and refuse. An open drain ran down the middle of the street, or down each side of the wider streets; but neither the rain nor the men employed as rakers succeeded in keeping them clear, helped though they were by the kites and crows that swooped down from the church towers to pick up bits of offal and fish-bones and carry them away to their nests.

The rakers carted the filth away to tip it into the great pits or lay-stalls that were dug outside the city gates or down to the river where boats were moored, waiting to ferry it away. But no sooner had a street been cleaned and its rubbish carted off than it was filled up again with kitchen refuse and excrement thrown out of doors and windows, with rushes discarded from hall floors and straw cleared out of stables, with rotting animals' heads and entrails from butchers' shops, with rubble from builders' yards, stale fish from fishmongers' stalls, and feathers from the poulterers'.

Orders were constantly being issued against these abuses, as against the pigs that still wandered about the streets grunting from door to door. But they seem to have had as little effect as the repeated orders about building materials and the regulations covering the height and length of ale-stakes, the long poles with bunches of leaves at their end, which stuck out from the sides of taverns at angles highly dangerous to horsemen who rode at night through streets dimly lit by the flickering light of candles stuck into grimy lanterns.

Not only the taverns but shops and business premises, and private houses, too, had their signs hanging overhead. Even the brothels in Southwark and Cock Lane, Smithfield, carried on business beneath painted boards depicting the Boar's Head, the Cross Keys, the Saracen's Head or the Swan; while a nobleman lodging in a house which was not his own would hang his escutcheon from a prominent window.

Although the poor still lived in ramshackle buildings of wattle and wood, lath and plaster, often inhabiting a cramped penthouse leaning against their workroom; although the indigent shopkeeper often still lived surrounded by his family and his stock in an attic above his shop – or in a cellar beneath it – there were by the middle of the fifteenth century many comfortable houses, built half of timber and half of brick, of three, four or even five storeys in height. Most of the bricks, narrow like Roman tiles, came from brickfields in the villages of Whitechapel and Limehouse, and the timber frames were often pre-fabricated by carpenters at Maldon in Essex and sent to London by boat.

Each floor in these houses overhung the smaller one below it. In this way space was saved in the increasingly crowded city, but light and air were lost in the lower storeys, and even in the street itself for sometimes the roofs almost touched overhead.

In such houses as these lived the families of the well-to-do craftsmen, the successful shopkeeper, and the minor merchant, families grateful for the comfort of coal fires without the choking smoke that so often filled the chimney-less rooms of the poor, and enjoying the pleasure of glazed windows which, since the reign of Edward III, had taken the place of the shuttered or linen-covered holes of Norman domestic architecture.

The vast mansions of noblemen and rich ecclesiastics were on quite a different scale. In front of them, on either side of the gate-house which commanded the approach to the courtyard, were rows of lodgings occupied by the officials of the household. Behind this screen of terraced lodgings, and facing each other across the courtyard, were two further rows of buildings for the men-at-arms, domestic servants, kitchen staff and stable-boys. Along the fourth side of the court was the mansion itself, elaborately ornamented with decorative plaster and stonework, armorial glass and intricately carved bargeboards.

The main feature of such mansions was the great carpeted hall, sometimes measuring up to fifty feet long, where the family dined and entertained their friends and neighbours, and where the servants also ate, but on a lower level than their masters, in a rush-strewn annexe known as 'the marsh'. Around the tapestry-lined walls were doorways leading to the smaller parlours whose projecting bay windows with their latticed panes overlooked well-tended gardens. Above were bedchambers, still-rooms and closets, and in some mansions even a private chapel.

The richest of the city's merchants, lived in houses quite as fine. Richard Whittington – like many other successful businessmen of his time, the younger son of a country gentleman – lived in a style befitting a man of his immense wealth and influence who between 1397 and 1419 was four times Mayor; while the house of the mercer and wool merchant, Sir John Crosby, known as Crosby Hall, occupied most of what is now Crosby Square, Bishopsgate, and was often rented by the French and Danish Ambassadors and their multitudinous suites.[1]

Although mansions like Crosby Hall were to be found in most parts of the city, rich merchants now tended to congregate in certain areas – in Alder–manbury, for instance, near the Guildhall, centre of the city's government.[2] Between Aldermanbury and the market in Cheapside – where the movable stalls of earlier times were now being replaced by permanent shops with houses above them – many more rich merchants lived, the houses of those who were officials of the city being marked by painted posts. In this area, too, were several of the halls of the city livery companies, the trade associations which had developed from the primitive guilds. Brewers' Hall, Girdlers' Hall, Haberdashers', Goldsmiths', Saddlers' and Grocers' Halls can all still be found in the area between London Wall and Cheapside.[3]

VERA EFFIGIES PRECLAR DOMINI RICHARDI WHITINGTON EQUI AURAT.

Huius sparsa viri totu benefacta per ... ...sa monstrant indice qualis erat

The true portraicture of RICHARD WHITINGTON thrise Lord Maior
of London a vertuous and godly man full of good Works (and those famous) he builded
the Gate of London called Newegate. which before was a miserable doung eon. He builded
Whitington Colledge & made it an Almose house for poore people Also he builded a
great parte of ý hospitall of S. Bartholomewes in westsmithfield in London. He also
builded the beautifull Library at ý Gray Friers in Londõ. called Christes Hospitall:
Also he builded the Guilde Halle Chappell and increased a greate parte of the East
ende of the saied halle, beside many other good workes.

R. Elstrack sculpsit

Sir Richard Whittington with his legendary cat.

Merchants whose business was centred upon the river front chose to live close to it, so that in Fish Street Hill the collapsible stalls under which the earlier fishmongers slept at night were giving way to the permanent, solid houses of a rising middle class. Owing to the lack of ground by the river, these houses were tall rather than extensive, with deep cellars, attics for servants, and a great chamber on the first floor instead of a hall at street level; but they were all comfortable and expensively furnished.

There were enclaves, also, of foreign merchants. None of these kept themselves more isolated from London life than the successors of those German traders whom the Saxon Kings had established in the area around Dowgate, a district known, from the big scales used in the weighing of imported goods, as the Steelyard. Holding themselves aloof from all unnecessary contact with other Londoners, drinking their own Rhenish wine from stone bottles, electing their own aldermen in their own guildhall, issuing their own currency, refusing to allow women within their walls or even to play games with Englishmen for fear of quarrels, these Hansa merchants held a monopoly of Baltic trade until, already impoverished by the competition of English merchant adventurers, they were expelled by Queen Elizabeth.

Opposite the Steelyard, across the river, lay the growing suburb of Southwark, its rows of taverns and brothels along Bankside an ever present temptation, its whores – Winchester geese they were called, for the Bishop of Winchester owned many of the houses where they worked – walking the streets provocatively painted. But Southwark, although its reputation was still well

The Triumph of Riches, a fresco by Holbein, now destroyed, for the Hansa Merchants' Banqueting Hall: from a copy by Jan de Bisschop, *c.* 1670.

deserved, was not entirely given over to drunkenness, lechery and the rowdy pleasures of those eager or compelled to escape from the stricter jurisdiction of the City. The Walnut Tree and the Tabard Inn, where Chaucer's pilgrims met, were both perfectly respectable; there were decent lodgings in Southwark, as well as at Westminster, for country gentlemen who came to attend parliament; two bishops and four abbots had large houses here; while several other substantial houses had been built around St Thomas's Hospital and by the walls of the Augustinian Priory which had been founded in 1106 on the site of the Saxon nunnery of St Mary Overy.[4] Moreover, Southwark's increasing trade was bringing to the town the families of numerous hard-working men who settled down by the glassworks and ironworks, tanneries and weavers' shops.

Although Southwark and Westminster were the only two important centres in their own right outside the walls by the fifteenth century, there were by now many other places around the City which were already laying the foundations of their future importance.

Upstream from Southwark was Lambeth where Stephen Langton, Archbishop of Canterbury between 1207 and 1228, had begun the palace which his successors have improved and extended into the rambling pile of red brick castellated buildings which remains their home and office.[5] On the northern bank, opposite the marshy ground between Southwark and Lambeth, were two other riverside palaces. One of these was the Palace of the Savoy, home in the thirteenth century of the Count of Savoy, uncle of Henry III's Queen, Eleanor of Provence,[6] a man much favoured by the King and a celebrated matchmaker who lodged there 'many beautiful ladies brought in 1247 from the courts of Europe and thereafter married to his wards, a large number of rich young English nobles'. The other was York Place, the London palace of the Archbishops of York, one of whom, Cardinal Wolsey, was later to live there in a state almost as magnificent as that of the King himself. Around both these big palaces, as around the Archbishop of Canterbury's palace at Lambeth and Kennington Palace, a royal residence up till the time of Henry VII, sizeable communities had gathered, attracted by the magnet of riches and the opportunities of service.

So also round the City itself, from St Giles and Holborn to Whitechapel and Wapping, new villages were developing and old ones expanding, most of them purely agricultural villages, for the nearby market of London saved them from the need of becoming industrialised themselves. At the same time, immediately outside the walls, the clusters of buildings by the gates were beginning to take on the appearance of separate villages. In previous centuries efforts had been made to keep the strips of land between the gates and the bars – the barriers pulled across the roads beyond the drawbridges – as clear of buildings as possible, so that an enemy force would be deprived of cover in its assault. But by 1450, between Bishopsgate and Bishopsgate Bars, for example, in addition to St Botolph's church, there was a line of almshouses, a tavern, a public latrine, and a graveyard; outside Aldersgate, as well as a church and a hermitage, where the anchorite, who would one day die there, held out his thin white arm through the grating for alms, there were several large country houses and a hospital; beyond Cripplegate there was a considerable suburb of craftsmen's huts and workshops; around Newgate a straggling outgrowth had been formed into the new ward of Farringdon Without; while outside Ludgate a long line of inns and taverns welcomed the hundreds of pilgrims who went that way to St Paul's to see the marvellous collection of relics it contained – an arm of St Mellitus, a crystal phial containing some of the Blessed Virgin's milk, a hand of Saint John the Evangelist, fragments of St Thomas à Becket's skull, Jesus's knife, St Mary Magdalene's hair, the head of St Ethelbert, and a jewelled reliquary that preserved the blood of St Paul.

As well as being a museum of relics, St Paul's was a meeting place for lawyers and their clients who could be seen at all times of the day discussing their affairs in the nave. There had once been a law school within the Cathedral precincts, but Henry III, in order to foster the schools he had founded at Oxford, in 1234 had forbidden the teaching of law within the city; and since then the lawyers had settled themselves outside the walls, conveniently halfway between the courts within them and the royal courts at Westminster.

There were at this period two country roads, with bridges across the

Lead badge of St Thomas à Becket found in the Thames, probably given to pilgrims leaving London Bridge for Canterbury; fourteenth or fifteenth century.

Wax impression of the seal of St Paul's; thirteenth century.

Fleet, joining the City to Westminster. The upper of these, now known as Holborn, led out of Newgate; the lower (Fleet Street and the Strand) led out of Ludgate. These roads were joined by two lanes running north and south: Fewter's Lane (Fetter Lane) and the Chancellor's Lane (Chancery Lane); and it was at the top end of the Chancellor's Lane that the lawyers first settled. The premises leased to them formed part of the inn of the then Chancellor, the Bishop of Lincoln, an inn in medieval terminology signifying a rich man's large household. Some years later, in about 1370, the legal Society of Lincoln's Inn was formed.

Other lawyers leased premises forming part of the inn of Lord Gray de Wilton, and so formed the Society of Gray's Inn; while yet others later moved into the nearby buildings once occupied by the Knights Templars whose order had been suppressed by Clement V in 1312, following accusations of blasphemous and homosexual practices to which confessions had been elicited by torture. The Templars' premises were made over to the Knights Hospitallers of St John of Jerusalem, who let all but the ecclesiastical precincts to the members of what soon became known as the Societies of the Middle and Inner Temple.[7]

Thus it was that by the end of the fourteenth century the four Inns of Court had established themselves in a legal quarter which, now greatly expanded, still separates Westminster from the City of London.

At the bottom of Chancery Lane the limit of the City's jurisdiction was

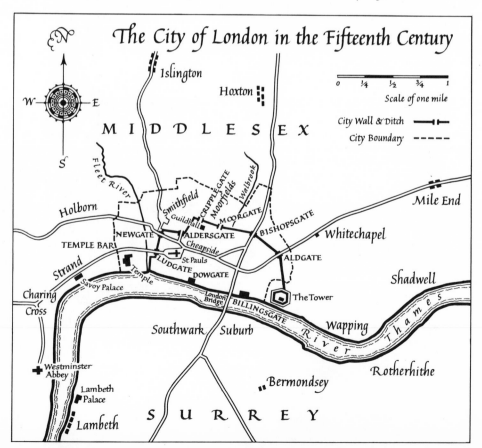

then marked by the posts and chains of Temple Bar stretching across Fleet Street. Around the Bar as around all London's Bars a small community had developed. But it was still an isolated community, as the Temple itself was isolated from Lincoln's Inn, as Holborn was still separated from Clerkenwell by open fields, and Clerkenwell from Shoreditch by the undrained Moor.

Fifteenth-century London, despite its spreading suburbs and expanding satellite villages, was still essentially a walled town of the middle ages in an open countryside. The first of its growing-pains were yet to come.

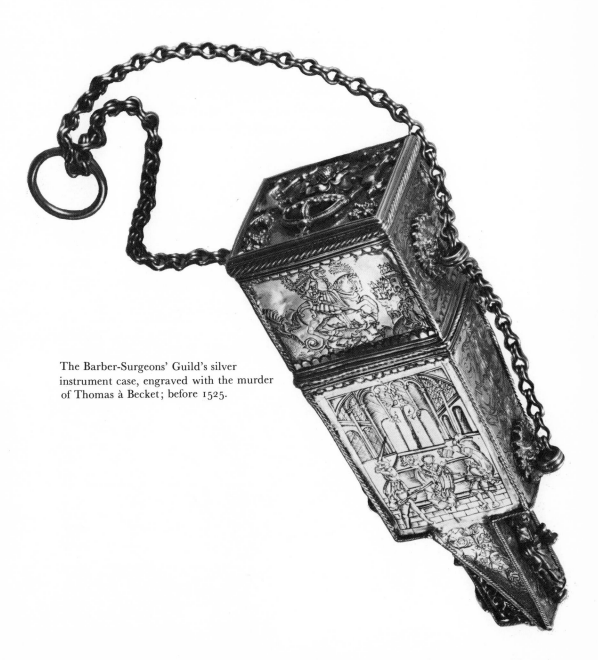

The Barber-Surgeons' Guild's silver instrument case, engraved with the murder of Thomas à Becket; before 1525.

4 *Tudor London 1485–1603*

Most mornings in the early 1530s a small boy carrying a jug could be seen leaving his father's house on Cornhill and walking down past Leadenhall Market to Aldgate. Outside Aldgate he made his way to Goodman's Farm, bought three pints of milk which cost him a halfpenny, and then returned home. His name was John Stow; his father was a tailor in a poor way of business, and he himself was apprenticed to the trade when his schooling was over. But tailoring was not to his taste. An antiquarian at heart, he wanted to be a writer; in particular he wanted to write a detailed history of the city in which he had been born. He began collecting materials for a book which would accurately record its past and minutely describe its present. Many years later his *Survey of London* was published.

The London in which John Stow was born, and the way of life of its inhabitants, had not greatly altered since the birth of his grandfather. There was the same marked contrast between rich and poor, splendour and squalor;

John Stow, tomb in St Andrew Undershaft.

'Tittle-Tattle; Or, the several Branches of Gossipping': detail from a broadside of the end of Elizabeth's reign.

there were the same pageants and processions, water sports and bonfires, quarrels, riots and plagues. Youths still tilted at the quintain on Cornhill, still practised archery to the uproarious accompaniment of drums and flutes in Moorfields and at Islington and Finsbury. Men still drank wine at the Pope's Head Tavern in Cornhill at a penny a pint (the bread was free); they still got drunk at Bartholomew Fair as they had done ever since the beginning of the twelfth century when Henry I had granted the right to hold a fair to the Prior of St Bartholomew's; and they still flocked to Southwark to enjoy the excitements of the brothel and the bull-ring. Pirates were still hanged in chains downstream from the Tower as they had been since Roman times; the heads of traitors were still displayed on London Bridge until blown into the river on a windy night; hundreds of beggars and footpads still roamed the streets keeping a close watch for simple countrymen and unsuspecting foreigners; the markets, bigger than ever, busy and rowdy six days a week, 'unmeasureably pestred with the unimaginable increase and multiplicity of market-folkes', still continued as before.

Cheapside was the largest of the markets, with crowds of country people standing shoulder to shoulder behind their trestle tables, displaying their goods in baskets on the ground or holding them out in their hands. The market was opened – at dawn in winter and six o'clock in the summer – by the ringing of a bell which was tolled again for half an hour in the afternoon to warn the shoppers that it was about to close; and between the first chime in the morning and the last chime in the afternoon all Cheapside was a blare of noise as men and women shouted the virtues and prices of their wares.

Further east was Leadenhall Market, the place to go for the best poultry and milk and – inside the central market building itself – for leather and cloth, kitchen pans and tools. The market here sprawled around Leadenhall in every direction, up towards Bishopsgate, across to Lime Street and down Gracechurch Street to the butcher's market in Eastcheap and the fish market on Fish Street Hill.

There were other markets at the western end of Cornhill where Prince's Street now joins Threadneedle Street; in Newgate Street where Pepys's coach was later to pluck down two pieces of beef into the dirt to the fury of the butchers; and on the quays at Queenhythe, Billingsgate and Bear Key, as well as at Smithfield, Southwark and in King Street, Westminster.

As John Stow grew up he became aware of marked changes in the London scene; and few of them pleased him. He did not approve of the way the gardens of so many big houses were being turned into bowling-alleys and dicing-houses, of the way so many rich men, instead of building almshouses as their forebears would have done, were encroaching upon common lands and open fields to put up houses for themselves 'like Midsummer pageants, with towers, turrets and chimney-tops'. He regretted the increasing interest in artillery, which was leading to a sad decline in the trade of the bowyers, fletchers and bowstring-makers in Grub Street and which was turning the archery grounds in Tassel Close, Bishopsgate Without into a smoky waste where the gunners from the Tower fired their brass cannon into butts of upturned earth. He regretted, too, that young men no longer practised with sword and buckler outside their masters' doors, for 'worsen practices within doors are to be feared'. Above all he complained of the insidious encroachments upon common ground, upon the precincts of churches, and even upon roadways, encroachments which were making the streets so narrow that they were constantly blocked by the ever growing numbers of wagons, drays, tumbrils and barrows. Much of the Walbrook, now 'worse cloyed and choken than ever it was before', had disappeared beneath buildings which stretched across the stream from bank to bank. The medieval ditch, although still deep and two hundred feet wide in places, was elsewhere a clogged and dirty channel – Houndsditch derived its name, Stow said, from the number of dead dogs thrown into it – and between Aldgate and the Tower, where once the water had been deep enough to drown a horse, the moat had been filled up completely and covered with carpenters' yards, kitchen gardens, bowling alleys and tenements. In the markets in Eastcheap and in Farringdon Ward the butchers had edged further and further forward, first building roofs over their stalls, and then replacing their stalls with

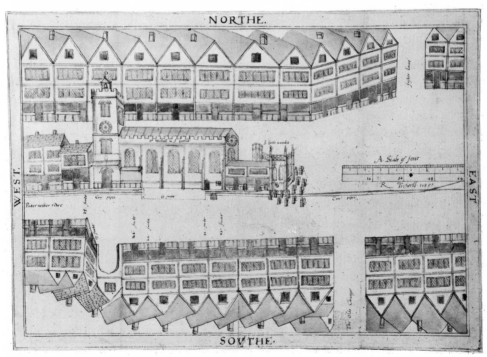

Westcheap at the west end of Cheapside, the principal London market; in the centre the Little Conduit surrounded by water-jugs. Drawing by Ralph Treswell, 1585.

Bowling; *c.* 1600.

bigger sheds, and finally building houses which stretched out over the road-way where their customers had formerly walked. In Knightrider Street the fishmongers had done the same thing.

The trouble was that the City had long since become so overcrowded that it would have to expand or it would suffocate. In the middle of the century the pressure had been relieved for a time by the Dissolution of the Monasteries which had not only opened up for development within the walls great tracts of land confiscated from the abbeys, but had also released the City from the constricting grip of the monastic lands that hemmed it in on every side. Numerous religious houses passed into the hands of rich laymen who converted them into palaces, selling part of the garden for building and either pulling down the chapels or turning them into parish churches. Thus, the premises of the Carthusian monks in West Smithfield, after being used for a time as storehouses for the King's tents, were granted to Sir Edward North, a successful lawyer, who used the medieval masonry to build himself a splendid mansion on the site of the cloister.[1] Thus, too, premises of the Crutched Friars came into the hands of Sir Thomas Wyatt, the poet who had been Keeper of the King's Jewels and a close friend of Anne Boleyn. Wyatt built himself a big house on the site and pulled down the church to make a tennis court. At the same time the Chapel of St Martin-le-grand was acquired by a speculator who demolished it to build a wine tavern; and much of the rambling Carmelite Priory of the Whitefriars was demolished, its materials carted all over London, and its site soon occupied by small tenements, taverns and poor men's shops.

But although the Dissolution provided the City with hundreds of new homes, there were many Londoners who had cause to regret the government's policy. One of these was John Stow's father, who lived in a small house near the Austin Friars in Throgmorton Street. Part of the Austin Friars' property had come into the hands of Thomas Cromwell, the brewer's son who became Henry VIII's secretary, Visitor-General of the Monasteries, and in 1539 Lord Great Chamberlain. Without giving his neighbour, the old tailor, any warning, or offering him any compensation, Cromwell had his house dug out of the ground, placed on rollers and pulled over twenty feet away from his boundary so that he could extend his garden further down Throgmorton Street.

Some of the friars whom Cromwell had displaced crossed over to the Continent to continue their life in foreign monasteries; but many more, released from their vows of celibacy, followed the example of hundreds of monks and nuns from other monasteries in and around London, settled down amidst the ordinary population, married, had children, and aggravated the already desperate problem of overcrowding. The problem was further aggravated by the numbers of foreigners who came year by year to London either to escape the persecution of the Catholic authorities at home or to enjoy the benefits of working in a town which had established itself as one of the leading centres of European trade.

The population of London and the surrounding district was perhaps no more at the beginning of Henry VIII's reign in 1509 than it had been at the end of Henry V's in 1422; but by 1563 it had increased to well over 90,000, twenty years later to about 120,000, and by the end of the century to almost 200,000. Much of this increase was contained in the expanding suburbs to the east of the White Tower, along the roads to Whitechapel and Stepney, Shadwell and Limehouse and down by the waterfront to Wapping. The development here was, for the most part, poor and squalid. John Stow wrote of continual streets and straggling passages, 'with alleys of small tenements or cottages . . . inhabited by sailors' victuallers' which had destroyed the once beautiful 'fayre hedges and long rows of elms'. He condemned the dirty ribbon of brick and wood which stretched all the way from Radcliffe, past Goodman's Fields to the 'filthy cottages' and laystalls round Aldgate, the 'horrid entrance to the City'.

In the next generation Stow's strictures were constantly repeated. All these villages to the east of London were being spoiled by the spread of noxious trades – like the alum works at Wapping – by the erection of ramshackle buildings which harboured not only the poor labourers who walked to work in the City each day, but also the 'beggars and other loose persons, swarming about the City'.

Further downstream were the two royal dockyards at Deptford and Woolwich, created by Henry VIII, on either side of his palace at Greenwich, to relieve the congestion in the medieval harbours of Queenhythe, Dowgate and Billingsgate; and at both Deptford and Woolwich, as at Gravesend, Dartford, Tilbury and Blackwall, small untidy towns were beginning to develop, towns which owed their existence and their future to England's growing trade, her expanding navy and mercantile marine. To the west of these towns, dotted about in the fields on the northern bank, were the damp, evil-smelling, crowded settlements where lived the sailors and shipwrights and all those who made their living from the river and the sea.

Pre-eminent amongst the new generation of London merchants whose capital, vision and adventurous trading companies had done so much to increase the trade of the port, was Thomas Gresham. His family came from Holt in Norfolk (where the school he founded still bears his name) but both his father and his uncle had settled in London, had become prosperous mercers and, each in turn, Lord Mayor. Thomas was sent to Cambridge before learning the mercers' trade; and in 1543, both in the interests of his family business and as agent for the King, he went to Antwerp, at that time the commercial and financial capital of northern Europe. Determined to transfer that centre to London, he offered to build at his own expense in the city a bourse like Antwerp's where merchants from all countries could meet and discuss their business.

His offer was accepted; the Corporation presented him with a site between

Sir Thomas Gresham, attributed to A. Key.

Wolsey in 1526 as Cardinal Archbishop of York.

Cornhill and Threadneedle Street, and in June 1567 after eighty houses had been demolished and four streets destroyed, the first stone was laid. Although there was a strike when Flemish bricklayers were brought over to work on it, the large building was roofed within six months. It was an impressive colonnaded structure, with rows of shops on the upper floor and an open courtyard in the middle. It was officially opened by Queen Elizabeth, who first dined with Thomas Gresham at his home in Bishopsgate, and thereafter it became known as the Royal Exchange.[2] Once the prosperity of Antwerp had declined as a result of the 'Spanish Fury' – in which six thousand of its citizens were killed and eight hundred houses burned by Spanish soldiers – London and its new bourse began to assume the importance of Gresham's dream.

The Royal Exchange which permanently transformed the aspect of Cornhill, was but one of many large sixteenth-century buildings which were changing London's face. Principal among these buildings were the halls and chambers of the new royal palace which now covered acres of ground on the river front between Charing Cross and Westminster Hall.

Here had once stood York Place, the London residence of the Archbishops of York, where Cardinal Wolsey had lived in the 1520s in a style as grandiose as that of the royal Court itself. Here the Cardinal had enjoyed the services of five hundred liveried attendants, including chaplains, clerks, heralds, physicians, apothecaries, minstrels, armourers, surveyors, secretaries, choristers, carvers, waiters and grooms, as well as a High Chamberlain, a Vice-Chamberlain, eighteen gentlemen ushers and forty gentlemen cup-bearers. The two huge kitchens employed a staff of over sixty men, not to mention the boy scullions and turnspits.

When he left to confer with the King at Greenwich, Wolsey would walk down the steps to his barge preceded by attendants carrying two silver crosses and two silver pillars, by the great seal of England and his cardinal's hat borne by a 'nobleman or some worthy gentleman, right solemnly, bareheaded'. The oarsmen would bring the barge into the bank before shooting under London Bridge because the huge stone starlings built round the bases of the piers forced the water into narrow and dangerously fast flowing channels. At Old Swan Stairs, therefore, the Cardinal alighted. He walked along Thames Street – magnificently clothed in his robes of crimson, sable-tipped satin, holding to his nose a scooped-out orange containing a sponge soaked in scented vinegar – and at Billingsgate he found the barge awaiting him at the foot of the steps.

When Wolsey fell from power, after failing to arrange a speedy divorce for Henry VIII from Catharine of Aragon, York Place, although it belonged to the See of York and not personally to the Cardinal, was taken over, like Hampton Court, by the King. Magnificent as it already was, Henry immediately set about making it finer. He bought additional land from the Abbot of Westminster and other neighbours, and extended the grounds behind the Palace to take in acre upon acre of land for his new gardens. He built a new flight of steps to the river, and since the various buildings of the Palace were split in two by the road from London to Westminster he built two splendid bridges across the roadway. The beauties of Whitehall Palace, as it now came to be called, were further enhanced by three lofty galleries – the Privy Gallery, which had been removed from Wolsey's mansion at Esher, the Stone Gallery, where the guests at royal banquets could look down upon the river, and the Long Gallery with a ceiling painted by Holbein. In the grounds below were four tennis courts, a bowling green, a cockpit and a tilt yard. Away to the west were the red brick walls of another of the thirteen palaces which the King owned within a day's ride of his capital.

This was St James's Palace, once a hospital for lepers, on whose site Henry had built himself a country house convenient for Westminster, yet without the discomfort of the ancient riverside palace there which was by now falling into decay. Westminster had still been the most important of the royal palaces during the time of his father; but there had been a fire there in 1512, and although the damage was afterwards made good, Henry had by then found his other palaces, at Eltham, Richmond, Windsor, Greenwich and Hampton Court, as well as Whitehall, more to his taste. In comparison with

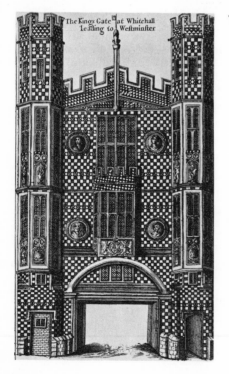

The Holbein Gate, Whitehall Palace.

Mayer, of alderman die
Mayer gheweest is.

Aldermā

Een
Lineu
ziet
folio

these St James's Palace was at first scarcely more than a hunting lodge surrounded by open fields and parkland, and by the gardens and orchards of Whitehall.[3]

Yet even at St James's it was clear to foreign visitors that the King lived in as splendid a way as any sovereign in Europe. His father had spent no more money than the traditional necessity for occasional displays of lavish entertainment and ostentation demanded; and by cutting Court expenses to a minimum had been able to leave his son a fortune of well over a million pounds.

For Henry VIII, with his gargantuan appetite for food, drink, women and all the pleasures of life, economy was neither possible nor necessary. At Court, where the number of attendants grew each year, there were constant dances, displays, tournaments, games, bull-baitings and banquets; vast and countless meals were daily consumed; extraordinary entertainments were provided by jesters, dwarfs, dancers and minstrels for the benefit of foreign ambassadors and of the suites of visiting noblemen and magnates. At all times the King took, and was expected to take, the centre of the stage.

Denied seclusion by the responsibilities of his rank, he was scarcely ever alone even in his Withdrawing or Privy Chambers; and in the Presence Chamber he was the principal if sometimes passive actor in a ritual that had long since taken over the qualities of a stylised drama. He was closely watched by curious spectators as he sat waiting to be served with his meal, as the board was brought in ceremonially and all food tasted before it passed the royal lips. To assay the salt, for example, the Carver uncovered the cellar, dipped a piece of bread inside, made a 'florishe' over it, and gave it to the Panter to eat. All the dishes had to be treated in the same way after they had been brought into the sound of trumpets, and always with an elaborate flourish of the hand.

The 'choreographic ceremonial of dressing and undressing his Majesty, observed at St James's as at Whitehall, was no less precise. Gentlemen and Grooms of the Bedchamber placed in position a chair upon which the King could sit and a cushion upon which he could rest his feet; they passed his garments from hand to hand, deferentially helping him into each according to their various duties; they placed a handkerchief over his shoulders before brushing his hair. At night time a similar and no less strict ritual was observed by attendants who helped him out of his clothes and solemnly bore away each discarded piece, who laid out a bowl of water for washing and a cloth for cleaning the teeth, put on the King's night cap, escorted him to his great bed – which had been made with the required motions and gestures by three Yeomen of the Chamber – and closed its curtains with a bow.

There were differences, of course, between the rules of Court procedure and their observance; and it seems from statutes issued in 1526 for the better

8. London Bridge with the Tower and Southwark Cathedral by Richard Garth, 1575; in the foreground a beacon

running of the royal palaces that servants had been known to wipe their greasy hands on the tapestries in the King's chamber and to put down dirty dishes on his bed after the Yeomen had made it; that 'vagabonds and mighty beggars', 'vile and unmeet persons', were often to be found loitering about the gates and courtyards in the hope of getting a meal of salmon tails or pigs' heads or of stealing a sack of bread chippings; that scullions had to be warned not to go about the royal kitchens 'naked or in garments of such vileness as they do now'; that the Knight Harbinger had been lax in keeping whores and lewd women out of the Household.

Maintaining order and discipline at Whitehall Palace was peculiarly difficult, for the rambling group of buildings was more like a village than a palace, a village whose inhabitants were all either in the King's service or had a claim upon his hospitality. The servants were granted not only lodgings but fuel, candles and a stipulated allowance of food – from the maximum of sixteen dishes at dinner enjoyed by the Lord Chamberlain to the relatively modest, but still substantial, four dishes allowed to the porters at the gates. A visiting duke had a right to expect to be provided with nine beds and stabling for twenty-four horses during his stay at Court; the chaplain in a nobleman's suite could demand two beds and stabling for three horses.

By the early 1530s so numerous had the Palace's staff and guests become that the buildings had once more to be extended by the addition of a number of further 'distinct, beautiful, costly and pleasant lodgings'.

Vast as Whitehall Palace was, though, by the time of Henry VIII's death, there were several palaces to the east of it which were almost as imposing.

Between the new Privy Stairs at Whitehall Palace and the mouth of the Fleet River, there was, in fact, by the beginning of the seventeenth century an almost continuous line of rich men's palaces for well over a mile. Adjoining Whitehall was Northumberland House, the immense town house of the Percys, Dukes of Northumberland, whose grounds sprawled to Charing Cross. Further downstream were the medieval walls of the Palace of the Savoy, and the huge Renaissance mansion built between 1547 and 1550 from monastic ruins by the Lord Protector Somerset in the rein of his nephew Edward VI. This mansion was later to become the home of Edward's sister, the Princess Elizabeth, of Anne, the Danish Queen of James I, and of the Queens of Charles I and Charles II. East of Somerset House were the palaces of the Earls of Arundel and Essex; then, before the banks of the Fleet were reached, appeared the rambling halls and courts of the Temple; and finally the dark red walls of Bridewell, once a Norman fortified palace, later rebuilt in 1523 by Henry VIII as 'a stately and beautiful house' for the accommodation of the Emperor Charles V and his suite, but since the reign of Henry's son a prison for vagabonds and troublesome whores.[4]

The courtyard of Arundel House: etching by W. Hollar, 1646.

Behind these riverside palaces, on the other side of the Strand, were the houses of other great men: Craven House, at the bottom of Drury Lane, home of the Craven family, whose immense fortune had been founded by Sir William Craven, merchant tailor and Lord Mayor of London; Exeter House, opposite the Savoy, the palace of Lord Burghley; and the extremely valuable Convent Garden estate, once the property of the Abbey of Westminster, now in the hands of the Russell family, headed by the Earls of Bedford.[5]

On the southern bank of the river, west of Southwark, there had been little development since the fifteenth century; and from his bedchamber window at Lambeth the Archbishop of Canterbury could look out upon an open countryside of meadows, marsh, woodland and market gardens. In Southwark itself, however, the face of Bankside had been transformed by the strange shapes of that new phenomenon, the London theatre.

The first theatre in London, known simply as The Theatre, was opened by the actor James Burbage in 1577 in Shoreditch. But although a second theatre, the Curtain, was built nearby a few months later, and although Burbage and his more famous son, Thomas, helped to start the Blackfriars in the refectory of the old Dominican friary, these theatres were under constant attack from the City authorities who condemned them as hotbeds of vice and plague, as rendezvous for the idle and licentious, for evil men excited by boys dressed up as women, and for all those who would rather answer the call of the trumpet to a play than the tolling of the bell to a sermon.

45

Southwark offered the players the opportunity to escape from the restrictions threatened by the City, yet was soon reached by boat or bridge. At the time of the Dissolution of the Monasteries, that part of Southwark which had formerly been owned by the monastery of Bermondsey and the priory of St Mary Overy passed into the hands of the King. In 1550 it was sold to the City for about £1,000. Excluded from the sale, however, were two areas which remained outside the City's jurisdiction. One was around the Clink prison, the other was known as Paris Garden; and it was in these two areas that the new theatres of Elizabethan London developed, free from City regulations and City censorship. The Rose, which first staged the plays of Marlowe and provided a setting for the flamboyant genius of Edward Alleyn, was built in 1587. It was followed by the Swan in 1596, by the Globe (in which Shakespeare owned a one-tenth share) in 1599, and by the Hope in 1613.

To these and other theatres Londoners were summoned in the afternoon by the loud blasts of trumpets and the waving of flags. Money for the seats was collected inside the door and placed in a box which was then locked and put in a little office – the box office. Then to shouts of encouragement from the noisy spectators, sitting on tiered seats all round the stage or on stools actually upon it, the play began. Interrupted by cries of indignation, rebuttal, abuse or satisfaction, the actors worked their way through to the end of the act, when dancers, acrobats and jugglers would take over the stage, men and women selling pies and pamphlets, herbal cures and fruit would struggle with their trays and baskets through the narrow aisles, apprentices would

The Globe Theatre: detail from Visscher's view of London, 1616.

make assignations with complaisant girls, and journeymen fill the air with clouds of tobacco smoke, not infrequently setting the wooden seats alight and sending the audience scampering for the doors. The Globe was burned out the year the Hope was opened, but the only casualty was a man whose breeches were set alight and he soon put out the fire with a bottle of ale.

Near the theatres were the bear gardens, the bull-baiting rings and the cockpits which attracted the rich and poor, the noble and vulgar, just as they had in the Middle Ages. Audiences, having enjoyed a performance of *Othello* or *Edward II* one night, might go the next to watch a bear being baited by mastiffs in Paris Garden or a cock flying at his opponent with spurs and covering the sand of the pit with blood and feathers, dogs being tossed high into the air by maddened bulls and being caught on sticks so that their fall was broken and they could fight again another day, or even men slashing at each other with swords and slicing off ears and fingers to the roared approval of the crowds in the galleries.

The northern suburbs were far quieter and less populous than Southwark. Moorfields, soon to be drained and turned into a public park, was still largely a marsh, crossed by embankments and dotted with ponds. Clerkenwell, Smithfield and Spitalfields, once constricted by the sprawling monastic lands, were all growing now – due in part to the arrival of so many Huguenot refugees – and there were rows of houses on both sides of the road at Hoxton. But large-scale building in the north was inhibited by problems which were less apparent on the other sides of London. The heavy clay upon which Holloway, Camden Town, Regent's Park, St John's Wood, and Notting Hill have since been built, made it impossible for householders to enjoy any cheap and satisfactory system of drainage. Also, and more decisively, there were what seemed insuperable problems of water supply: elsewhere in London rainwater falling on to a gravelly subsoil was retained above the impervious underlying clay and could be raised through a shallow well; but where the clay came to the surface no rainwater could be stored and no wells sunk. These geological peculiarities of the northern London district insured that the direction and intensity of its development had to wait upon the provision of an improved water supply.

For centuries most of London's water had been drawn from the Thames, carted up to the streets in water wagons, and sold from house to house in buckets by the water carriers. This far from pure supply from the river had been augmented in the past by the numerous wells and pools in and around the city – though many of these, like Holywell, 'much decayed and marred with filthyness', were now contaminated – and, since the early thirteenth century, by water piped from the streams and springs to the north.

A banqueting house had been built at the beginning of the pipe line which carried the water from the Tyburn springs down to the City, and here the mayor and aldermen dined each year after inspecting the conduit. From the banqueting house, on the site of the present Stratford Place, Oxford Street, the conduit ran down through Conduit Street, along the north of the Strand and Fleet Street, across Fleet Bridge to two leaden cisterns in Cheapside. In later years other conduits and cisterns were put into use, bringing water from the springs of Hampstead and Highgate and from the Muswell at Muswell Hill, while reservoirs were constructed on the Fleet. Also, leases were granted for pumping up water from the Thames to tanks in Leadenhall and elsewhere. In 1581 a Dutchman was given a 500-years' lease of the first arch of London Bridge where he erected a huge water wheel which, driven by the tide, pumped water to numerous houses between Thames Street and Eastcheap; and in 1593 an Englishman, Bevis Bulmer, who was lent £1,000 by the City and allowed to use part of Leadenhall to assemble his engine, erected a horse-driven pump just west of Queenhythe at Broken Wharf.

But neither of these machines was capable of pumping the water very far from the river bank; and householders who were granted the right to let in quills to the main pipes for their own private supply were often extremely wasteful. The household at Essex House, for instance, used almost to empty the conduits by using hundreds of gallons of piped water in the laundry and for swilling out the stables. Furthermore, although new cisterns were constantly appearing in various parts of the City, there were never enough for the crowds of people who needed to use them; and so rough and provocative were some of the water carriers, who elbowed and pushed their way through to fill their buckets, that an order had to be issued forbidding anyone to approach a cistern armed with a club.

The City authorities were well aware of the need for a fresh and continuous supply of water to meet the growing needs of the population, particularly in the northern suburbs where wells and water-carriers were rare; but they were reluctant to face the problem of its expense. So it was left to a private individual to put forward proposals to solve their dilemma for them.

At the end of the sixteenth century Edmund Colthurst of Bath had suggested that he should be allowed to tap certain springs in Hertfordshire and Middlesex and so divert their waters into a new river which he would dig across country to a reservoir to the north of London. The suggestion was adopted. Colthurst, though, was not a rich man, and by 1605 he had managed to bring his river forward no more than three miles. He asked the Lord Mayor and Aldermen to help him with the cost; but nothing was done until, four years later, a wealthy entrepeneur named Hugh Myddleton took the scheme over as the City's deputy.

Myddleton, like so many London merchants of his and his father's time, was a younger son of a country gentleman. Born about 1560 he followed one of his eight brothers to London from North Wales and was apprenticed to a goldsmith. Within a few years, a successful goldsmith in his own right, he had made both a name and a fortune for himself, and the City were delighted to have found so talented and solid a businessman to act for them in the New River venture.

Myddleton, however, was soon as deep in difficulties as Colthurst had been. The fundamental problem was not one of money: 130 labourers were being regularly paid for digging the canal. But the work was forced to a halt by the objections of the landowners through whose property the excavations had to pass. Generous compensation was offered them, yet they demanded more; bridges were guaranteed where the canal cut across established paths, yet they continued to insist that Myddleton was destroying public rights of way. The New River, they protested, would ruin their pasture, turning fields into quagmires; their cornfields would be trampled down by workmen and workmen's carts; their servants, their tenants and their cattle would all be drowned in a river which was being dug for the private profit of a Welsh interloper. When King James, riding in Theobald's Park, was thrown from his horse and fell head first into the frozen river, it seemed to Myddleton's opponents an awful forecast of worse horrors to come.

But James I was on Myddleton's side. He had become interested in the river as he watched its progress through the Park, and he recognised its importance to those 'pore people [who were] enforced to use foule and unwholesome water which breedeth great infections'. So when Myddleton,

Sir Hugh Myddleton: engraving after Cornelius Johnson.

abandoned by the merchant bankers who had become alarmed by the rising cost of the scheme, offered the King a half share in the future profits in it if he would contribute half the expense, James readily agreed. Myddleton, for his part, was thankful to get the King directly concerned in the scheme, for he believed that once the New River was known to be a royal venture the objections of the landowners would be more easily overcome.

In this he was quite right. By March 1613 the New River had passed Hornsey, Newington and Holloway; the following month Myddleton's labourers were digging in Clerkenwell where the huge reservoir was eventually built thirty-eight miles from the river's source.

From this reservoir, the New River Head, the water flowed in hollowed out elm trunks, strengthened at the joints with iron collars and pierced in places by brass ferrules into which the branch pipes were screwed. These branch pipes took the water to tanks and barrels in the houses of those prepared to pay the quarterly rent which ranged between 5s. and 6s. 8d. Although this rent was modest enough, few people could be found to take advantage of the new supply at first. There was a strong prejudice against piped water which continued into the early nineteenth century, when water-carriers still went from house to house calling out, 'Fresh and fair river water! None of your pipe sludge!' Often, indeed, in the early days of the New River, its water, while being far from sludge, was not as pure as it should have been. Vandalism was common: the river's banks were frequently cut and its bridges pulled down, dead dogs and cats and rubbish were thrown into the water, washerwomen used it for their laundry, builders

The Waterhouse at the New River Head: etching by W. Hollar, 1665.

let sewers into it, thieves stole the taps; and the water-carriers spread the rumour – widely believed – that a wise man had warned that all this tapping and piping of water would soon flood all London and everyone would be drowned. Furthermore, householders discovered that although the turn-cocks were supposed to ensure that all subscribers were supplied with water on at least two days a week, it was often necessary to bribe them to open the valves even to fill up the cisterns.

Gradually the worst of the problems were overcome; month by month more and more Londoners began to recognise the convenience and quality of piped water; and the numbers of subscribers to the New River Company increased to such an extent that the supply from the original Hertfordshire springs, at its height capable of yielding four million gallons of water a day, had to be supplemented by a further supply from the River Lea.

But although Hugh Myddleton's money and determination had at last ensured a water supply which made possible a large-scale development of London's northern suburbs, both the City and the Government were now more than ever anxious that no such development should occur, either in the north or indeed anywhere else.

It was feared not only that all the open spaces around the City would soon disappear but also that an increase in population in the areas outside the control of the City authorities could not but increase the dangers of plague and riot, beggary and crime, even of famine and rebellion. Far too many strangers, both from other towns in England and from abroad, were coming to settle in London's suburbs; in the thirteen years between 1567 and 1580, the foreign population had doubled – from about 20,000 to 40,000 in a total population of about 120,000 – and many of the newcomers were living in the most squalid conditions. Pestilence was rife in the sea ports, and would be rife in London, too, spread by those who frequented brothels and 'unchaste plays', unless development were checked. So in the summer of 1580, a proclamation was issued prohibiting, within three miles of any London gate, the building of any new house where no former house was known to have been within living memory. From that date onwards for over a hundred years similar proclamations and orders were repeatedly issued, prohibiting new buildings or the division of existing ones, laying down rules as to the materials to be used in renovations or extensions, defining punishments for householders and builders who transgressed the law, providing for the pulling down of houses put up without licence.

In 1593 an Act of Parliament confirmed the proclamation of 1580; in 1602 a further proclamation was issued after the Council had many times reiterated their concern at transgressions of the former one; the next year a severe outbreak of plague followed the Queen's death, killing thirty thousand people in London alone, and one of James I's first acts was to condemn the overcrowding which had caused the outbreak. But it was impossible for the authorities to prevent overcrowding; and the policy of prohibiting new building in the hope of keeping down the population served only to cram the poor into houses that already existed. Nor, despite their constant efforts, were the authorities successful in preventing new buildings being erected.

No attempt was made to interfere with the building of new stabling and outhouses at St James's or with the work on the royal mews at Charing Cross; and when Salisbury House was being altered in 1608 no objection was officially raised to the carting to London of sixty or seventy tons of stone from one of Canterbury's partly ruined gates – although Lord Salisbury was advised to take the stone from the inside of the gate where its disappearance would not be so easily noticed, for 'the townsmen keep so much ado'. Yet the repeated attempts which *were* made to prevent building by the less privileged were quite unsuccessful.

In 1607, after once again condemning the 'filling and pestering of houses with Inmates and several dwellers (and those of the worst sort) almost in every severall roome', James I issued a new proclamation, which repeated many of the previous prohibitions, increased the punishments which could be inflicted, decreed that houses built in contravention of the law could be pulled down as late as seven years after their completion, and disallowed any additions covering more than a third of the area of the original site. Special licences might be granted for the building of new houses in particular circumstances, but these houses must all be of brick or stone and in a uniform style approved by the Aldermen.

This proclamation, like its predecessors, seems to have been largely ignored; and in 1615 the King was obliged to appoint a special body to deal with its infringements. He wrote at this time of his ambition to be able to say, like the Roman Emperor who found a city of brick and left it of marble, 'we had found our Citie and suburbs of London of stickes, and left them of bricke'. But so long as his repressive policy remained in force his ambition was unlikely to be achieved. Knowing that they might, if they were lucky, escape with a fine, builders continued to put up unauthorised houses; yet knowing, too, that if they were not lucky, their buildings might be pulled down, they took care to use the cheapest materials and to expend as little money as possible. Some builders went so far as to erect screens to hide their illicit buildings from the authorities: one man in Cursitor's Alley, Chancery Lane, built high walls round a field where he claimed to be keeping tame rabbits, but where, in fact, he had put up a row of squalid tenements; many other builders selected the narrowest, darkest, most out of the way alleyways and courts to put together any sort of jerry-built shelter which could command a rent. Also, since additions to existing buildings were allowed, it became common practice to patch up a derelict house, add the permitted extension and dig out beneath it a large cellar to let as a shop, a gaming room, a 'tippling house', or, even as lodgings to some improvident family.

Although proceedings were taken against the 'poorer and meaner sorte of offenders', the richer builder usually managed to escape, for it was rarely that action was taken against people of 'better qualitie and worth'. In any event few substantial houses which had been built without a licence were ever pulled down, it usually being possible to satisfy the authorities by paying compensation instead. By 1637 the owners of 1,360 houses in the London area, all of them built outside the walled City contrary to the law, had compounded for their offence in this way. Most of them, and most of those which were to follow within the next thirty years, were to be found in the west and north in an area stretching from Westminster through St Martin's-in-the-Fields to Bloomsbury, Holborn, and Clerkenwell. For it was here that the people of 'better qualitie' now chose to live.

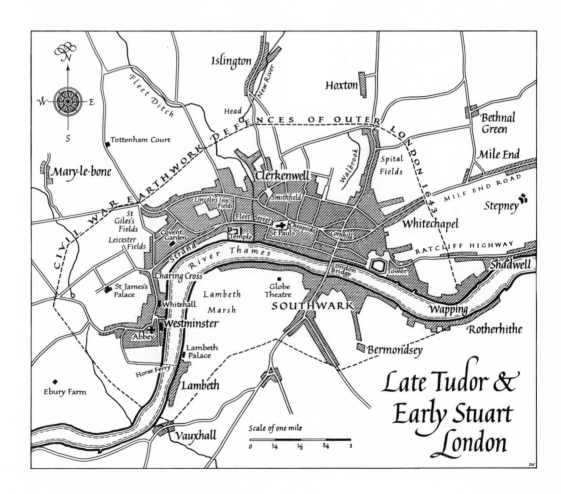

5   *Noble Speculators 1603–1665*

Despite the gradual westward migration of the richer households, Westminster itself was not much favoured except by those who worked at Court or in one or other of the Government's offices. It was true that there were no rows of squalid hovels immediately adjoining the royal palaces, for the King's proclamations against such development were always strictly enforced there; but elsewhere in Westminster there were slums as squalid as any in London. The long absences of the peregrinating Court reduced those who made an uncertain living from its presence to poverty and crime; while the temptations offered by rich courtiers and unwary foreigners as well as the security afforded by the Sanctuary, drew hundreds of dangerous criminals to the narrow streets around the Abbey: Thieving Lane derived its name from the character of its inhabitants long before its prison was built to incarcerate those unlucky ones who were caught. Also, the marshy ground upon which much of Westminster was built made its residents uncommonly susceptible to the plague.

Further north the ground was more open and healthy, and so here it was, outside the City gates and away from the clutter of Westminster, yet within easy reach of both, that the best houses were built. They were built in St Martin's Lane behind the Church; in Long Acre and Great Queen Street (named after James I's Queen, Anne); in Lincoln's Inn Fields and on the Earl of Bedford's estate in Convent (now Covent) Garden.

The St Martin's Lane development was carried out by the Earl of Salisbury, – at the time Lord Treasurer – both to the annoyance of King James and the owners of nearby cottages on the estate. For Salisbury had compelled his tenants to surrender their rights to hang out washing and to graze their cattle on five acres of land on the west side of St Martin's Lane, and then had built a row of houses in Swan Close. To do so he had filled in a draining ditch which resulted in cascades of water flowing unchecked into the Palace of Whitehall. The King retaliated by having a sewer built to drain this water into the Thames and by having the cost of it distributed amongst the owners of property along its route, which to all intents and purposes meant Lord Salisbury.

'The English Gentleman and English Gentlewoman': engraved titlepage, 1641.

In 1630 Salisbury's neighbour, the Earl of Leicester, wanting to make some money too, decided to develop part of his estate in Leicester Fields in the same way as Salisbury had done in St Martin's Lane. But the country people living in the area, warned by what had become of the open lands on the Salisbury estate, protested that Leicester Fields should not be taken from them. The Privy Council thereupon appointed a body of commissioners who decided that while the Earl of Leicester could build a house along one side of the fields, the fields themselves must be kept open, planted with trees and provided with walks. So the history of Leicester Square began.

The proposed development of Lincoln's Inn Fields also met with strong opposition from the local residents, the lawyers, who angrily protested when, in 1638, William Newton, a builder from Bedfordshire, was granted a licence to build thirty-two substantial houses in a field behind the White Hart Inn on the corner of Drury Lane and High Holborn. The Society of Lincoln's Inn insisted that this and another two fields, 'commonly called Lincolnes Inn Fields [ought to be] converted into walkes after the same manner as Morefieldes' which had by then been made into a public park. But the representations of the lawyers were ignored, and by 1641, Newton's houses were finished. A few years later houses had appeared in the other two fields, and Lincoln's Inn was enclosed on three sides by tall brick houses.[1]

The most attractive and ambitious of all these early seventeenth-century developments was the transformation of the Earl of Bedford's estate in Covent Garden.

Francis Russell, who had succeeded his cousin as the fourth Earl in 1627, was a gifted man of independent spirit, outspoken yet shrewd, who was much disliked at Court. Anxious to make money as a building speculator, as the Earl of Salisbury and others had done, and encouraged by the £500 a year his estate was already bringing in from tenants along the Strand and Long Acre, he had hoped to extend his developments there but had been prevented.

A fee of £2,000 paid in 1631, however, secured him a licence for the building in Covent Garden of as many houses and buildings 'fitt for the habitacions of *Gentlemen* and men of ability' as he liked. The long-standing prohibition against building except on old foundations had been confirmed by a Proclamation issued six years before; but this Proclamation had provided for the appointment of four commissioners, including the King's Surveyor of Works, who were clearly intended to approve any schemes which would improve the lay-out of areas where development had already taken place, which would add to the 'uniformitie and Decency' of the neighbourhood, and for which substantial fees could be obtained for licences.

The King's Surveyor at this time happened with good fortune to be an architect of genius, Inigo Jones.

Inigo Jones: engraving after Van Dyck.

Francis Russell, fourth Earl of Bedford: engraving after Van Dyck.

Jones was the son of a Smithfiéld clothworker. Born in 1573, he had been apprenticed to a joiner in St Paul's Churchyard, but showing exceptional talents as an artist and designer he had gone to Italy to study the works of the great masters of design. He came home to England with a deep admiration for the style associated with the name of the brilliant Paduan architect, Palladio, and with an established reputation as a designer of scenery and costumes for the court entertainments known as masques which he had seen so skilfully performed at the Medici court in Florence.

He entered the service of the English court on his return home, and was soon not only providing the exotic settings for such entertainments as Ben Jonson's *Masque of Beauty* (plate 11), but also designing buildings in various parts of London.

These buildings reveal how strongly the classical lines of Palladio had inspired his own genius. Few of them now remain, but his graceful drawings for such structures as the New Exchange in the Strand, a counterpart to Gresham's Royal Exchange in Cornhill, indicate the style of classical façade which was soon to dominate the London scene, replacing the irregularities and informalities of Tudor and Jacobean vernacular. Later designs of his which were put into execution, and whose realisation can still be appreciated today, were the Queen's House, built for James I's Queen in the grounds

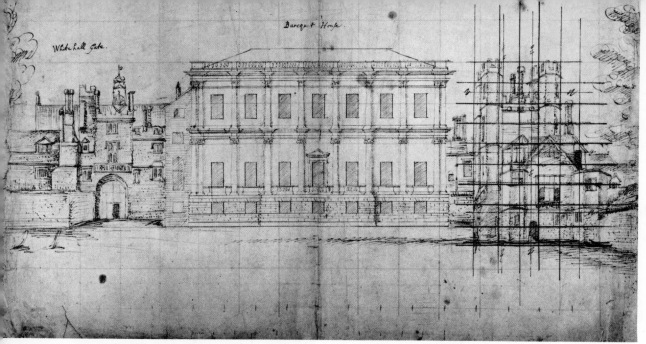

A drawing for a masque scene by Inigo Jones, showing his own Banqueting House and Whitehall Gate; executed for Ben Jonson's *Time Vindicated*, performed in the Banqueting House 19 January 1623.

of the Palace at Greenwich,[2] the Queen's Chapel at St James's,[3] originally intended for the Spanish princess whom Prince Charles had hoped to marry in Spain in 1623, and the Banqueting House in Whitehall,[4] an imposing if small-scale Italianate *palazzo* which it was hoped would one day serve as a model for a whole new range of buildings in place of the Tudor palace (plate 9).

Indeed, the contrast between Inigo Jones's new buildings and their Jacobean neighbours was startling; and to many a Londoner the new style, blossoming under the patronage of the Court, was thoroughly distasteful. The average citizen far preferred the old familiar gables and mullions, brackets, barge-boards and idiosyncratic masonry and carpentry to all these foreign ideas of construction which seemed to him 'like Bug-beares or Gorgon heads'.

The new square which Inigo Jones designed for the Earl of Bedford seemed particularly strange (plate 10). The idea of a church and a square of terraced houses looking inwards on to a large open courtyard was nothing unusual to those who had travelled abroad; but to the Londoner who had never left England it appeared almost shocking. Even John Evelyn, who had visited Leghorn in 1644 and recognised that the church and the 'very fair and commodious piazza' there had given 'the first hint to the building of the church and piazza in Covent Garden with us', thought that the London version was a very inferior copy.

The Covent Garden church, the first new church to be built in London

9. Detail of Rubens's ceiling for the Banqueting House, 1634.
10. (*overleaf*) Covent Garden in the 1740s, by Samuel Scott.

since the Reformation, was begun in 1631. The Earl considered it merely as a focal point of his development, a necessary appendage to the community of houses he intended to create. He did not want to spend much money on it, and, being a low churchman, he wanted nothing elaborate. 'In short,' as he told Inigo Jones, 'I would not have it much better than a barn.' 'Well, then,' replied Jones, 'you shall have the handsomest barn in England.'

And this, at a cost of nearly £5,000, is what he was given. A Tuscan pastiche, at once plain and majestic, it was placed on the western side of the square, its three doors (two of them since moved) looking out through the smooth, tall columns which supported the huge eaves of the roof, towards a sundial, surrounded by newly planted trees and painted benches, in the middle of the piazza.[5] Facing it on the east side of the square, and extending from it on the north, were fine terraces of stuccoed houses whose front doors opened onto vaulted arcades in the manner of the Italian architect Sebastian Serlio and whose backs overlooked pleasant gardens, coach houses and stabling.[6] There were no houses on the south side of the square which was bounded by the garden wall of Bedford House.

Once the square itself had been established, streets of new but rather less expensive houses were built around it, James Street leading north to Long Acre, Russell Street in the east linking Covent Garden to Bow Street, King Street and Henrietta Street extending back on each side of the church to Bedford Street which led down into the Strand. Like the houses in Great Queen Street and Lincoln's Inn Fields, with their regular fresh red brick or stuccoed fronts, their well-defined cornices, and pilaster orders rising from first-floor level to roof, the houses here bore the hallmark of Inigo Jones's taste. They were not all individually designed by him, but as the King's Surveyor he had an overriding responsibility for their outward appearance. He probably gave the craftsmen a drawing and a few general instructions, leaving it to them and to the controlling contractor to provide the detailed finish.

When building in Covent Garden had been completed, a licence was obtained by the Earl of Bedford for the setting up of a regular fruit and vegetable market for the convenience of the inhabitants of this extensive new neighbourhood. The market was started along the Earl's garden wall where for generations gardeners had been selling fruit and vegetables which their families could not eat themselves.

As it grew and prospered the Market overwhelmed the earlier character of the district, finally persuading all those who could afford to do so to move further out into the country west of Whitehall or into Bloomsbury.

As the relations between the Puritan merchants of the City and the Court deteriorated during the years that led up to the Civil War, this gradual

11. Inigo Jones's design for the costume of a torchbearer in Ben Jonson's *Masque of Blackness* performed on 6 January 1605.

The cold, not cruelty makes her weare
In Winter, furrs and Wild beasts haire

Winter

For a smoother skinn at night,
Embraceth her with more delight.

'Winter': etching by W. Hollar, 1643, of a lady in winter clothes walking in smoky Cornhill.

movement of the rich and fashionable out of London and its northern and eastern suburbs, and into the newly developed estates farther away to the west, was accelerated.

In Elizabeth's time many noblemen and courtiers still lived in the City: the Earl of Essex and Sir Francis Walsingham both had houses not far from the Lord Mayor's mansion in Mincheon Lane; Drake had a house in Thames Street; Lord Bryndon had one in Farringdon Without; the Earl of Cumberland lived for long periods in Bishopsgate; the Earl of Kent in Cripplegate. But now there were few such men and their households left in the City. The exodus had been hastened by the industries which were now proliferating in the City and in the inner suburbs to the north and east of it, more particularly along the waterfront. In these areas the increasing use of coal in industry even then darkened and poisoned the London air with smoke and soot.

At the beginning of the seventeenth century there were several wealthy families still living in Whitechapel and Shadwell, but fifty years later most of them had left. Also in 1620 Clerkenwell had been a fashionable country village, despite the smell of the brewery and the noise of the forge in St John Street which, so the Earl of Exeter complained, made his dining-room uninhabitable. Aristocrats and rich City magnates, who travelled by coach to their counting-houses each day, both lived there in pleasant harmony. As the century progressed, however, and the village grew, as the spaces between the houses on the way into London gradually became filled into an almost continuous line over which the smoke hung heavily, Clerkenwell's aristocratic residents, including at one time the Earls of Essex, Carlisle and Ailesbury, abandoned its now displeasing atmosphere for more attractive places to the west.

Also, there was a growing feeling amongst the well-born that it was somehow degrading to live too close to tradesmen, however rich – an impossible concept in earlier times before the religious, constitutional and economic disputes of the middle years of the seventeenth century had established a firm barrier between the Puritan merchant and the landed proprietor, between the City Fathers and the Court. This new form of snobbery was demonstrated when the Marquess of Winchester sold the large house on the site of the monastery of Austin Friars which had been granted to his family at the time of the Dissolution of the Monasteries. Included in the sale was a dower house occupied by the Countess of Shrewsbury who received a letter in which her neighbour expressed his regret that, now the Winchester house had been acquired by 'one Swinnerton merchant', she presumably would be moving herself. For he could not conceive that her ladyship would 'willingly become a tenant to such a fellow'.

The withdrawal to the west of London of such households as the Marquess of Winchester's and Lady Shrewsbury's was accelerated by the approach of the Civil War when the City was to become a parliamentary stronghold defended by twenty-four forts and eighteen miles of linked trenches.

The War brought nearly all building in the City and suburbs to a halt; men did not care to risk their money at a time of such uncertainty, when so many houses lay empty, deserted by the families of those who had gone away to fight. Shopkeepers who had made their living from the custom of noble families in the Strand and around Whitehall were ruined; while in Whitehall Palace itself weeds grew in the Courts. It was 'a Palace without a Presence', according to a pamphleteer of 1642. 'You may walk into the Hall, for surely there are no strong smells out of the kitchens to delight your nostrils withal.' In Charles I's time cooks in these kitchens prepared in a year over three thousand carcasses of beef, seven thousand sheep, nearly seven thousand lambs and twenty-four thousand birds, not to mention the vast quantities of pigs, fish, game, boars and bacon which were sent into the hall to fill the eighty-six tables laid each day for those who chose to avail themselves of royal hospitality. Now, not a single greasy scullion was to be seen 'head and ears in a kettle full of kidneys, nor anything else to stop your progress into the house. You may walk into the Presence Chamber with your hat, spurs and sword on. And if you will presume to be so unmannerly, you may sit down in the Chair of State.'

Only the year before, the King had entered London, after a visit to Scotland, to the acclamations of the people. The houses had been hung with banners and flags; fountains had spurted wine; guards of honour had lined the streets; after a banquet at Guildhall the King had been escorted back to Whitehall by citizens lighting the way with flaming torches. Charles had felt confident that the City would support him if there were to be a struggle between himself and Parliament.

He had soon been proved wrong. Trade in London in the autumn of 1641 had been badly depressed; and on all sides the King's government had been blamed. By December the reversal of the City's feelings towards the King was complete. Out-of-work mariners and dockers, hawkers and oyster-women roamed the streets around Westminster shouting anti-Royalist slogans. Encouraged by their Puritan masters, apprentices insulted bishops in their coaches and stormed Westminster Abbey. When Charles attempted a *coup* against Parliament by entering the chamber of the House of Commons, where no King had set foot before, to arrest five of his leading opponents, the crisis was reached. The five Members escaped from the House and took refuge in the City. Charles bravely entered the City to demand that they should be handed over to him; but his words were greeted with shouts of 'Privilege of Parliament!' 'Privilege of Parliament!' And on his return to Whitehall the shouts were repeated, as crowds of people surrounded his coach, shaking their fists at him.

In the days that followed, feelings in London rose to a new pitch, almost to panic, as rumours flew about that the Royalists were about to launch an attack on the City. A Committee of Public Safety was appointed and a Puritan soldier given overall command of London's Trained Bands. Barricades were erected in the streets; cauldrons of water boiled to pour down on the heads of any Cavaliers who dared to invade; cannon were dragged into position; armed boats patrolled the river; citizens flew to arms.

There was no immediate attack, though. The King and his family fled from Whitehall Palace to Hampton Court, and it was not until several weeks later that the Civil War began. When the Royalists did move on London, when the King's nephew, Prince Rupert, charged into Brentford with his cavalry, throwing its defenders into the river, the citizens backed by the Trained Bands stood firm on Turnham Green, and the King was obliged to turn away.

Yet within a few months elation turned to gloom as the citizens of London fell victims to the privations forced upon them by the war. Money had to be found for the fortifications and for Parliament's army; horses and wagons were requisitioned; supplies of food were intercepted by the King's patrols; the shipping of coal from blockaded Newcastle came to a sudden end. With fuel short and food expensive, with beggars and crippled soldiers at every street corner, Londoners began to long for an end to the war and to develop a lasting resentment against the man who had launched it.

In January 1649 when Charles I, 'Traitor, Tyrant and Public Enemy', was executed on a black-draped scaffold especially erected outside the Banqueting House in Whitehall, not a single citizen risked his life to save him.

After the execution of the King, the policy of Oliver Cromwell's government towards new buildings in London followed that of the Stuart kings. Cromwell confirmed the rule against the erection of any structures on new foundations, reaffirmed the law that required all houses built on old foundations to be of brick or stone, and imposed fines of one year's rent on all those who had built a house on new foundations on a site of less than four acres within ten miles of London since 24 March 1620. Specifically excluded from the prohibition against new building were three developments which were already under way or which had been planned: the Earl of Bedford's still unfinished scheme in Covent Garden; a similar, though more modest, development by the Earl of Clare who proposed to build houses and a market on the site of his big garden between Lincoln's Inn Fields and the Strand; and a development by Sir John Barksted on the site of Bangor House and its grounds in Shoe Lane, between Holborn and Fleet Street.

In 1660 these new developments to the west of London were given fresh

KING CHARLES II
triumphal Entry into the
City of London at his
Restoration.

Charles II's entry into the City at his Restoration, 1660: a later engraving.

impetus by the Restoration of Charles II. John Evelyn, the diarist, was in the Strand the day the King returned and described the joyful scene: 'This day, his Majesty, Charles the Second came to London after a sad and long exile . . . This was also his birthday, and with a triumph of above 20,000 horse and foot, brandishing their swords, and shouting with inexpressible joy; the ways strewed with flowers, the bells ringing, the streets hung with tapestry, fountains running with wine; the Mayor, Aldermen, and all the Companies, in their liveries, chains of gold, and banners; Lords and Nobles, clad in cloth of silver, gold, and velvet; the windows and balconies, all set with ladies; trumpets, music, and myriads of people flocking . . . '

Within a few months a royal proclamation was issued reducing the radius of the prohibited area for new buildings from ten miles to two, and it soon became clear that within this two-mile limit licenses could fairly easily be obtained – by those who could afford them – for schemes which recognised the principles of planning established by the Earl of Bedford and Inigo Jones in Covent Garden.

Within the walls of the City, however, there were vast areas which had long been overdue for demolition and reconstruction, acres covered with small ramshackle lodgings which had been erected inside the walls, because of the prohibition so often repeated between 1580 and 1661 against building outside them, mazes of alleys and courts, crumbling hovels and rotting tenements where families lived with rats in appalling and shameful squalor, close to starvation and close to death. It was here that the bubonic plague of 1665 killed most of its twenty thousand victims; it was here that the Great Fire took strong hold.

6　The Great Fire and the Rebuilding of The City 1666–1710

The fire, which began in a baker's house in Pudding Lane near London Bridge in the early hours of Sunday 1 September 1666, seemed nothing remarkable at first. For an hour after the baker with his wife and servant had fled from his burning staircase onto his roof, the flames did not spread far. Even when the gusts of a sharp north-east wind blew a shower of sparks across Pudding Lane and into the coachyard of the Star Inn on Fish Street Hill, setting fire to the heaps of straw and hay piled up against the wooden galleries, there seemed no cause for special alarm. The Lord Mayor was called at his home in Gracechurch Street; but, looking out upon the localised conflagration delivered himself of this contemptuous opinion: 'Pish!' he said, 'a woman might pisse it out.' Samuel Pepys was also called; and he, too, dismissed the fire as of little danger. He had seen so many in his time; they usually soon burned themselves out; he went back to bed and to sleep.

It had been a hot dry August, though. The coating of pitch that covered so many of the wooden buildings down by the river was peeling off in black flakes. Soon the flames, wafted by the rising wind, were carried across the jumble of old houses that lurched towards each other across the cobbles of Pudding Lane, and down towards the timber sheds and stalls of Fish Street Hill, to the littered alleys that led from Thames Street to the river, the stacks of wood and coal on the wharves, the bales of goods in the warehouses, the barrels of tallow, oil and spirits in the cellars.

Attempts were made to check the blaze by forming chains of fire-fighters armed with leather buckets full of water, but the water merely hissed in the flames. The few, primitive fire-engines that London then possessed were brought into use, but the piles of furniture and household effects which had been pulled out into the streets and the crowds of frightened, shouting people allowed them no room in which to move and play. The Lord Mayor was urged to order the wholesale pulling down of houses in the path of the fire, but he dared not give the order for fear of the claims for compensation that would ensue. Soon the fire was out of all control.

By Monday night the whole of Thames Street from Fresh Wharf to Puddle Dock had been destroyed; and the fire had spread as far north as Cornhill,

The City viewed from Southwark, before, during and after the Great Fire.

burning down the Royal Exchange, and roaring west towards Cheapside. The next day St Paul's and the Guildhall were both burning fiercely; and the flames were leaping on past Newgate to the Temple. Nothing that the King and his Council, or the Lord Mayor and his advisers could suggest or do seemed capable of halting them, until the seamen, brought up from the dockyards, insisted that the only way to save what remained of the City now was ruthlessly to blow up with gunpowder whole rows and streets of buildings, and thus create an open gap so wide that no burning embers could be thrown across it by even the strongest wind. This answer to the danger, wild and reckless as it appeared, was indeed the only hope remaining. Its adoption, and the merciful dropping of the wind late on Tuesday night, brought the fire under control at last.

By then, three hundred and ninety-five acres of the City had been completely devastated. In addition to St. Paul's, eighty-seven parish churches had been effaced; in addition to the City's loss of the Royal Exchange, the Guildhall and the Custom House, forty-four of the City Companies had lost their halls; over thirteen thousand houses had disappeared; ton upon ton of smouldering debris, ash, and tumbled masonry lay beneath the pall of smoke; and almost a quarter of a million people were homeless.

The disaster was appalling, the opportunity unique. The problem of the refugees, tens of thousands of whom had been driven out into the open fields towards Islington and Hampstead, was relatively simple. The King and Council gave orders for tents and temporary sheds to be erected, for the

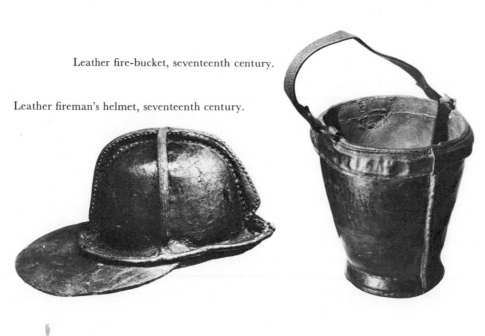

Leather fire-bucket, seventeenth century.

Leather fireman's helmet, seventeenth century.

care of the old and the ill by outlying parishes, for schools and churches to be turned into storage places, for new markets to be set up to take the place of those which had been lost. Soon the worst privations were over.

The problems presented by the rebuilding of the City were far more complex. The debris, which was still smouldering hotly in March 1667, lay so thick that it was impossible to tell any more where houses had been and where streets had led; water pipes and sewers had been cut. With wharves, warehouses, markets and counting-houses all destroyed, trade was at a standstill; contracts could not be fulfilled nor rents collected. The City authorities, anxious to ensure that life returned to normal as soon as possible, were determined that reconstruction should start without delay. If it did not do so the citizens might well decide to remain in the outer suburbs where they could work beyond the control of the Companies, escaping both their fees and responsibilities.

Charles II, on the other hand, a man with a well-developed taste for neatness, order and grace, was concerned that the new London should be as solid as any town in Holland, as imposing as the Paris which Louis XIV hoped to give to France. The need for a quick recovery must not overshadow the need for a comprehensive plan, must not lead to haphazard, uncontrolled building which would result in a town as susceptible to fire and disease as its predecessor.

On 13 September, in the King's name, a proclamation was issued which set out certain immediate principles: new buildings must be of brick or stone; new streets must be wide enough for the convenience of passengers and vehicles alike; a survey would be prepared which would define the ownership of land so that, although 'every man must not be suffered to erect what buildings and where he pleases, he shall not in any degree be debarred from receiving the reasonable benefit of what ought to accrue to him'; unauthorised buildings would be pulled down; but those whose claims to sites were undisputed might build on them provided they did so in conformity with the general plan.

In the event unauthorised buildings were rare, for it took almost two months to clear away the charred ruins and the rubbish, and then the severe winter weather made it impossible to build on sites which had been cleared. But although granted this respite, the planners were unable to take full advantage of it. The competing interests of those involved, the difficulties of raising money in an age which had not developed the techniques of long term borrowing, and of tracing the various interests in the land when so many deeds and leases had been lost and so many landlords and tenants had died during the plague, all made the fulfilment of an overall plan virtually impossible.

There were plans and proposals enough. Sir William Petty, the economist and statistician, provided one; so did the City Surveyor, Peter Mills; so did Robert Hooke, Curator of Experiments at the Royal Society; and so did Richard Newcourt, a map-maker, who suggested that the city should be reformed in the shape of an exact parallelogram with numerous perfectly square blocks of buildings all facing inwards on a piazza and a church. John Evelyn proposed that all the public buildings should be placed along the river front beside a wide embankment, and laid particular emphasis on the need for ridding the city of the 'horrid smoke', which, as he had complained in his *Fumifugium: or the Smoake of London dissipated* (1661), 'obscures our Churches, and makes our Palaces look old, which fouls our Clothes, and corrupts the Waters'.

A fourth plan was submitted by a young professor of Astronomy who had displayed a talent for architecture in his designs for the Sheldonian Theatre at Oxford and Pembroke College chapel in Cambridge. The plan recommended that the entire area should be cleared and a fresh start made with wide straight streets and large open spaces, with a new Royal Exchange and St Paul's serving as the principal of several focal points, with a huge piazza in Fleet Street, and with a spacious embankment on both sides of a widened Fleet River.

The professor who submitted this plan was Christopher Wren, a modest

John Evelyn: engraving by R. Nanteuil.

Evelyn's plan for rebuilding London after the Fire.
Wren's plan for rebuilding London after the Fire.

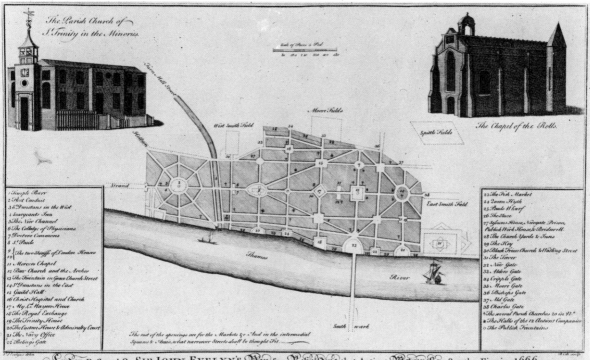

The Parish Church of S.ᵗ Trinity in the Minories.

The Chapel of the Rolls.

London Restored Or SIR IOHN EVELYN'S Plan for Rebuilding that Antient Metropolis after the Fire in 1666.

A PLAN FOR REBUILDING THE CITY OF LONDON, AFTER THE GREAT FIRE IN 1666, DESIGN'D BY THAT GREAT ARCHITECT S.ᵗ CHRISTOPHER WREN, AND APPROV'D OF BY KING, AND PARLIAMENT, BUT UNHAPPILY DEFEATED BY FACTION.

EXPLANATION.

and practical scholar who had been born in a Wiltshire rectory thirty-three years before (plate 12). He had but recently turned to architecture, yet the reputation he had already made for himself and his imaginative yet practical plan assured his appointment as one of the three Crown Commissioners for the Rebuilding of London, the other two being Sir Roger Pratt, a lawyer who had studied design in Italy and become a distinguished advocate of the neo-classical school, and Hugh May, a senior official of the Office of Works, who designed the new wing known as the Star Building at Windsor.

At the same time that these three Crown Commissioners were appointed, the City Corporation nominated their own three representatives – Peter Mills, the City surveyor, Edward Jerman, one of his associates, and Robert Hooke, the clever quarrelsome Professor of Geometry whose plan for rebuilding had the support of the City fathers.

The Commissioners began their difficult task in an atmosphere which the Secretary of the Royal Society described as 'very perplext'. 'Some are for a quite new model, according to Dr Wren's draught,' Dr Oldenburg continued in a letter to Robert Boyle; 'some are for the old, yet to build with bricks; others for a middle way, by building a [quay] and enlarging some streets, but keeping the old foundations and vaults. I hear this very day [2 October 1666] there is a meeting of some of his majesties councill, and others of the nobility, with the leading men of the citty, to conferre about this great work, and to try whether they can bring it to some issue, before the people that inhabited London doe scatter into other parts. The great stresse will be, how to raise money for carrying on the warre [against the Dutch], and to rebuild the citty at the same time.'

The stress, as it happened, proved too much for any of the plans submitted to be adopted in their entirety. The urgent demands of impoverished shop-keepers, of impatient tradesmen, merchants and City officials, the plight of the homeless, the cost of the war and the difficulty of raising large sums of money for reconstruction and compensation, the anxiety of the trustees of charities whose bounty was financed by rents, the disputes between planners and owners, between landlords and tenants, between Parliament, King and City Corporation, all continued to disappoint those who had hoped to see a new model town rise upon the ashes of the old. King Street and Queen Street were formed, opening up a new highway between the Guildhall and the river by Vintners' Place. Yet, for the most part, the old plan was restored, the houses being built, as can be seen from the official map prepared by Ogilby and Morgan, on narrow frontages. This certainly conserved space and saved on road-building by getting as many buildings as possible into one street; but it condemned the occupants and their descendants to a reliance on staircases which was unknown in Paris and other European capitals, to a life which one French visitor later described as like that of a bird in a cage, running up and down steps, perching on different storeys like a canary on a stick.

Yet the rebuilding was not all disappointment. Much was done of lasting benefit. Rules were made and enforced regarding the types of houses which could be built and the materials of which they could be constructed. Houses were to be of four types, 'for better regulation, uniformity and gracefulness'. Except for those of the 'greatest bigness' – which would be set back behind courtyards – in the six 'high and principal' streets the houses were to be of four storeys; in lesser streets of three storeys; in by-lanes and alleys of two storeys. Façades must be flat and straight, and although balconies were permitted for houses with forecourts, there were to be no more bows or jutties; while the offensive water spouts of the past were to be replaced by drainage pipes to convey waste water down the side of buildings and into the gutters in the streets. Shop fronts were to be subject to regulation, and all signs were to be set back against the wall rather than hung out where passers-by might knock their heads against them; the huge water cisterns, so great an obstruction to traffic in the past, were not to be replaced in the main streets; the responsibility for paving passed to the central control of the City.

Although there was to be uniformity, there was in the event to be no dullness. For most houses were designed by the craftsman in charge of its building, and, as Roger North was told by an experienced builder, it was easy to tell what was the contractor's particular craft. If the front were 'set out with fine brick-work rubbed and gaged' then he was a bricklayer; if the stone were 'coyned, jamb'd, and fascia'd' then he was a mason; if the building were 'full of windoe, with glass in compass, and reliev' then a glazier had been in charge; if balcony and balustrading were much in evidence you could be sure a carpenter had had control.

The regulations which these craftsmen had to observe were contained in the Rebuilding Acts; and these comprehensive Acts provided also for two important projects for the improvement of the river front – the building of a new canal along the course of the Fleet and of a long, wide quay along the north bank of the Thames.

The Thames quay, a feature in both Wren's and Evelyn's plans, was to run from the Tower to the Temple. A handsome paved open space, lined with houses and with stone steps down to the river, it was to be both useful and beautiful, to sweep away once and for all the jumble of tumbledown, decaying sheds and jetties, steps and laystalls, the rotting flotsam that each low tide revealed in the noisome mud, to make the London waterfront as handsome as that of Genoa or Rotterdam. But this scheme, like so much else planned in high hope that year, was never fully realised; and no trace of it survives.

The Fleet Canal was a more successful enterprise. Over the years the Fleet, never a fast-flowing river even in Roman times, had become a shallow, silt-choked, rubbish-filled abomination, 'very stinking and noisome', no longer navigable, little better, indeed, than a sewer. As early as 1290 the White Friars had complained that the stench arising from it, impossible to deaden with the strongest incense, had been responsible for the death of several of their brethren. Three centuries later Ben Jonson painted a sickening picture of a voyage up the Fleet on a hot summer's day when the seat of every privy was 'fill'd with buttock and the walls do sweate urine and plaisters'. Each stroke of the oars 'belch'd forth an ayre as hot as the muster of all your night-tubs' when they clustered to discharge their 'merd-urinous load'.

The Fire presented the City with the opportunity to do something at last about this disgusting pestilence on its western border. Planned and supervised by Hooke and Wren, a new canal slowly took shape. The course of the Fleet was straightened; the banks were levelled for new wharves; drains and gratings were installed; breaches were repaired; tons of silt were dredged; rubbish, the garbage of slaughter-houses, and the debris of builders' yards continually thrown into the works and piled upon the wharves, were patiently removed; booms were placed across the channel to prevent lighters and barges from forcing their way in and interrupting the work; the City wall which ran along part of the east bank was underpinned; the brook above Holborn Bridge was arched over as far as the City boundary. Then at last, thanks largely to Thomas Fitch – the capable, conscientious and determined carpenter who had contracted to carry out the work – the canal, nearly fifty feet wide, cleared and once more navigable with broad wharves, was finished at the end of October 1674.

Unfortunately the canal did not enjoy a long life. A few ships used it, but not enough; and one critic disgruntled by its immense cost, complained that its only use was 'to bring up a few chaldrons of coles to two or three Pedling Fewel-Merchants'. Within a few years it was as choked as the old river had ever been. The cutlers, dyers, butchers, brewers, tanners and millers, all of whom found it either convenient or necessary to establish themselves beside a stream of water, were making use of it as a rubbish tip. The Tatler in 1710 wrote of

> *Sweepings from butchers' stalls, dung, guts, and blood,*
> *Drown'd puppies, shaking sprats, all drenched in mud,*
> *Dead cats, and turnip tops, come tumbling down the flood.*

The stone wharves, used for rubbish dumps and dust-heaps as well as for public thoroughfares and carriage parks, were as ill-used as the stream itself, so in 1733 it was decided to arch the canal over up to Fleet Bridge; and in 1766, soon after a drunken butcher had fallen in and, unable to extricate himself from the mud, had frozen to death, the rest of the Fleet was covered over and so became an underground sewer instead of an open one.

Slow as the construction of the Fleet Canal had seemed, there was much else of the city's reconstruction which was even slower. For years London had been full of workmen, who had been drawn there from all over the country, in search of steady work and high wages; and of foreign craftsmen, mainly from France and the Rhineland, whose work can still be seen in the City churches and the halls of the Livery Companies; the streets had been clogged with carts carrying bricks and tiles, slate and lime, Norwegian timber and Portland stone.

Over fifty thousand tons of Portland stone were required for St Paul's alone, in addition to the twenty-five thousand tons of other kinds of stone, the five hundred tons of rubble, the five hundred and sixty tons of chalk, the eleven thousand tons of ragstone, the wagonloads of marble, timber, sand, copper, lead and iron.

St Paul's, not begun until 1675, was not finished until thirty-five years later when a St Paul's workman had become a synonym for slowness. More than half the fifty-one churches rebuilt by Wren were not started until as late as 1676; and although work on the Guildhall and the Royal Exchange was by then almost complete, the plans for the new prison at Ludgate, the Compters in Wood Street and the Poultry, as well as numerous other public buildings and rows and squares of private houses had not even been approved three years after the last cellar had ceased to smoulder.

The Rev Samuel Rolle, author of *London's Resurrection*, reported how displeasing was the appearance of the city in 1668 with streets half built, the houses standing 'so scatteringly' and so many of them 'let out to Alehouse-keepers and Victuallers to entertain workmen imployed about the city'.

But at least these houses and those others which were eventually joined to them in neat terraces, the shops and offices, warehouses and workrooms, the churches and the halls of the Livery Companies, were all built of strong and durable materials to carefully regulated specifications.

Some builders evaded the rules; a few were punished, others escaped. Anthony Selby, a rich draper with valuable property in Mincing Lane, for example, refusing to be controlled by the new building line, had put up property which was not only built of forbidden materials but also overlapped the line by five feet. The offending parts of the building, after a good deal of argument and litigation, were pulled down, and the City bought the rest together with the land on which they stood. Such infringements as Selby's were not common, however. For the first time in over a thousand years the streets of London were, if not as wide as they had once been, fairly straight and regular, and the buildings in them sound and handsome.

Edward Jerman was chosen to design several of the Livery Companies' Halls and the Royal Exchange (plate 16); Robert Hooke had a large share in the important replanning of the area around the Royal Exchange, and was afterwards to become, like Hugh May and Roger Pratt, one of the most sought-after architects in late seventeenth-century England; but of the Commissioners it was Christopher Wren whose name has become most closely associated with the new London, mainly because of those ubiquitous churches whose stone and lead steeples rising above the surrounding roofs so dramatically altered the city's sky line.

Assisted by his pupil, Nicholas Hawksmoor, by his friend, James Gibbs, and such brilliant craftsmen as Grinling Gibbons, the wood carver, Strong, Kempster and Pearce, the master masons, and Jean Tijou, the smith, Wren provided the new city with a succession of masterpieces, enduring tributes to his genius.[1] The finest of them all was St Paul's.

The old Cathedral, bigger than any in England, bigger, indeed, than any in Europe except Milan, Seville and St Peter's, Rome, had lost its great spire in 1561 when an old plumber left a pan of coals burning inside it while he went to have his dinner. He returned to find a raging fire sending gouts of

The Mercers' Chapel and adjoining shops as rebuilt after the Fire.

flame through the roof, from which the cross and eagle were soon dislodged and sent blazing down in a shower of sparks through the roof of the south transept.

The fabric had been repaired in the 1630s by Inigo Jones who had cased most of it with ashlar masonry at a cost of about £100,000, and who, by providing it with a new and magnificent (though to modern eyes incongruous) portico, 'contracted the Envy of all Christendom', as John Webb put it, 'for a Piece of Architecture, not to be paralleled in these last ages of the World'.

But since then the Cathedral had been continuously neglected; and by the time of the Restoration in 1660 had been sadly in need of fresh repairs. The central tower was leaning dangerously owing to the settlement of one of the piers; pigeons, crows and jackdaws had made their nests in the wooden roof and behind the parapet where they came under constant attack from young boys with catapults; the interior, dirty and crumbling, was used on weekdays not only as a meeting-place for lawyers and their clients, as an employment exchange and advertising agency, but even as a market, a haunt of touts encouraging the sale of the obscene prints displayed on the bookstalls outside, a promenade for fashionable youths and courtesans, and a short-cut for porters carrying casks of beer and loads of fish and vegetables between Carter Lane and Paternoster Row.

Repairs were begun once more in 1663; but three years later the Fire so devastated 'the great Pile' that it appeared 'like some Antique Ruine of 2000 years continuance'. Wren, who had already prepared a rather fanciful design for a new cupola before the Fire, now set about designing a completely new cathedral. He provided his first suggestions in the form of 'a most curious Model' of wood in November 1672. This modest design, condemned by Roger Pratt, was followed by a far more elaborate one which was approved by the King in November 1673 but was also condemned, this time by the clergy. Having spent a great deal of time and energy on this new design, which he exemplified in a wooden model costing £600 (now to be seen in the Trophy Room at St Paul's), Wren was so dismayed when it was rejected that he burst into tears. His next design was so extraordinary, so inferior to the previous one, that it was afterwards suggested that he had presented it, overworked as he was, in a fit of pique to show how silly were the requirements of the clergy when set out in architectural terms. This, none the less, was the design which received the Royal Warrant in May 1675.

Over the course of the thirty-five years in which the Cathedral was being built, however, Wren constantly modified this design and improved upon his original drawings; so that when his son laid the highest stone in the lantern in 1710, the masterpiece which was then completed bore so little resemblance to its early plans that it was recognised as being one of the finest churches in Europe.[2]

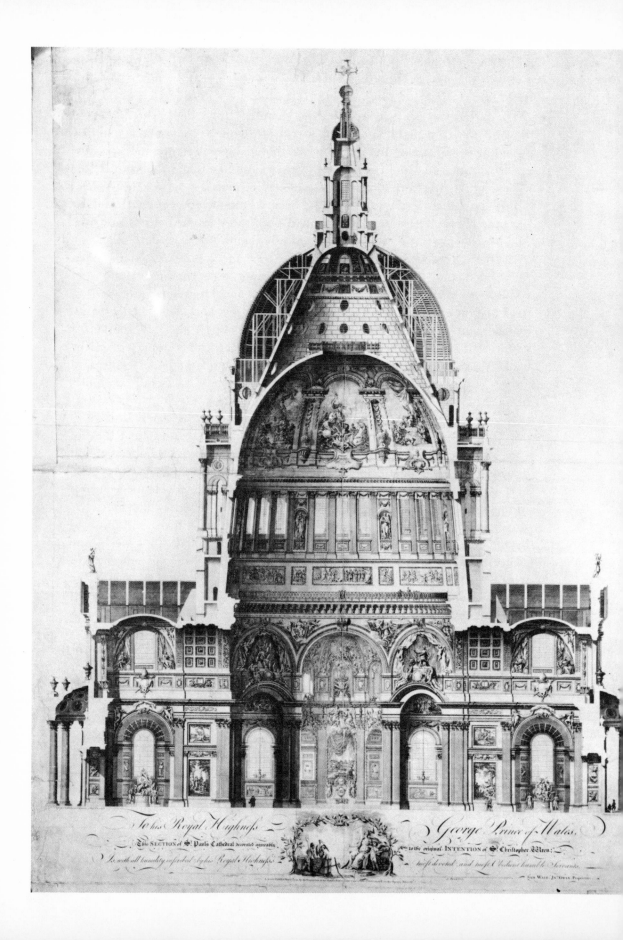

To his Royal Highness

George Prince of Wales,

This SECTION of S.t Pauls Cathedral decorated agreeable, to the original INTENTION of S.r Christopher Wren;

Is with all humility inscribed by his Royal Highness's most devoted, and most Obedient humble Servants.

Sam Wale Jn.r Gwin Proposers.

Magnificent as so many of the new buildings were, it proved impossible to persuade all those whom the Fire had driven from London to return to live within close view of them. The poor worker could not afford the new rents, the shopkeeper preferred to make his living in the suburbs, the craftsman chose to remain where he was less restricted and more gently taxed, the merchants had acquired a taste for country life in Stoke Newington or Islington, the rich and the noble had established to the west of London new centres of fashionable life.

Orders compelling Aldermen to return to the city, reductions in the fees demanded by the Companies and less severe restrictions upon entrance into them, temporarily checked but failed permanently to reverse this alteration in the structure of London's population, this change in the City's character.

Detail from the cover sheet of Ogilby and Morgan's map, 1677.

Section through St Paul's: engraving of 1755.

7 *Fashionable* Faubourgs
1660–1695

Outside the City walls the transformation of the western suburbs was quite as complete as the changes being wrought in the City itself. Around the Earl of Southampton's house in Bloomsbury, in the fields to the north of St James's Palace, along the road which led to the village of Knightsbridge, and around the Haymarket, rows and squares of new houses, built in the style made fashionable before the Fire by Inigo Jones, were appearing year by year.

The development in St James's Field had been started soon after Charles II's return in 1660. It was inspired by the King himself (plate 14) and by one of his most accomplished and most devious courtiers.

On his return to St James's, Charles had immediately set about the improvement of the park so sadly neglected during his years of exile on the Continent when its trees had been cut down to provide fuel for the citizens. Advised, so it has been said, by André Le Nôtre, Louis XIV's garden designer, he planted it with fruit trees, stocked it with deer, made a lake on which he could feed his ducks and round which he could walk his spaniels, and built an avenue, lined with trees and covered with powdered cockleshells, where he could play pall mall, a game something like croquet that had originated in Italy as *palla a maglio* (ball to mallet) and had become a fashionable craze in France.

This royal pall mall alley was built just inside the park wall only a few yards away from an existing one in St James's Field on the other side of the road. The site was unfortunately chosen for, as the King soon discovered, the clouds of dust set up by carriages and carts rattling along the road to and from St James's Palace, were highly irritating to the players; so, rather than move the new pall mall alley south, it was decided to move the road north, to block the existing thoroughfare and make another one between the two lines of elms on the old pall mall alley in St James's Field. This new road, paved in 1662, was called Catherine Street in honour of the Queen, Catherine of Braganza; but those who used it chose to retain the original name by which it is still known today.

Thus Pall Mall became the new south boundary of St James's Field which

The development of the West End: St James's Palace, Pall Mall and St James's Square (bottom right): view of *c.* 1714–22.

Charles II and Catherine of Braganza being presented by Ogilby with the
subscriptions for the official survey of London.

was enclosed on the north by the road to Knightsbridge and on the other
two sides by St James's Street and the Haymarket. And it was on these forty-
five open acres that Henry Jermyn, Earl of St Albans, had the notion of
building an estate of aristocratic houses looking inwards onto a large central
square.

Henry Jermyn was well-known, not to say notorious, yet a rather mysterious figure. His father, Sir Thomas Jermyn, had been a Privy Councillor
and Vice-Chamberlain, but his own influence at Court was far greater than
Sir Thomas's had ever been. Henry Jermyn owed this influence to his intimate
friendship with the King's mother, Henrietta Maria, whose secret husband
he was, in fact, widely rumoured to be. After a time spent as English
Ambassador in Paris he had been appointed Henrietta Maria's Vice-
Chamberlain in 1628, and had never thereafter lost her favour. His seduction
of one of her maids of honour, whom he refused to marry, seems to have
increased rather than lessened her fondness of him; and in 1639 he was
appointed her Master of Horse. Four years later he became her secretary
and the colonel of her bodyguard; and during the Court's exile he enjoyed
the complete management of her finances which enabled him to afford a
carriage and an excellent table, while other, more scrupulous, courtiers were
living in penury.

Although he inevitably aroused widespread jealousy and distrust, Henry
Jermyn's lack of conscience and principle was useful to the King, who
rewarded him accordingly. He was appointed Lord High Admiral, although
he had as little knowledge of the sea and as little interest in seamen as most

12. Sir Christopher Wren by J. B. Closterman.

CHRISTOPHER WREN K.ᵗ
...DENT of the ROYAL
SOCIETY

of his predecessors in that office; and at the time of the Restoration he was created an Earl and sent as English Ambassador to Paris where he seems to have found opportunities to increase his already substantial fortune.

A man with 'drayman's shoulders' and 'butcher's mien', in the words of one of his numerous enemies, the poet Andrew Marvell, he returned to London with an unimpaired appetite for good food, gambling, intrigue and money, 'more a Frenchman', in the King's opinion, 'than an Englishman'.

Persuading the King to grant him a lease of part of St James's Field for its development, he had obtained by 1665 the freehold of half the field, including the central area where St James's Square was to be built. He later obtained a lease of the rest of the field till 1740.

In cooperation with various associates, including Sir Thomas Clarges, a doctor turned courtier and financier who had come to the King's attention when in the service of General Monck, the Earl of St Albans had soon developed the whole area around the central piazza by letting plots on build-ing leases to various speculative builders prepared to put up houses for aristo-cratic tenants. He made several new roads behind his graceful terraces of houses – naming the principal ones Jermyn Street after himself, King Street and Charles II Street after his patron, Duke Street and Duke of York Street after his patron's brother, and Babmaes Street after his patron's faithful servant, Baptist May – he established a market, St Albans Market, though more commonly known as St James's Market, and he had a church designed by Wren, to face onto Jermyn Street with its northern windows overlooking the road to Knightsbridge, soon to be known as Piccadilly.[1]

Although the St James's development was well conceived and executed, it was not so much in the Square that the rich aristocrats, for whom St Albans had intended it, chose as yet to live, nor in St James's Street, which the King had had paved in 1661, but along Pall Mall where the houses along the southern side could enjoy an open view across St James's Park. Here lived the Countess of Ranelagh, whose husband the first Earl owned houses in King Street and St James's Square as well as a large country house with beautiful grounds in Chelsea, being a most extravagant man who 'spent more money, built more fine houses, and laid out more on household furnishing and gardening than any other nobleman in England'. Here also lived the King's mistress, the vivacious and disarmingly vulgar Nell Gwyn, whose house was – as it still remains – the only freehold one on the south side of Pall Mall since, as she saucily told her lover, she had 'always conveyed free under the Crown, and always would'. It was a charming house with a garden running down to St James's Park, and the King could often be seen talking to its pretty little owner over the wall. John Evelyn was walking with the King in the Park one March day in 1671 and 'both saw and heard a very familiar discourse, she looking out of her garden on a terrace at the

13. One of the earliest pieces of English chinoiserie: the Saddlers' Com-pany's ballot box made for the Court of the East India Company in 1619.

Nell Gwyn and two of her royal bastards.

top of her wall and [Charles] standing on the green sward under it.'

'I was heartily sorry at this scene,' Evelyn continued. 'Thence the King walked to the Duchess of Cleveland, another Lady of pleasure and curse of our nation', the acknowledged mother of six of the King's numerous illegitimate children.

A few doors away from Nell Gwyn's house was Schomberg House, later the property of the Duke of Schomberg, whose father had acted as second-in-command to William of Orange during the Glorious Revolution of 1688. The dark red brick façade of Schomberg House can still be seen amidst the grey and yellow nineteenth-century premises of the clubs which now occupy so much of the southern side of Pall Mall.[2]

Here also, at the St James's end of Pall Mall, separated from the Palace by Marlborough Road, was where Sarah, the tiresome Duchess, chose to build the sprawling Marlborough House where, later, King Edward VII came to live as Prince of Wales, and where his son's widow, Queen Mary, spent the last years of her life.[3]

While St Albans was busy in Pall Mall and St James's Field, increasing the fortune which was to pay for the heavy gambling that occupied so much of his time in his blind old age, other courtiers were making money for themselves or building mansions further to the north along St James's. Henry Bennet, Earl of Arlington, for example, was presented by the King with a parcel of land at the top end of St James's Street, and, having a large house not far away on the other side of the Palace and disinclined to become a speculator himself, sold it to a builder. This builder, a Mr Pym, put up a number of houses so quickly and so badly that within a matter of months all the windows were 'wry-mouthed', the door lintels had cracked, and the chimneys had fallen down bringing the roofs and the upper floors with them. The rubble was soon cleared nevertheless, and Arlington Street and Bennet Street became as fashionable as St James's Square and St James's Place.

In St James's Place, indeed, there were so many mansions by the end of the seventeenth century, that the plots available for purchase were becoming increasingly narrow. Thomas Coke, a Member of Parliament, choosing to live there, was obliged to build so close to the garden wall of his neighbour, Charles Godolphin, that the infuriated Godolphin stormed out into his garden, with pistol cocked in his hand, and threatened to shoot any workman whose head appeared above the top of the wall.

Along Piccadilly, as well as along St James's, big houses were now going up apace. One of the earliest and largest was Clarendon House, built by the Earl of Clarendon, on·a large and valuable site on the north side of Piccadilly which he had been granted by the King in 1664. Here his architect, Roger Pratt, built a vast mansion at a cost of between £40,000 and £50,000. It was known as Dunkirk House by his contemporaries who believed Clarendon had paid for it out of his share of the profits on the sale of Dunkirk to the French King.

Although unpopular both at Court and with the people, Clarendon had a good friend in John Evelyn, who came to visit him at Clarendon House the day before the Earl fled into exile to escape impeachment for high treason. 'I found him in his garden at his new-built palace, sitting in his gout wheel-chair, and seeing the gates setting up towards the north and the fields,' Evelyn wrote in his diary. 'He looked and spake very disconsolately.' The palace, Evelyn thought, 'a goodly pile to see' and 'placed most gracefully'; and he was deeply distressed when Clarendon's son sold it – for half what it had cost – to the Duke of Albemarle, an improvident young man whose debts compelled him in turn to put it up to auction. The highest bid – of £36,000 for the house and its twenty-four acres of land – came from a consortium of bankers and speculators, headed by Sir Thomas Bond, a denizen like St Albans of the Queen Mother's court. In 1680 Bond, and his associates – who included John Hinde, a goldsmith, and Richard Frith, a builder whose name is more closely associated with Soho – began the development which was soon to cover its gardens with the buildings of Bond Street and Albemarle Street.

When the Earl of Clarendon had first been granted the land by the King, he had disposed of wide and deep strips, on either side of the part he retained for himself, to two friends, Lord Berkeley of Stratton who in 1664 built Berkeley House on his right, and Richard Boyle, Earl of Cork and Burlington, who, between 1663 and 1668, built Burlington House on his left.

John Evelyn dined at Berkeley House, which he was assured had cost nearly £30,000, soon after it was finished; and he thought it more like a stately palace than a house. Designed by Hugh May with a huge Palladian portico, it contained many noble rooms, but they were 'all rooms of state, without closets'. 'For the rest,' Evelyn noted, 'the forecourt is noble, so are the stables; and, above all, the gardens, which are incomparable by reason of the inequality of the ground.' These attractively undulating gardens stretched back to Hay Hill Farm; and when Berkeley Street, Stratton Street and Berkeley Square were built, the streets to the west of the Square – Hay's Mews, Hill Street and Farm Street – all commemorated the farm whose fields they covered.

The gardens of Burlington House were almost as extensive as those of Berkeley House and Clarendon House, but the red brick mansion itself was more modest, for it was not until 1716 that the third Earl, helped by his architect, Colen Campbell and inspired by Palladio's Palazzo Porto at

Burlington House, Piccadilly, and its gardens, built 1663–68.

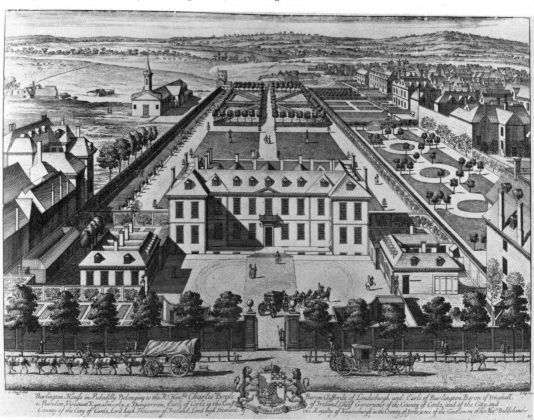

Vicenza, replaced his great-grandfather's house with the magnificent building which became a model for so many other houses in the neo-classic taste.[4]

Although most of the more spectacular building by rich aristocrats in the late seventeenth century was in Piccadilly, Pall Mall and St James's, many fine houses were also erected at this time in Bloomsbury.

The principal landowner in Bloomsbury was the Earl of Southampton, the son of Shakespeare's patron, who lived in a splendid house, with Wren and Kneller as near neighbours, on the north side of what is now Great Russell Street, his gardens covering the present Southampton Row. As Lord Treasurer, Southampton tried unsuccessfully to stop the Earl of St Albans from developing St James's Field, concerned that houses there might draw purchasers away from the plots he himself intended to offer for sale around a square he had formed in front of Southampton House. Southampton's fears were unjustified; his influential scheme for a self-contained unit with market, shops and smaller houses around the central square was a success. Bloomsbury was 'esteemed very healthful', and the good dry air attracted many rich men who did not want to live too close to the river, preferring to build themselves houses on higher ground. There was no finer house in Bloomsbury than Montague House, finished in 1676, 'a stately and ample palace', in Evelyn's opinion, 'built after the French pavilion way by Mr. Hooke'. Ten years after its completion it was burned to the ground; and in 1754 its successor was bought to house Sir Hans Sloane's collections of antiquities, works of art, and curiosities of natural history which formed the nucleus of the British Museum.

The Earl of Southampton died in 1667 and, having no sons, his property eventually came into the hands of his daughter, Rachel, whose son was Wriothesley, second Duke of Bedford and grandson of the man who had developed Covent Garden. The Duke and Duchess, their fortune enormously increased, decided to move to Bloomsbury. So in 1704 they demolished their house in the Strand and moved to Southampton House which became known thereafter as Bedford House.

Less aristocratic developments than those in Bloomsbury, St James's Fields and along Piccadilly were meanwhile being carried out nearer to the City's boundaries. Around what is now Piccadilly Circus itself there had been no buildings at all until, in the early years of the century, a tailor and collar-maker named Robert Baker, in a good way of business in the Strand, had bought one and a half acres near the windmill and built himself a house there. This house was referred to by the local wags as Pickadilly Hall, a pickadil or piccadill being a high ruffed collar, the sale of which was supposed to have been largely responsible for Robert Baker's fortune.

Pickadilly, at first applied to the tailor's house, was eventually used to describe the whole area around it, and, in particular, to denote one of the most famous gaming-houses of the early seventeenth century: Shaver's Hall, so called since it was run by a man who had been the Lord Chamberlain's barber.

The extensive grounds of Shaver's Hall, including bowling-alleys, tennis courts, orchards, formal gardens and tree-lined walks, struck the shrewd eye of one Colonel Panton, a reformed gambler who having won £1,500 in a single night never gambled again. The profits of Shaver's Hall slumped during the Civil War, disappeared altogether during the Commonwealth and did not recover at the Restoration, so Colonel Panton was able to buy the site at a reasonable figure in 1664. He also bought some land belonging to the Baker family which ran along the north end of his new property; then, having obtained a licence to build, began a development which was so successful that his neighbours were soon induced to follow his example. By the end of the century houses had been built all around Pickadilly Hall, not only by Panton but also by Henry Coventry, a Secretary of State under Charles II, and by the Wardour family, whose name like Panton's and Coventry's is still commemorated in the area.

East of Wardour Street, development had by this time been started by Thomas Neale, Master of the Mint, who in 1693 began that star-shaped pattern of streets which was to become the notorious slum district known as Seven Dials; building had also begun in the area which was known as Soe Hoe, the name being derived from the hunting call so often heard in the open fields here. Two of the principal property owners in Soe Hoe were Charles Gerard, Earl of Macclesfield, and Sir Francis Compton, both of whom took part in the development of the area and gave their names to its streets. The most active speculators in Soho, however, were Richard Frith – the rich builder who helped Thomas Bond make Bond Street and gave his name to Frith Street – and Dr Nicholas Barbon.

Barbon was the son of Praise-God Barbon (or Barebones), the leather merchant and Fifth Monarchy man who, being nominated by Cromwell and his council of officers as Member for London, gave his name to one of the Commonwealth's parliaments. Nicholas was born about 1640, studied medicine in Holland, and was admitted as an Honorary Fellow to the College of Physicians in 1664. He was an ambitious, shrewd, persuasive and masterful man whose arrogant demeanour gave way on occasions to an insinuating charm. Although better known as the founder of fire insurance companies and as an economist quoted by Marx, he was also the most active and ambitious of all the property dealers of Restoration London. He explained that it was worth his while to engage in small ventures: '*That* a bricklayer could do. The gain *he* expected was out of great undertakings, which would rise lustily in the whole.' His name constantly reappears in the

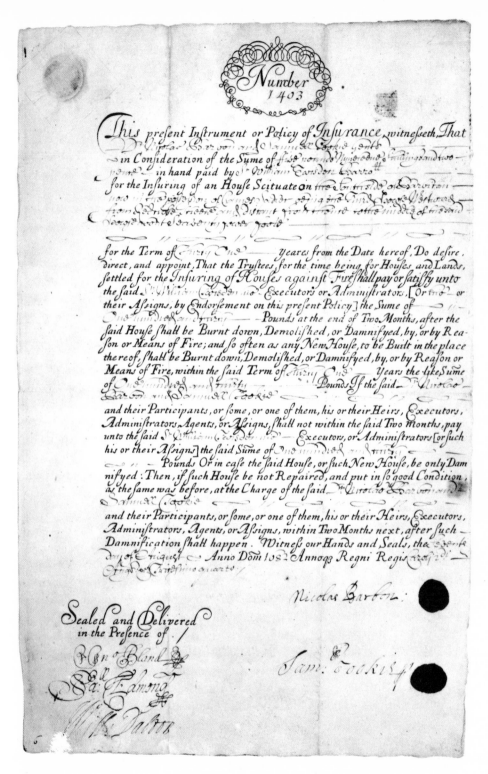

Nicholas Barbon's signature on a fire insurance policy for a house in the Barbican, 1682.

records, buying, selling, building, leasing, renting; sometimes as the controller of immense sums of money, at others as the defendant in a suit for the recovery of unpaid debts, at one time as the owner of a small house in Theobalds Row, at another the builder of several large houses on the Earl of St Albans' estate in St James's Field, in 1683 as the purchaser of the great Tudor mansion at Osterley, once the home of Sir Thomas Gresham, ten years later as a bankrupt.

Some of his schemes were successful, others not. Many of the houses his contractors built were sound, a few fell to pieces. His methods were frequently questionable, on occasions actually criminal.

When he wished to redevelop an area part of which was already built on, he would invite the various owners and tenants to his house in Crane Court where he lived in the grandest style, keep them waiting in a beautifully furnished drawing-room beyond the appointed time, and suddenly appear as richly dressed, so Roger North said, as a 'Lord of the Bedchamber on a birthday'. Then, with a combination of deceit, cajolery, veiled threats and bonhomie, he would persuade them to agree to his suggestions. If any of their number proved unresponsive to both blandishments and financial inducements he had a simple and brutal remedy: he pulled the stubborn fellow's house down over his head. He was often in trouble with the law, of course, but he so wearied his opponents with appeals, counter-claims, non-appearances, apologies, withdrawals, specious arguments, disingenuous excuses, lies and incomprehensible speeches, that more often than not the case was finally abandoned in despair. He appeared to be quite without either conscience or malice; he smiled agreeably when called a fraud, a cheat and a mountebank; he nodded consolingly when an outraged client berated him. He was a humbug, dishonest and unscrupulous; but his flair amounted almost to genius.

One of Barbon's first speculations was to the south of the Strand which the noble families who had once lived there were now abandoning for new houses further out in the country to the west. In 1674 he bought Essex House from the executors of the Duchess of Somerset into whose possession it had come after the death of Robert Devereux, the third and last Earl of Essex in the Devereux line. When the sale was completed, King Charles offered to buy the property at a higher price than Barbon had paid for it as a reward for Arthur Capel – recently created first Earl of Essex in the Capel line – for his good work as lord-lieutenant of Ireland. But Barbon refused, pulled the house down, and began to rebuild smaller houses on its site, selling to the Society of the Middle Temple parts of the eastern end of the garden, and transforming Milford Lane (which divided Essex House from the adjoining Arundel House) from a squalid alley of brothels and tippling-rooms into a respectable lane of handsome houses, cook-shops, taverns and vaulting-schools, with a new wharf at its lower end for brewers and woodmongers.

Further west along the Strand, on the far side of the Savoy, Barbon bought the Duke of Buckingham's house which was known as York Place, having formerly been the London residence of the Archbishop of York. This also he pulled down to build new houses on its site.

The Duke, to dramatise his quarrel with the Government and Court, moved to a house in the City, but before he left he insisted on being remembered in the Strand, not merely by the preservation of the gate which led from his garden to the river steps,[5] but also by having his Christian name and family name and every syllable of his title used in the naming of Barbon's new streets. They are all still there – George Street, Villiers Street, Duke Street, Buckingham Street, even Of Alley, although this last has now been renamed by an unamused authority to 'York Place formerly known as Of Alley'.

Barbon's most ambitious scheme was the development of a group of open fields between Gray's Inn and the Earl of Bedford's Covent Garden estate which were then known as Red Lyon Fields.

The new Red Lion Square was to be a most attractive area, with terraces of fine houses 'occupied by gentry and Persons of Repute' and a pleasant

King's Square in Soe Hoe, now Soho Square: early eighteenth-century engraving.

piazza of lawns and gravelled walks. But Barbon's high-handed methods in the building of it annoyed both the King – whose private way to Newmarket along Theobald's Road was very roughly treated – and the lawyers of Gray's Inn who foresaw that they would lose the countryside around their Inn in the same way as their fellow-lawyers on the other side of Holborn had lost the unrestricted use of Lincoln's Inn Fields.

A hundred gentlemen of Gray's Inn accordingly moved in mass against Barbon's workmen who, for a time, kept them away by hurling bricks at them. Soon, however, the lawyers overwhelmed the labourers, two of whom were carried off as hostages. The next day Barbon retaliated by marching around the fields – where foundations for his houses were already being dug – at the head of two hundred of his workmen who followed him shouting threats and waving their hats by way of challenge. In a moment of quiet Barbon himself announced that if there were any further opposition he would bring out a thousand more men to enforce his rights.

Evidently intimidated and somewhat placated for the time being by the indisputably attractive result of his speculation in Red Lion Square, Barbon's opponents were once more up in arms against him when he began building, to the east of the Square, on land he had persuaded the Corporation of Bedford to sell him. The houses in Bedford Row itself were satisfactory enough, though rather coarsely and cheaply finished;[6] but some of those in North Street, East Street and Lamb's Conduit Street bore all the evidence of hasty, ramshackle construction.

The trouble was that Barbon had over-reached himself, and was in difficulties with his creditors. Unable to sell numbers of unfinished houses he was forced to let the contractors keep them as payment for their bills. By 1694 his finances were strained beyond recuperation; and four years later he died. He left instructions in his will that none of his debts should be paid. While Barbon and his associates were concerning themselves with development in more or less fashionable districts, cheaper and more transient houses, factories, shops and taverns were now spreading fast to the north and east of the City. Clerkenwell, now almost completely deserted by the rich families which had once lived there, trebled its population within the twenty-five years following the Fire of 1666. Spitalfields and Soho, already crowded with foreign immigrants, absorbed thousands more after 1685 when Louis XIV's revocation of the Edict of Nantes drove his Huguenot subjects to seek refuge abroad. Southwark also greatly increased its population when the Bishop of Winchester moved his London house to Chelsea and the park of Winchester House became available for building.

Bethnal Green expanded quickly, too, after Lady Wentworth obtained permission to build small houses there for 'mariners and manufacturers'. Merchants who had prospered since the Fire built modest houses for themselves in Hackney, Clapham, Camberwell and Streatham. At Stoke Newington the manor house was demolished in 1695 and replaced by terraces of cottages.

All these places, though, were still essentially villages from which open countryside could still be seen from the bedroom windows. Only such dockyard towns as Woolwich and Deptford were industrialised in the way that the City and its immediate suburbs were. Kensington was still surrounded by market gardens; Chelsea, which was to remain a small country village for another century yet, was but a group of isolated houses amidst six hundred acres of arable fields and pasture, common land, orchards, gardens and riverside meadows, a small country village, like scores of others within three miles of Charing Cross.

Howland Great Dock near Deptford: engraving of *c.* 1707.

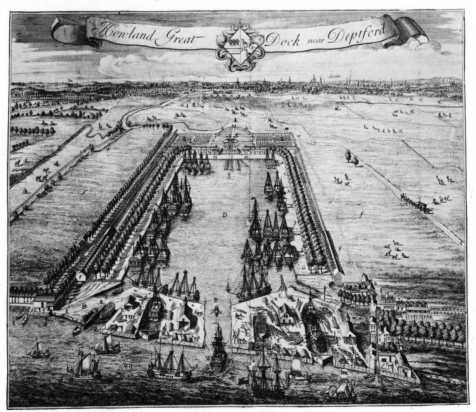

94   Samuel Pepys: engraving after Kneller.

8   *Pepys's London 1666–1703*

A generation after the Fire, although there was much rebuilding still to be finished, the visitor to London in search of pleasure, excitement and surprise was sure to be satisfied. The streets were as noisy and full of life as they had ever been, and quite as crowded, for the population of London and its suburbs had rapidly increased since the beginning of the century from a figure of about 350,000 at the time of the Fire to some 650,000 towards the end of the century when, according to Sir William Petty, it was doubling itself every two generations, partly because of a greatly increased birthrate and a slightly lower rate of infant mortality, but mostly because of the thousands of immigrants still crowding into the City and its inner suburbs year by year.

Tradesmen and hawkers shouting 'Pancakes!' and 'Dumplins! Dumplins! Diddle, diddle, dumplins ho!' 'Hot Baked Warden Pears and Pippins!', 'Flag-brooms! Flag-brooms!', 'Sweep! Sweep!', 'Knives to Grind!', 'Cucumbers to pickle!', or 'Here's your rare holland socks, four pairs a shilling!' walked up and down, crying their wares and skills in a wonderful variety of plain-song and ditty. In Long Lane, people on their way to see the workmen clambering over the huge, half-finished walls of St Paul's were set upon by the sellers of second-hand clothes leaping out of their shops to pull at the hands of passers-by, grab their shoulders and shout in their ears.

In the street market, which had sprung up along the banks of the river by Fleet Bridge, evil-looking men stood by barrows piled high with nuts and gingerbread, oranges and oysters, while old trulls in straw hats or flat caps offered socks and furmety, night caps and plum pudding. At Coles Child's celebrated shop at the sign of the Blue Boar on London Bridge, much frequented by tourists, customers could buy anything from a pair of whalebone stays or a tooth brush to a patch box or a squirrel chain; and at New Exchange in the Strand they could buy clothes and hats and trinkets, toys and fopperies, gloves and fans, silk stockings and bottles of scent.

The New Exchange, designed by Inigo Jones, had been built by the Earl of Salisbury on land he had bought for the purpose adjoining his garden wall. First opened by James I in 1609 it was a long and elegant building with about a hundred small shops lining the corridors on the ground

Cries of London, 1680: 'Knives or Cisers to Grinde' and '4 Paire for a Shilling Holland Socks'.

and upper floors. It had not at first been a success and the first floor had had to be converted into private apartments as Lord Salisbury could not find tenants for the shops; but once the Lincoln's Inn Fields and Covent Garden developments were completed and after the Great Fire had destroyed so many City shops, the New Exchange came into its own as a fashionable parade for ladies and dandies and as a shopping centre where 'you may fit yourself with ware of all sorts and sizes'.

There were a number of excellent book shops on the lower floor of the New Exchange, though the most celebrated were still to be found around St Paul's and Paternoster Row, and, for law books, near the Temple and Westminster Hall. In these shops the new books on sale were all unbound, lying on tables and shelves in loose sheets, so that the purchaser could choose the style and colour of the binding, having his entire library, if he wished, bound in green and gold-blocked calf. If he was not sure that he wanted to commit himself to buying a particular work by asking the bookseller to bind it for him, he could read the loose sheets in the shop, sitting down at one of the reading desks in the window, or he could take them home and read them there before making up his mind.

Shopping in London for goods other than books was, however, a mixed pleasure. The goods displayed on the shop-board were usually attractively

The Monument erected to commemorate the Fire: engraving of *c.* 1680.

and invitingly arranged; but the interiors of the shops were often dark and smelly. The tradesmen's wives, who sat on seats outside the doors of the more expensive shops and politely invited the passers-by to inspect their husband's wares, were superficially a good deal more gracious than the husbands themselves who haggled over the price of every item, demanded that worn silver coins should be placed on the scales and their true weight made up, and often enough gave customers from out of town change in counterfeit money.

The energetic tourist in Restoration London would rise early and breakfast, perhaps, on cheese and bits of toast softened in a mug of ale in one or other of the numerous taverns. Two of the best known of London's taverns were the Rose in the Poultry, which had been there since early Tudor times, and Locket's Tavern at Charing Cross, an extremely expensive establishment 'much frequented by gentry'. An excellent meal was also served at the Eagle and Child in St Martin's Lane which seems to have specialised in pigeons, mutton steaks and Westphalia ham; and at more than one inn in Black Horse Alley it was possible to eat a good dinner for threepence, though at Pontack's towards the end of the century the price of the *table d'hôte* could be as much as two guineas a head. There were taverns, in fact, to suit every taste and every pocket.

The landlord stood behind the bar which was always placed close to the front door so that he could take the orders of his customers as they came in and despatch the pot-boy or the maid to the room they had entered; for most taverns had once been private houses, and contained several small rooms rather than a few large ones. The Mouth tavern in Bishopsgate had eight drinking-rooms each one of which was provided with screens so that they could be divided up into partitions for the benefit of customers who required privacy for the pursuit of love, intrigue, important conversation or private business.

The good tavern-keeper's profits were considerable; but he had to work hard for them. His house was open all day, every day, and for most of the time he was expected to be on duty, not merely as barman, kitchen manager, and sometimes waiter, but as business agent, procurer, banker and messenger-boy. The visitor could expect him to provide him with wine, food, fire and comfort, change his money, give him advice on the pleasures of the town, take messages for him, and then hire him a coach to speed him on his way.

It was easy enough, however, for the stranger to find a coach for himself in London. There were rows of hackney-coaches standing in ranks at the May-pole in the Strand, as well as in Palace Yard in Westminster. But they were all hideously uncomfortable. Instead of glass windows they had sheets of tin

14. Charles II on Horseguards Parade *c.* 1680 (detail).

perforated with small holes which the passenger could pull up to stop too much rain or dust falling on him; and instead of springs, they were equipped with leather straps which did little to prevent the occupants being shaken up and down, like peas in a rattle, over the stones and cobbles. In the winter there were the added discomforts and inconveniences of getting stuck in the mud, for although the streets were better than they had been before the Fire, many of them were almost impassable in bad weather. Mud was not the only hazard. Every year there were more vehicles on the road, and the congestion was appalling. In addition to about seven hundred public hackney-coaches – or Hackney Hell Carts as they were commonly called – there were, according to one estimate, as many as five thousand privately owned coaches, a relatively new innovation, since, up to the middle of the century in London, coaches had been considered suitable only for ladies. Many of these coaches were prodigiously cumbersome vehicles pulled by six horses and followed by luggage carts and pack-horses; and when such caravans, followed by public passenger wagons carrying twenty passengers drawn by eight horses, were making their way down a narrow street while an array of sedan chairs, carrioles, hackney-carriages, butchers' wagons, dung carts, brewers' drays, herds of cattle and droves of turkeys were moving impatiently in the opposite direction, a traffic jam was inevitable.

If he preferred to go by water, the visitor would be greeted by groups of watermen who came running towards him as soon as he came into sight at the top of the stairs, shouting 'Oars! Oars! Will you have any oars!' More than one visitor has recorded his embarrassment at being asked 'such an abominable question' in public, before realising that he was being offered something quite different from what he had at first supposed.

Once on the river the stranger might be further embarrassed by the custom, already old and long to continue, of greeting the passengers in all passing boats with the most outlandish and fanciful insults, threats, abuse and derision which the mind could conceive. Those too shy or inarticulate to reply to this River Wit, as it was called, could fortunately rely on the waterman to return the shouts with his own accusations, selected from a store of rudery preserved in his memory and learned by heart for such occasions.

Both watermen and hackney-coachmen, like tavern-keepers, were prepared to give advice on what the curious traveller should see during his stay in London. One sight which all agreed should not be left off any itinerary – since it could be reached by both road and water – was the Tower.

For, although no longer occupied now as a royal palace, the Tower was still a prison – the Earl of Strafford, Archbishop Laud, and the Duke of Albemarle were all here in the 1640s; several regicides and William Penn, the Quaker, in the 1660s; Samuel Pepys, on a charge of complicity in the Titus Oates plot in 1679 (plate 15); Algernon Sidney, the Duke of Mon-

15. Titus Oates in the pillory outside Westminster Hall, 1687: detail from
   a painting by an imitator of Jan Wyck.

mouth and Judge Jeffreys in the 1680s – and there was always a chance of catching a glimpse of a celebrated face at one of the barred windows. Also at the Tower was the famous Traitors' Gate where, as the tide fell, visitors looking down into the moat were deafened by the roaring waters, falling like a cataract; and here too was still the royal menagerie, the lions, the hell-cats called tigers, eagles, horned owls, leopards and a dog with only two legs.

As curious as the beasts in the Tower were the strange objects on display in the museum of the Royal Society, 'the entire skin of a Moor, tanned with the hair on', 'a tooth taken out of the womb of a woman, half an inch long', and 'a piece of bone voided with his urine by Sir William Throgmorton'.

Those with a taste for inspecting living curiosities of nature might choose to go to Newgate Prison to look at the inmates awaiting trial or execution; to Chick Lane where giant carriers and drovers ate vast hunks of meat in public, 'stuffing their insatiate appetites with greasy swine's flesh, till the fat drivelled down from the corners of their mouths'; to the kitchen door of a large house to look at the crowds of ragamuffins, calling themselves members of the City Blackguard, who loitered there at meal times; to a Billingsgate night-cellar to listen to the red-faced fish-wives, with baskets on their heads, rings on their thumbs, and glasses of warm ale and brandy in their hands, loudly discussing the affairs of the day in an atmosphere redolent of stale

The Tower engraved by W. Hollar, 1647.

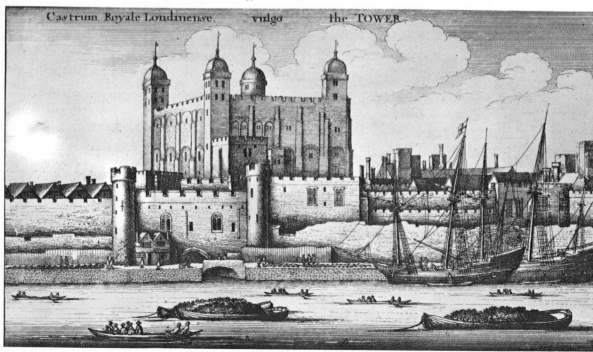

sprats and tobacco smoke; or to Bethlehem Hospital, built in 1676 as a madhouse, and the home of numerous lunatics whose strange antics could be observed and whose ravings could be heard for the price of the twopenny entrance fee. Among the most popular of the Bedlam exhibits in the late seventeenth century were a man in a straw cap who claimed to command an army of eagles and would declare war on the stars if only he could have a bottle of claret; a man who talked of nothing but bread and cheese, of how 'bread was good with cheese and cheese was good with bread, and bread and cheese was good together and abundance of such stuff'; and a former scholar of St John's College, Cambridge, whose 'frenzical extravagancies' were peculiarly diverting.

If it were a Sunday the visitor would find drama, as well as consolation and uplift, in a church where the congregation would show its approval of a particularly passionate or zealous sermon by a continuous, and mountingly loud appreciative hum. Bishop Burnet was often so overwhelmed by this humming that he would sit down to enjoy it, rubbing his face with his handkerchief.

After church the visitor might choose to refresh himself in a coffee-house, to take a glance at the latest news in the *Flying Post*, a look at the interesting letters from foreign places and the advertisements which the proprietor had stuck on the wall, to have a chat with a fellow customer, perhaps, and a dish of coffee – 'Politician's Porridge' – sweetened with sugar no doubt, but never whitened with milk. Already there were scores of chocolate and coffee-houses in London – though they had been unknown before the Civil War – most of them with a reputation for accommodating one particular type of customer: there was Man's Coffee-House, behind Charing Cross – known also as The Royal Coffee-House and as Old Man's – which catered for stockjobbers; there was Will's Coffee-House on the corner of Bow Street and Russell Street, Covent Garden, where men of letters were to be found in the company of those who fancied themselves as wits. Lawyers and scholars met at the Grecian close by the Temple and at Nando's above the Rainbow Tavern in Inner Temple Lane; clergymen at Child's in St Paul's Churchyard; artists at Old Slaughter's in St Martin's Lane; authors at Button's in Bow Street; military men at the Little Devil Coffee-House in Goodman's Fields and in Young Man's; men of fashion and politicians at the Cocoa Tree, at Ozinda's in Pall Mall, and at various establishments in St James's including White's; shippers, merchants and marine insurers at Lloyd's, one of the oldest coffee-houses of them all, which was in existence in Tower Street in 1688. Frenchmen went to Giles's, Scotsmen to the British. Altogether, by the time Queen Anne came to the throne in 1702, there were at least five hundred such places in London (plate 18). Some were highly exclusive, already taking on the atmosphere and peculiarities of private clubs; others were far less reputable establishments where the snapping of snuff-box lids was lost in the noise made by men arguing, puffing at pipes or chewing wads of tobacco, where the atmosphere stank of tobacco worse than 'a Dutch barge or a boatswain's cabin', and the walls were plastered with so many advertisements for patent medicines, dentifrices, beautifying waters, golden elixirs, lozenges, drops, 'Popular Pills', 'Liquid Snuff', and 'Doctor Case's Pills for the Speedy Cure of Violent Pains without Loss of Time or Hindrance of Business', that they seemed more like mountebanks' parlours than coffee-houses.

Some coffee-houses were fronts for brothels like the 'widow's coffee-house' which Ned Ward, the convivial landlord of the King's Head Tavern, Gray's Inn, described in his *London Spy* in 1698.

This coffee-house was approached from a dark and antiquated entry by means of an almost perpendicular staircase which the visitor pulled himself up by clinging to a rope nailed to the wall. Inside the coffee-room, where a pint coffee-pot stood before a handful of fire in the rusty grate, there was a muddled array of phials, gally-pots, long bottles of Rosa Solis, advertisements for pills and for a rare whitewash for the face. On the long table were two or three stone bottles, a quartern pot, a roll of plaster, a pipe of tobacco, a pair of spectacles, and a Bible. Around the walls were displayed a grenadier's

A coffee house, a coffee plant and a vine: illustration to a broadsheet of 1674.

bayonet, musket and cartouche-box, a head-dresser's block, 'an old fashioned clock in a crazy case, but as silent as a corpse in a coffin', a print of 'The Seven Golden Candlesticks', a lady's hat with a scarlet topknot, and an extract from an Act of Parliament against drinking, swearing and all manner of profaneness. The floor was broken like the floor of an old stable, the windows were mended with brown paper, and 'the bare walls were full of dust and cobwebs'.

Down the stairs from the attic there appeared during his visit, so Ned Ward said, a couple of airy youths who by their cropped hair, stone buckles in their shoes, broad bold hatbands, and lack of swords, he took to be merchants' sons or 'the apprentices of topping tradesmen'. 'They stayed not above a minute in the coffee-room,' Ned Ward commented, 'but, Magpie-like, asked what o'clock, then made their bows after the newest fashion and so departed. My friend by this time (knowing the entertainment of the house) had called for a bottle of cock-ale [ale, supposedly aphrodisiac, in which a cock and other ingredients had been boiled], of which I tasted a glass but could not conceive it to be anything but small beer and treacle.'

While Ward was drinking instead a glass of Nantes brandy, which the old widow assured him would restore 'an old man of three score to the juvenility of thirty', two of the girls of the house came down the stairs in white dimity under-petticoats, embroidered like turkey-work chairs, pin-up coats of Scotch plaid adorned with bugle lace, and gowns of printed calico. Their faces, covered in paint, powder and patches, looked as though they were made of wax; and their heads were 'dressed up to the best advantage like a vintner's bar-keeper'. They joined Ward and his friend for a time, but when a 'seemingly sober citizen in cloak and band, about the age of sixty', came into the room, they went upstairs to join him in their 'secret work-room'. Ward then left and went outside where 'each jack-a-lanthorn [watchman] was croaking about the streets the hour of eleven'.

Ward was a connoisseur of such establishments, and a reliable guide to the various places in and around the metropolis where prostitutes could be found. According to him, a head-dresser's shop was seldom to be found without a harlot who could be seen sitting inside, expensively dressed in velvet and with as many patches on her face as there are spots on a leopard's skin. These were 'first-rate love-birds of about a guinea purchase'.

Men who could not afford so high a price would find a cheaper prostitute in Whetstone Park, between Holborn and Lincoln's Inn, in Bankside, Southwark, around St Bartholomew's Hospital, in Gray's Inn Walks, or at any of the fairs – at the Mayfair held every year in Brook Field, between Piccadilly and the Oxford road, until suppressed in 1708 because of the 'drunkenness, fornication, gaming and lewdness' it always provoked; at Horn

Fair, to which parties sailed down from London to Cuckold's Point, Rother-hithe, and then, wearing horns, walked to Charlton, where the fair was held; and at Bartholomew Fair, where the music-houses were full of women 'who by their want of stays, the airiness of their dress, the improvement of their complexion by paint, and the multitude of patches' could quickly be recognised for what they were.

If a mistress were required rather than a whore, Ward advised a visit to Duke Humphrey's Walk, St James's Park, a good place also for a lady to furnish herself with a gallant whose faithfulness could be assured for a suit of clothes, three meals a day and a little money for an occasional glass of usquebaugh. Alternatively, Covent Garden Church was a recognised rendezvous for the wife who was looking for a lover and the husband for a mistress; and most evenings on the Grand Parade in the Temple women could be seen frisking in and out of staircases, carrying rolls of parchment, papers and band-boxes, their faces hidden by masks, rumpled hoods and scarves. The best place of all, perhaps, for assignations were the two Exchanges, the one in the Strand for the more fastidious, the Royal Exchange for the less particular.

The new Royal Exchange, indeed, a far more elaborate building than the one destroyed in the Fire, was a sight (plate 16) which drew every visitor to the City, as did St Paul's. The paved interior courtyard was crowded with merchants and shoppers, tourists and idlers, Dutchmen in thrum caps with their hands in their pockets, Spaniards in short cloaks with their moustaches full of snuff, Scotsmen and Irishmen, Jews and parsons, maid-servants looking for places advertised on the notices stuck to the pillars, and sharp-faced ruffians keeping a watch for victims to kidnap and carry aboard a boat sailing for the American plantations, all standing about, talking, arguing, laughing, frowning, swearing, smiling, staring, strolling up and down the various walks, making their way to one or other of the 160 shops which were arranged above the surrounding portico, or pushing their way outside amongst the crowds of hawkers, porters, sellers of mandrake and pippins, cordials and balsams, chestnuts and oranges, and the numerous decrepit old men offering glass eyes, ivory teeth, corn plasters and spectacles.

After dining on calves' heads, geese and Cheshire cheese in a tavern, or on roast pork in the famous cook-shop in Pie Corner at the Smithfield end of Giltspur Street, the tourist might choose in summer to walk or drive out into the country – perhaps to have his fortune told by the gipsies who lived in the woods at Norwood, or to have an *al fresco* meal at the Cherry Gardens in Rotherhithe.

Although the open countryside was being pushed gradually farther and farther away from the City walls, it was still easy enough to reach. It was no

London Curtezan
la Putain de Londres
Cortegiana di Londra

M Lauron delin:

P Tempest excud:
Cum Privilegio

London prostitute of 1680.

105

longer possible to hunt at St Giles's and Soho, or in Gray's Inn Fields as Lord Berkeley had done every day a century before; but the sportsman had to go only a mile or so farther afield to hunt at Hampstead, or to the ponds in St George's Fields and Islington for shooting duck. Islington, famous for its cream and cakes and fresh syllabub, also offered pleasant walks across the fields to Canonbury, or across the River Lea to Wanstead where, at Mob's Hole, Dame Butterfield provided dancing to the music of bagpipes, fiddles and trumpets, and a feast of Essex calf and bacon roasted on a wooden spit.

Nor did the visitor have to go as far as Islington or Wanstead in search of pleasure in the open air. Vauxhall Gardens, laid out in Lambeth in 1661, had already become a popular and pleasant retreat, whose success induced Boydell Cuper, an old servant of the Howard family, to open Cuper's Gardens, which he decorated with leaden statues from Arundel House. Cuper's Gardens, or Cupid's Garden as it was more generally called, was opened in 1691, on the south bank of the river opposite Hungerford Stairs, and served as a rendezvous for clerks and apprentices, seamstresses and maids, a place where they could flirt and sing, talk and laugh and drink bottle-ale in the privacy of the arbours. There were also floating house-boats on the Thames which provided music and dancing; and there was music and dancing, too, at the various wells encircling the city, none more popular now than those discovered in his garden by Mr Thomas Sadler, a surveyor, whose charge of threepence for water included entrance to the dance room at no extra charge, and whose theatre was soon as popular as his 'spa'.

If exhausted on his return the tourist could retire to a Sweating House where in an atmosphere as hot as a pastry-cook's oven he sat and sweated until the rubber came to scrub and slap him with a gauntlet of coarse hair camlet before allowing him to lie down for an hour's sleep.

Thus refreshed he could go out to enjoy the night life of the town, with some hope after 1685 – a slender one perhaps – of not falling over in the dark, for by then one William Hemming had been granted a monopoly of street lighting on condition that he put a lamp outside every tenth house in the main streets between six o'clock and midnight. An evening might be enjoyed at the Groom-Porter's gaming-house, at the Hockley-in-the-Hole bear-garden, at the Theatre Royal in Drury Lane opened by Thomas Killigrew in 1663, or at a tavern on London Bridge.

London Bridge, as many a foreign tourist agreed, was one of the most fascinating of all the sights that London had to offer. It seemed astonishing that the ancient, top-heavy structure had not long since collapsed under the weight of the carts and carriages that rattled continuously across it between the bulging houses and haberdashers' shops whose projecting backs, over-hanging the water, were supported on great wooden beams and whose upper

16. The courtyard of the Royal Exchange *c.* 1725 (detail).
17. (*overleaf*) A frost fair on the Thames by Temple Stairs, 1683–84.

Advertisement for the King's Bagnio, or bath-house, in Longacre, 1686.

storeys were joined together by iron tie-bars to prevent them toppling backwards into the river.

The roadway beneath the tie-bars was scarcely twelve feet wide so that the carts frequently scraped the houses on each side as they squeezed past each other, and pedestrians were often trapped and seriously injured. Their shouts and the raucous bawling of the carters was as constant an affront to the ears as the roaring of the torrent below and the rushing noise of the great water-wheel.

A man had been employed to keep the traffic on the move ever since the bridge had become almost impassable during the years of rebuilding after the Fire, but neither he, nor the two other men who later came to reinforce his efforts, could keep the roadway unblocked for long. Yet the building of a second bridge further upstream was constantly opposed both by the City who feared a drop in their trade, and by the powerful company of watermen who made their living by plying the fleet of wherries, coracles, ferry-boats and barges that filled the river at all hours of the day and for most of the night.

There were, so claimed John Taylor, the Gloucestershire man who became one of their number and their champion, as many as 40,000 people along the waterfront whose livelihood depended on the river. He included, no doubt, the stevedores and boat-builders, fish-wives and porters, hawkers and scavengers, as well as the watermen and their apprentices whose numbers were so often reduced by the forays of the press-gang.

The press-gang was but one of the hazards of the watermen's life. The oarsmen who ferried passengers from bank to bank in comfortable eight-oared wherries with cushioned seats and awnings, the skullers of the smaller passenger boats, and those who manned the big tilt-boat that carried passengers up the Thames from Gravesend, all these were rarely in danger. But the poor fishermen, whose only possessions were their coracles and tackle and the waterside hovels in which they lived, their ill-fed and ill-clad apprentices who slept in the boats to stop them being stolen in the night, and the 'bridge-shooters' who took their craft between the piers of London Bridge where the rushing water rose to an intimidating height, all these watermen led a hard and dangerous life.

Most passengers preferred to get out of their boat at the Three Cranes in Upper Thames Street, before the waterman shot the bridge, and then to rejoin him at Billingsgate, knowing that the Duke of Norfolk's boat had once collided with a breakwater and that many of his suite had been drowned, that scarcely a year had passed since then without a similar accident being recorded. As Pepys said, his friend Salisbury 'could not by any means be moved to go through the bridge' on a river trip to Whitehall, and so he was fain to go round by the Old Swan. Those who braved the passage sometimes found the experience exhilarating; and one Frenchman, so one of Pepys's other friends told him, 'when he saw the great fall, he began to cross himself, and say his prayers in the greatest fear in the world; though as soon as he was over, he swore, "Morbleu! c'est le plus grand plaisir du monde".'

On occasions, however, the water was too turbulent for even the most experience of the 'bridge-shooters': an average of fifty watermen were drowned by the bridge each year. Other watermen and their passengers died after having been tipped into the water and having swallowed too much of it. For although in summer, seen from the pleasant green gardens on its banks, it glittered and sparkled in the sunlight, a closer inspection revealed a dirty brown scum, with bits of sewage and rubbish floating about in it, giving off a putrid smell. The Englishman on the Grand Tour complained of the filthiness of the Continent's waterways, how clothes washed in Rome stank of the Tiber; but there were few big European rivers dirtier than the Thames, and the German Paul Hentzner's complaint, that his clothes once washed in the Thames at London never afterwards lost the smell of its slime, was one which subsequent travellers echoed. Most watermen, of course, became so accustomed to the fumes and vapours of the river that they no longer noticed them, and their children even swam in it, as young men did in the Fleet even after it had become once more a sluggish sewer.

During a hard winter there were less insalubrious pleasures; for then the river froze over from bank to bank and the young could slide and skate on it, and if it had previously flooded – as it often did before the embankments were built in the nineteenth-century – they could also skate over acre upon acre of ice at Chelsea and above the marsh between Lambeth and Kennington. In the winter of 1683–1684 there was so hard a frost that not only streets of booths were put upon the frozen Thames and oxen roasted on the ice, but horses and carts and carriages were driven over it from bank to bank. There were 'divers shops of wares quite across as in town', said Evelyn who walked across from Westminster Stairs to Lambeth to dine with the Archbishop and, after evening prayers, walked back again to the Horse Ferry at Millbank (plate 17).

The Frost Fair continued throughout the month of January with more and more booths and tents, cook-shops, barbers'-shops and drinking-sheds erected beneath the bridge. Teams of apprentices played football and hockey while their girl-friends cheered them on, eating mince pies and keeping their hands warm with baked potatoes. A printer put up a press and for sixpence sold a bordered card with the buyer's name and date inscribed on it together with the certification: 'Printed on the river of Thames being frozen. In the 36th Year of King Charles II.'

'Coaches plied from Westminster to the Temple,' Evelyn noted in his

Boys bathing in the Fleet in the early eighteenth century.

journal on 24 January, 'and from several other stairs to and fro, as in the streets, sleds, sliding with skates, a bull-baiting, horse and coach-races, puppet-plays and interludes, cooks, tippling and other lewd places, so that it seemed to be a bacchanalian triumph, or carnival on the water.'

There was another prolonged frost in 1698; an even longer one in 1740, although on that occasion there was a sudden thaw in the middle of it and the stalls and booths were carried downstream on the melting flows before their owners had had time to pack them up. The Frost Fairs only just survived the eighteenth century, however, for in 1825 work on a new bridge, designed by John Rennie, began. Seven years later the old one was demolished, and the Thames, now allowed to flow much more freely, did not freeze over so solidly again.

The heyday of old London Bridge had, in any case, by then long since passed. At the beginning of the eighteenth century the buildings put up after the Fire had already been deserted by the merchants who had formerly lived in them and had been taken over by impoverished artists and the keepers of cheap lodging-houses. In 1745 George Dance built two new terraces with an attractive colonnade running beneath the upper storeys on either side of the roadway. But a few years later the older houses at the Southwark end were sagging noticeably while the still narrow roadway was as frequently blocked as ever – despite the opening in 1750 (to the fury of the watermen) of a second bridge across the river at Westminster (plate 20). So it was decided to pull all the houses down and what had once been one of the most remarkable sights in Europe was no more.[1]

Another of London's most famous landmarks had also by now disappeared. For one night during the great frost of 1698 a Dutch maidservant at Whitehall Palace had left her master's clothes hanging up to dry too close to a charcoal brazier. The clothes caught fire, and within half an hour the whole of that part of the Palace was in flames. There had been countless other fires, large and small, in various parts of the enormous rambling complex of courts and chambers, galleries and theatres, cockpits, woodyards and spiceries during the past century. In the November after the Great Fire there was what Pepys described as a 'horrid great Fire' which entirely destroyed the guard house which had been built in 1649 on the site of the present Horse Guards; and a few years later a maid, throwing away a candle-end which had not been properly extinguished, started a fire that consumed a labyrinth of old buildings along the river front.

Although Cosmo III of Tuscany, one of Charles II's Medici relatives, had condemned the Palace as little better than a jumbled collection of two thousand rooms, all small, 'badly arranged and without doors', it had been improved since his day. Charles's brother James had preferred St James's,

but he had nevertheless spent a good deal of money on alterations to Whitehall, replacing the Privy Gallery by a tall building designed by Wren, with
fireplaces by Grinling Gibbons and ceilings by the Italian artist Antonio
Verrio, and building a new chapel nearby which was also decorated by
Gibbons and Verrio. A few years later Wren built a new riverside Terrace at
a cost of over £10,000.

All this, together with nearly every other building in Whitehall Palace,
was destroyed in the fire of 1698, only Inigo Jones's Banqueting House
and the two gates which had been built by Henry VIII being saved. The
Banqueting House still survives; but the two Tudor gates have been demolished, King Street Gate in 1723 and Holbein Gate – two of whose medallions
of Roman Emperors were removed to the gateways at Hampton Court – in
1759, at a time when all the gates of the City were being pulled down to ease
the congestion of traffic at these by then traditional bottlenecks.

The site on which Whitehall Palace had stood was leased in plots for private
building; and during the next century several large houses appeared on it.
Montagu House in 1733, Pelham House in 1755, Pembroke House in 1757,
Carrington House in 1764 and in 1772 Gwydyr House.[2] The first four of
these have disappeared, but Gwydyr House still stands not far from the only
remaining room of the Tudor Palace – the seventy-foot long brick-vaulted
wine cellar – which is preserved, twenty feet lower than its original position,
beneath the labyrinthine ramifications of the Ministry of Defence.[3]

London Bridge before and after its houses were destroyed; on
the left is the tide-driven pumping machine. Eighteenth-century engraving.

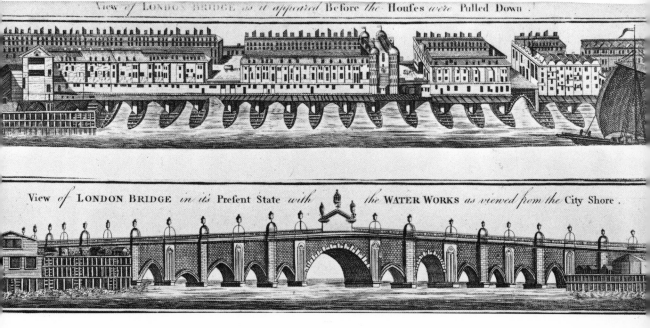

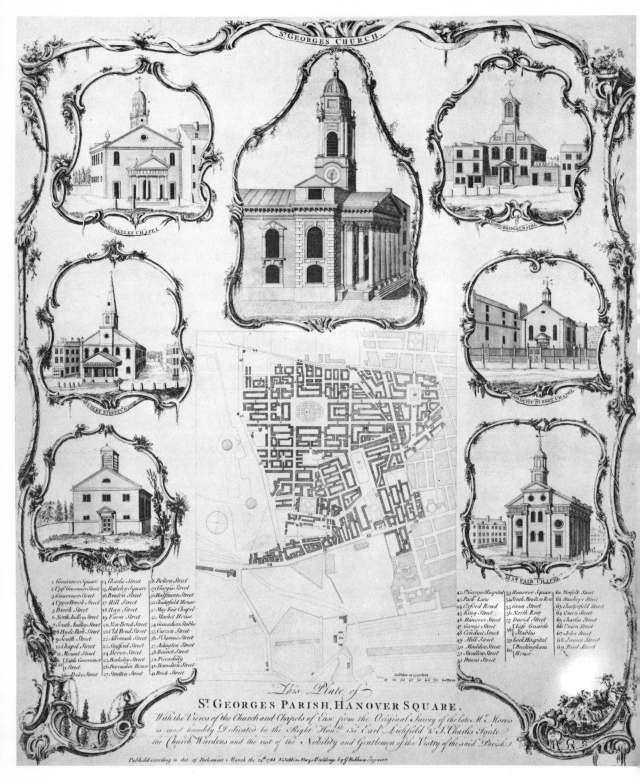

The Parish of St George's, Hanover Square, 1768.

9   *Georgian Growth 1710 – 1783*

In 1710, the year that St Paul's Cathedral was finished, a general election swept to power a High Church Tory Government which celebrated its victory by bringing in an Act for the building of fifty new churches 'in or near the Cities of London and Westminster or the suburbs thereof . . . churches of stone and other proper Materials with Towers or Steeples to each of them'. To many it seemed that the Act had come none too soon, for scores of London's old churches were either tumbling into disrepair or were becoming inadequate for the growing parishes they were intended to serve.

Although the number so confidently inserted into the Act proved far too ambitious, several fine new churches were built as a result of it, six of them by the architect who had risen to fame as Sir Christopher Wren's most gifted and original pupil.

Nicholas Hawksmoor was born in a Nottinghamshire farmhouse in 1661 and, at the age of eighteen, obtained a humble appointment on Sir Christopher's

The Royal Stables at Charing Cross and St Martin's in the Fields: engraving of 1753.

staff. His exceptional talents were soon recognised, and before long he had risen to be deputy-surveyor of the works at Chelsea and Greenwich Hospitals and clerk of the works at Whitehall, St James's, Kensington Palace and Westminster Abbey. So close, indeed, was his association with Wren's later work that much of it seems to be imbued with the spirit of the younger man's genius, just as much of Hawksmoor's own work was inspired by the dramatic verve of John Vanbrugh his near contemporary and, after 1699, his intimate collaborator.

Three of Hawksmoor's six beautiful churches, all displaying a thrilling fusion of sombrely classical grandeur and gothic fancy, are in Stepney: St George's-in-the-East, Christ Church Spitalfields, and St Anne's Limehouse. One is at Greenwich, St Alphege's; one in Bloomsbury, St George's; and the sixth, St Mary Woolnoth, is in the heart of the City, just east of the Mansion House.[1]

While these churches were being built, Hawksmoor's colleagues, as Commissioners for Churches under the Act of 1710, were busy supervising the construction of others. Two of these, St Mary-le-Strand and St Martin-in-the-Fields, remain among the most distinctive monuments of the London scene. Both were designed by James Gibbs, a Scottish Roman Catholic who had once considered becoming a priest and who, on a long visit to Rome, had conceived that admiration for contemporary Italian architecture which found expression in the baroque overtones of the church which stands serenely massive in the middle of the Strand.[2]

James Gibbs's other church, St Martin-in-the-Fields, was more restrained, far more in tune, despite its tall, elaborate steeple, with the spirit of academic Palladianism.[3]

Finished in 1726, St Martin-in-the-Fields was in sharp contrast to two churches, St John's Smith Square and St Paul's Deptford, previously built by Thomas Archer, an admirer, like Gibbs, of Italian architecture, yet one whose extreme devotion to baroque led to designs far more fanciful and bold than Gibbs had attempted in the Strand.[4] A safer and less flamboyant architect in contemporary eyes was Henry Flitcroft, the son of William III's gardener, a protégé of Lord Burlington – he was known as 'Burlington Harry' – and the man chosen both for the rebuilding of St Olave's in Southwark and for St Giles-in-the-Fields.[5] Safer and more reliable, too, in contemporary opinion was John James, the clergyman's son who replaced Gibbs as a Commissioner for Churches and was given the task of building St George's in the new Hanover Square, a church whose imposing columned portico was much admired and widely imitated.[6]

Hanover Square had always been intended by its originators as a fashionable centre. Conceived in the period of peace and stability that followed the end of the War of the Spanish Succession in which the Duke of Marlborough had so signally distinguished himself – and at a time when the death of the childless Queen Anne had brought a new dynasty to the English throne – Hanover Square was laid out between 1717 and 1719. It was built on land partly owned and partly leased by the first Earl of Scarbrough, an old general whose devotion to the new royal house is evidenced not only by the name of the Square, the dedication of its church (St George's), the wide street (George Street) which leads up to it from the south, but also by the German style of the grand houses which were built in it.[7]

While Hanover Square and its surrounding streets were taking shape, three other landowners were developing their estates to the south, east and north of it. The first of these was the young Lord Burlington whose magnificent house in Piccadilly, designed by himself and Colen Campbell on the site of his ancestor's far more modest one, was a noble memorial to the genius of Palladio.

Behind Burlington House its gifted owner let out plots on building leases to those who shared his tastes and were prepared to endorse the general scheme he had in mind for the area. Thus, in addition to buildings for which he himself made the drawings in his chosen manner, there appeared in Old and New Burlington Streets, in Cork Street and Savile Row, houses by

Hanover Square in 1787.

Henry Flitcroft ('Burlington Harry'); by Giacomo Leoni, the Italian compiler of a luxurious edition of Burlington's bible, Palladio's *I quartro libri dell' architettura*; by William Kent, who had met Lord Burlington in Italy where he had been sent to study the arts of the Renaissance; and by Colen Campbell who, too, had known Lord Burlington in Italy and who built a small *palazzo* for his own occupation in Old Burlington Street.

Colen Campbell was also concerned with the development of the Grosvenor Estate, a large block of land east of Park Lane and south of the road to Oxford, which had come into the possession of Sir Thomas Grosvenor, the third baronet of Eaton Hall in Cheshire, on the occasion of his marriage to the heiress of a rich London merchant named Audley.

In 1710 Sir Thomas's son, Richard, obtained an Act to develop part of his family's recently acquired estate by granting building leases around the large square which bears his name and in the two new streets – Audley Street and Grosvenor Street – that were constructed to give the Square access to the road to Oxford (Oxford Street) in the north and to New Bond Street in the east.

Colen Campbell was called upon by the Grosvenors' agent, Robert Andrews, to give his advice on the lay-out of the six-acre square; and in

Grosvenor Square looking north across the fields to the villages of Hampstead and Highgate: engraving of 1754.

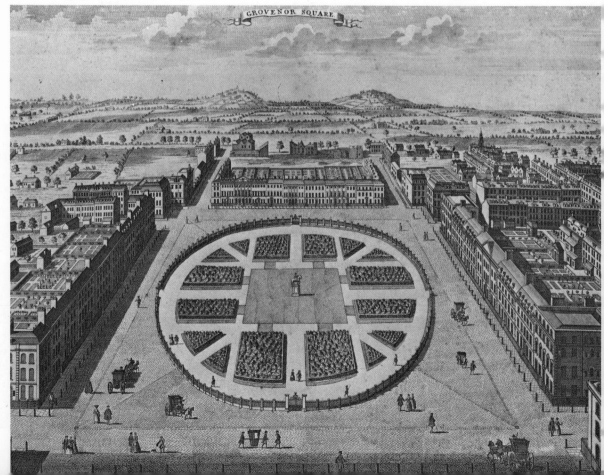

1725 John Simmons, a builder, began work on its east side by constructing a terrace of houses all of them identical with the exception of a larger house in the middle, whose pediment broke up the straight roof line, and two taller houses at either end. The other sides of the square were less symmetrical, some of the houses in them being big neo-classical mansions – for which, since the rich now preferred to spend their money on their country estates, there was little demand – others, like No. 43 – once the home of George I's exceedingly tall mistress, the Duchess of Kendal, nicknamed the Maypole – being less pretentious and far more comfortable.[8]

Dominated now by Eero Saarinen's impressively grand United States Embassy, Grosvenor Square – almost entirely rebuilt within the last forty years – seems more than ever to deserve its epithet, 'Little America', by which it has long been known. John Adams, America's first representative at the Court of St James's, lived at No. 9; while the Grosvenor Chapel in South Audley Street, built in the early 1730s, has seemed to many generations of Americans curiously reminiscent, as indeed it is, of many small parish churches in Massachusetts, New Hampshire and Maine, which were built on similar lines.[9]

A few years after Sir Richard Grosvenor had begun to develop his inheri-

A club of artists portrayed by Gawen Hamilton in 1735: the engraver George Vertue is on the left, James Gibbs fifth from the left and William Kent last on the right.

tance south of Oxford Street, his near neighbour Edward Harley, second Earl of Oxford – whose wife, Henrietta, was the daughter of the Duke of Newcastle and heiress to her father's rich estates – decided to follow his example. With the help of his agent, John Prince, and his architect, James Gibbs, Harley planned the development of that part of his estate known as Marylebone Fields, inducing several rich noblemen, who had served in his late father's Government, to enter into building leases with him.

Cavendish Square was soon the centre of a new fashionable suburb which spread outwards in a network of streets, most of them, like the Square itself, still bearing the names of various members of Harley's family and friends, of his family's country estates – Welbeck and Wimpole – and, later, of the man his daughter, Margaret, married, William Bentinck, Duke of Portland.

This later development of the Harley Estate did not take place until the 1770s. By then a neighbouring estate had been built upon by Henry William Portman, an extremely rich landowner with a country house at Bryanston in Dorset; and it was on the Portman Estate, more particularly in Portman Square, that the new style of architecture associated with the name of Robert Adam was displayed in its early flowering.

By the time of the Peace of Paris which in 1763 ended the Seven Years War, the older generation of architects which had centred round Lord Burlington at the altar of Palladio was beginning to pass away. Yet they, and their immediate successors, continuing and implementing the work of Inigo Jones, had ensured the maintenance of the classical tradition, both in the design of private houses and public buildings, and had bequeathed to London some of its most famous monuments.

George Dance, the Elder, had begun work in 1734 on the designs for the Lord Mayor's Mansion House, which took its final massive shape on the site of the old Stocks Market in 1753;[10] at about the same time the Governors of the Bank of England accepted the unmistakably Palladian plans of George Sampson for a new building in Threadneedle Street;[11] through the influence of the Earl of Pembroke, whose Palladian tastes were well known, the Swiss engineer and architect, Charles Labelye, was commissioned to design the new stone bridge which, at a cost of nearly £400,000 and after nine years' work, gracefully spanned the Thames at Westminster in 1750 (plate 20); and Lord Burlington's protégé, William Kent, was chosen, the following year, to build the new military headquarters of the Horse Guards in Whitehall, whose Venetian windows and sixteenth-century Italian façade look down proudly towards St James's Park.[12] After Kent's death the completion of the Horse Guards was entrusted to John Vardy who, with General Gray, was also responsible for the uncompromisingly Palladian Spencer House in St James's Place.[13]

A couple strolling in Marylebone Fields, *c.* 1750.

The other great houses built in these years – Kent's Devonshire House in Piccadilly, James Stuart's Lichfield House in St James's Square,[14] Chester-field House in Park Lane designed by Isaac Ware, Cambridge House in Piccadilly,[15] and No. 44 Berkeley Square[16] – were all in this elegant classical tradition, as, indeed, were the Foundling and Middlesex hospitals in their necessarily more plain and institutional way.[17]

By the end of the Seven Year's War, however, a new style was beginning to soften the rigidities of Palladianism. Sir Robert Taylor and James Paine, who, in the words of a younger architect, 'nearly divided the practice of the profession between them', designed many buildings which, while still Palladian in principle, display a rejection of the almost hidebound rules that had lately governed the less imaginative of the master's disciples. But it was Robert Adam and his rival Sir William Chambers who were really responsible for the fresh face which London architecture now began to display.

Sir William Chambers was the less revolutionary, the more staid and authoritative of the two men. The grandson of a rich merchant who had helped to finance the armies of Charles XII, he had been born in Stockholm and, at the age of eighteen, after an English education, had joined the Swedish East India Company in whose service he travelled to China where his interest in architecture was first aroused. Having the means to indulge his fancy, he decided to make a thorough study of architecture in Italy; and on his return to England in 1755 he was an authority on the buildings of the Renaissance.

Within a few years of his return, he had established himself as one of the most gifted architects of his day. He was employed by Lord Bessborough to design a country house at Roehampton,[18] by the Princess Dowager of Wales for works at Kew,[19] and later by Lord and Lady Melbourne for their town house in Piccadilly which, early in the next century, was converted into those 'residential chambers for gentlemen' known as Albany.[20] In 1755, after being appointed Surveyor-General of Works, Chambers was appointed architect of Somerset House.

Intended as a splendidly imposing home for various administrative offices and institutions including the Navy Office, the Ordnance Office, and the Royal Academy of which Chambers was treasurer, Somerset House was built around a huge courtyard laid bare by the ruthless demolition of the Tudor and Stuart buildings that had formerly covered the site. It is dignified, imposing, admirable and rather stolid.[21]

Robert Adam's buildings, in contrast, were rarely if ever stolid. To Chambers's own disapproving eye, indeed, they often appeared flippant. The most ambitious of them in London was the Adelphi which Robert, with the help of his brothers (hence its name), began to bring into being in 1768.

Robert Adam had then been back from his prolonged Grand Tour for some years and had established his reputation with the same speed as Chambers, two years his senior, had done. In 1764 when he published his *Ruins of the Palace of Diocletian* he was architect to both George III and the Board of Works, and had been entrusted with the design of the much admired Admiralty screen in Whitehall.[22]

The Adelphi, however, was a private venture, though a highly ambitious one. South of the Strand and east of the streets that Nicholas Barbon had formed out of the Duke of Buckingham's gardens, now leased by the Adams from the Duke of St Albans, Nell Gwynne's great-grandson, the brothers planned to build a little town within a town which would carry echoes of the Diocletian ruins Robert had so much admired at Spalato – then part of the declining Venetian republic, now Split in Yugoslavia.

The ground sloped sharply down from the Strand to the river and Robert Adam's idea was to build his houses upon a riverside terrace raised to the level of the Strand and supported by immense arches – in places standing in double tiers – by catacombs and vaults. Although the scheme was beset by all sorts of difficulties, and although Robert and his brothers were almost driven into bankruptcy by their own miscalculations and the prejudice of others, it was realised in the end; the Adelphi became the most dramatic

The Adam brothers' Adelphi Terrace on the Thames.

and distinctive feature of the river front between the Savoy and Westminster Bridge.[23]

The houses were gaily decorated and gracefully embellished in a way which would have amazed Lord Burlington but which was to become the essential characteristic of Robert Adam's art (plate 21). Those of his later London houses which can still be enjoyed – Chandos House in Chandos Street, 20 St James's Square and 20 Portman Square – all bear witness to his originality, the stamp of his idiosyncratic genius.[24] No architect who designed a building during the rest of the century could fail to be influenced by his work. The younger men who succeeded him, Henry Holland, James Wyatt, and George Dance the younger, were all to some extent in revolt against what Chambers had castigated as the 'affectations' of the Adam style; but none of them could wholly escape from its enduring spell.

Dance who, as City Surveyor, was responsible for the restoration of All Hallows, London Wall,[25] as well as the starkly impressive Newgate Prison;[26] Henry Holland, 'Capability' Brown's son-in-law, who built Brooks's Club[27] before turning his hand to indulge the extravagances of the Prince of Wales; and James Wyatt, whose fantastic Oxford Street Pantheon was, in Walpole's opinion, 'the most beautiful edifice in England' (plate 19), were all indebted in their various ways to Robert Adam's genius.

While Robert Adam and his followers were encouraging the ornamentation of buildings, the authorities were endeavouring to have them made plainer. For many years limitations had been imposed upon exposed woodwork for fear of fire. In 1707 an Act of Parliament outlawed the wide, overhanging eaves-cornices which had been common to most town houses a generation before; and in 1709 a complementary Act forbade builders to insert wooden window frames flush with the brickwork – sash-windows were by then beginning to replace the earlier casements – requiring them to be set back four inches from the surface of the wall. These two Acts were followed in 1774 by a Building Act which aimed at further reducing the hazards of fire by establishing firm rules for each of four types, or 'rates', of houses categorised in the Act: a 'first rate' house – that was to say one worth more than £850 – being required to conform to higher standards than the 'fourth rate' house – worth less than £150 – but all of them being required to eschew every kind of external wooden ornamentation. Even shop fronts were required to extend no more than ten inches from the wall.

The inevitable tendency of the rules laid down in the 1774 Building Act was to impose a boring uniformity on those terraces built without the advice of trained architects and skilful craftsmen. The loss of individual character in certain streets was accentuated by the standardisation in such external fixtures as doorways, the Restoration doorway being the product of an individual woodcarver's skill, while the Georgian doorway was, more often than not, no more than the faithful reproduction of a design copied from a carpenter's pattern book.

Monotonous standardisation was far less oppressive, however, in the streets which were evolving in the later Georgian period to the west of London than it was in those to the east, where row upon row of cheap, impermanent, box-like structures were being erected with little regard to anything but the profit of the speculator and landlord.

Indeed, on both the Portman estate, where in 1776 the Duke of Manchester built himself a house in what became known as Manchester Square,[28] and on the extension of the Bedford estate, where work on Bedford Square also began in 1776, the influence of Adam was strong.

Soon after Bedford Square was finished, the Bedford lands were still further developed around Bloomsbury Square which Lord Southampton had begun at the end of the previous century. This development was carried out by a Scottish builder from Southwark who began work by building houses in Russell Square and then, having pulled down Bedford House, filled in the north side of Bloomsbury Square.

This builder, James Burton, the most ambitious London builder since Nicholas Barbon, had made his first foray into property development in the fields surrounding the Foundling Hospital where the Governors of the

19. 'The most beautiful edifice in England': James Wyatt's Pantheon in Oxford Street, by William Hodges; the figures are perhaps by Johann Zoffany.
20. *(overleaf)* The City, south London and Westminster Bridge, by Robert Griffier, 1748.

Hospital had proposed to put up around two squares, Mecklenburgh and Brunswick Squares, 'all classes of Building from the first Class down to Houses of Twenty-five pound pr. annum without the Lower Classes interfering with and diminishing the Character of those above them'. Of these houses Burton eventually built almost six hundred. Within a few years, having moved on to other estates, he was said to have built houses worth in total almost £2,000,000.[29] Eventually, with a large fortune at his command, he was one of those who helped to ensure that the majestic plans which the Prince Regent and his advisers had conceived for the improvement of his capital did not meet the sad fate that seemed at times inevitable.

21. Robert Adam's design for a section of the drawing-room of Northumberland House.

IO   *Memorials of the Regency*
1783–1830

When the Prince of Wales reached the age of twenty-one, his father agreed that he should be provided with an establishment of his own; so, in November 1783, the emotional, charming and wayward young man excitedly took possession of Carlton House.

It was a large house towards the Haymarket end of Pall Mall, with extensive gardens, complete with bowers and grottoes, which had formerly belonged to Henry Boyle, Lord Carleton, and more recently had been the home of the King's mother, the Princess Dowager of Wales. The Princess had increased its size by adding to it the house next door which she had bought from George Bubb Doddington.

Since the Princess's death, however, the house had fallen into disrepair, and was by no means fine enough, nor yet even large enough, for the ornate and extravagant tastes of her grandson, who immediately set about its enlargement and enrichment, a process which was to continue, at a cost

Carlton House in 1800.

The Great Fair in Hyde Park, August 1814.

which the improvident Prince himself admitted was 'enormous', for almost thirty years.

The architect chosen to carry out the work, under the Prince's general direction, was Henry Holland who imposed upon it a classical dignity, an 'august simplicity' which, in Horace Walpole's opinion, made 'Mr Adam's gingerbread and sippets of embroidery' seem decidedly meretricious.

Inside, instead of 'only painting it and putting handsome furniture where necessary' according to his father's instructions, the Prince of Wales succeeded in producing the most magnificent palace in London. Approached from the Corinthian portico was a splendid hall, decorated with Ionic columns, leading to an octagon and a graceful double staircase. Above were the state apartments, music room, Chinese drawing-room, and the Prince's splendid bow-windowed bedroom, his dressing-room and bathroom. Below was a whole new range of domestic quarters, larders, sculleries, pantries, kitchens and cellars. Outside in the gardens, the old elms now looked upon flower beds, statues, a waterfall, a temple with an Italian marble floor, even an observatory.

Each year new splendours were added to Carlton House until it was considered finer than any other house in England, worthy, in Robert Plumer Ward's estimation, to stand comparison with Versailles and in Count Münster's with the palace at St Petersburg which was not its equal 'in elegance or richness'.

To some, indeed, it was altogether too rich, almost vulgar in its opulence. This was emphatically the opinion of Robert Smirke, the conscientious architect of the British Museum, who condemned the apartments as 'overdone with finery'. Yet the Prince continued to lavish money upon it, making it more majestic than ever, building on a whole suite of new rooms, some Gothic, others Corinthian, until it was quite dazzling in its magnificence.

Splendid levées were held here, balls and banquets, private parties and public receptions; and the Prince wandered from room to room, floridly handsome, bulging out of his exquisite clothes, charming some, repelling others, cultivated, exotic, replete. One fête which reputedly cost £120,000 was attended by two hundred guests, the men in court dress or uniform, the women in 'elegant variegated dresses', and provided amongst other delights a dining-table down which a stream of water, '*real* water had been made to flow in a meandering channel, with proper accompaniments of sand, moss and rocks in miniature, and bridges across. Gold and silver fishes frisking about the stream, exhibited the brightness of their scales, reflecting the light of 500 flambeaux, to the infinite delight of the guests.'

For three days afterwards the public were admitted to inspect the decorations in Carlton House's magnificent apartments. On the last day there was a stampede and ladies were to be seen 'all round the gardens, most of them without shoes or gowns; and many almost completely undressed, and their hair hanging about their shoulders'. People were thrown down and 'trodden underfoot – arms and legs were fractured . . . as to shoes no lady pretended to keep them; and after the event they were swept in heaps and filled several hogsheads'.

In 1810, the year that he was sworn in as Regent, the Prince discussed with his architect the possibility of making his marvel of a palace the *fons et origo* of a new road which would sweep up from it towards Marylebone Park, an expanse of open land north of Portland Place which had just reverted to the Crown from the noble families to whom it had formerly been let. The new street, as well as providing a grand route, a *Via Triumphalis*, between Carlton House and Marylebone Park, would cut a convenient swathe between the new and fashionable building developments to the west and the poorer district of Soho to the east. The scheme had been suggested some time before by John Fordyce, the Surveyor-General of His Majesty's Land Revenues, who had envisaged an extensive development in the Park which could scarcely be expected to be profitable were its inhabitants not to be provided with a new road down which they could drive to the town centre.

Nash's first plan of 1812 for the Regent's Park development with its terraces, villas, markets and canals.

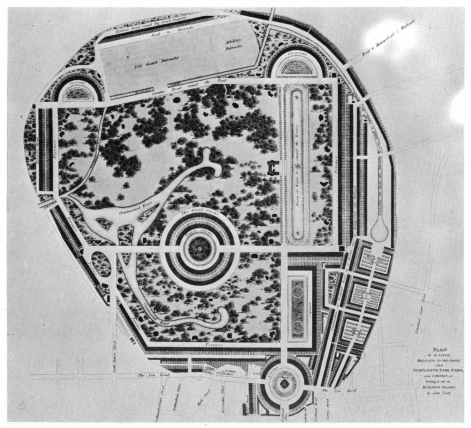

The Prince Regent's principal architect at this time was John Nash (plate 22), Henry Holland having died in 1806. In fact, Nash had been advising the Prince for several years before that; and there were many who believed there was a secret bond between them which went far deeper than their relationship as artist and patron.

Nash, the son of an impoverished Lambeth millwright who died when he was a child, had first appeared in the architectural world – no one seemed sure quite how – as an articled pupil in Sir Robert Taylor's office. An unsuccessful venture into speculative building in Bloomsbury, which resulted in his bankruptcy, was followed by a brief partnership with Humphry Repton, by a period spent designing country houses, and in 1798 by his marriage to a woman much younger than himself. This woman, so rumour had it, was the Prince Regent's mistress. Certainly after 1798 Nash was much more successful and appeared to be considerably richer than he had been before, arousing a good deal of jealousy and dislike by his self-satisfaction and display, his snobberies and affectations. A 'great coxcombe', Robert Finch recorded in his diary. 'He is very fond of women . . . attempted even Mrs Parker, his wife's sister. He lives in Dover Street, has a charming place in the Isle of Wight and drives four horses.'

Coxcomb or not, Nash was an architect of uncommon talent whose emergence as the Prince Regent's favourite architect was fully justified by his performance. His designs for the new Regent's Park were at once carefully conceived, practical and artistic. Between the terraces along the eastern and north-western sides, the open Park was to be dotted with groups of trees, with individual villas like Parisian *hôtels*, as well as a pleasure pavilion for the Prince Regent, and was to be broken in the south-eastern corner by the shores of a lake (plate 33) whose curving arms would stretch around a graceful garden. Spaces were provided for a shopping centre and an area of smaller houses; and at the south-eastern corner of the Park the handsome new Park Square was to be overlooked by a great sweep of houses in Park Crescent which would join the square to Portland Place and Regent Street. The new terraces were to be faced with stucco, an exciting change in a city still largely walled in brick.

Although Nash's visionary hopes were never realised in full, enough of his conception of what Regent's Park should be remains even now for us to realise how fine it might have been, and in patches actually was. For all their extravagance, occasional absurdity and audacious – sometimes even outrageous – panache, Nash's buildings round the Park, Terraces, Crescents, Gates, Lodges and Villages, are a continuing delight.

The same kind of verve inspired Nash's plans for Regent Street. As in the Park, so here, the original scheme was much altered in practice. Nash's early hopes for a perfectly balanced street came into collision with the

individual requirements of those who undertook to build in it. The Church
Building Commissioners could not be expected to content themselves with
a façade which would have also suited the requirements of James Burton
who intended to put up a row of shops. But although sites were eventually
disposed of for a great variety of purposes – houses, chambers, shops, offices,
a concert hall, an inn, a restaurant, a coffee-house, and two churches – Nash
did succeed in imposing upon the whole street a kind of unity.

His difficulties were extreme and at times seemed insoluble. For long periods
expanses of frontage remained unlet. Frequently James Burton stepped in
when no other lessee could be found; and Nash himself, when even Burton's
finances were stretched to the limit, took over the whole of the Quadrant,
that sweeping curve which swung the street round after it had crossed
Piccadilly. Although the negotiations were exhausting, Nash took trouble to
ensure that all the sites were developed with artistry, particularly at important
junctions. He found for the commanding site to the north of Piccadilly Circus
a rich insurance company promoter who was taken with the idea of giving
his office – the County Fire Office – a façade like the river façade of the old
Somerset House of Inigo Jones. He ensured that the Theatre Royal, Haymarket, was furnished with a handsome Corinthian portico which would
delight the eye of those coming into Regent Street from St James's Square.

Nash's church of All Souls, Langham Place.

And where Regent Street curves round to the west, north of Cavendish Place, he induced the Church Building Commissioners to take a site on which he built a delightful church – All Souls', Langham Place – whose circular columned porch took the eye round to the Adam charm of Portland Place.

At the other end of Regent Street, Nash had once more to make adaptations to the original scheme. For Carlton House could no longer be its closing vista as he had originally intended: its owner, now George IV, had decided to move. He complained that Carlton House, despite the vast sums of money which had been spent upon it, was antiquated, run-down and decrepit. His father had died in 1820 and now, as King himself of the greatest power in the world (plate 23), he must have something new. Parliament was persuaded to pay for a huge new palace, south-west of St James's Palace, on the site of Buckingham House which his father had bought in 1762 at a cost of £28,000. George III, a man of strongly domestic taste and habits, had conceived a dislike for St James's, where quiet family life was impossible, and had bought Buckingham House from Sir Charles Sheffield – a kinsman of John Sheffield, first Duke of Buckingham and Normanby, who had built it in 1703 – as a retreat from ceremonial and as a more suitable home for his numerous children. When the children were grown up it was assigned to Queen Charlotte as a dower house; and since her death it had become known as the King's House, Pimlico.

While adequate for his parents it was by no means so for George IV, and to help pay for the far more magnificent structure with which he intended to replace it, it was decided that Carlton House must be pulled down, and that new terraces should be built on its foundations and in its gardens.[1]

So Regent Street, instead of sweeping up from the Corinthian portico of Carlton House, dipped away down a flight of wide and shallow steps between Nash's huge new blocks of Carlton Gardens and Carlton House Terrace towards St James's Park.

With George IV's encouragement and support, Nash and his colleagues transformed St James's Park, planting trees, making new walks, turning its canal into a gracefully curving lake. Also, when Regent Street was finished, Nash, although by then well on into his seventies, conceived a plan to link its southern end – through an extension of Pall Mall running across the bottom of Haymarket and through a big new square by Charing Cross – to a new road leading up from Whitehall to the growing developments in and around Bloomsbury.

This new square Nash planned to build on the site of the Old Royal Mews where row upon row of stables surrounded the noble and lively bronze statue of Charles I, which had been made by Hubert Le Sueur in

1633.[2] The square planned by Nash was eventually to be dominated, however, not by Charles I – though his statue still sits astride its horse looking down Whitehall towards the scene of his execution – but by Nelson, whose greatest victory gave the square its name and whose column rises in its centre lifting *his* statue a hundred and fifty feet above Charles's head.[3]

Trafalgar Square, which Nash did not live to see completed, is bordered on its northern side by William Wilkins's domed and turreted National Gallery.

The formation of a national collection of pictures had been a venture close to the King's heart. There were numerous fine private collections in the country, many of them created by young men who had been inspired by the Grand Tour; there was an increasingly valuable royal collection which Charles I had begun and which, after the dispersal of many of its treasures during the Commonwealth, was now rising to a new glory. But there was no national collection to compare with those to be found in Italy and France. To form the nucleus for such a collection the King urged the Government to buy the thirty-eight fine pictures which had belonged to his friend, John Julius Angerstein. The Government did so; the pictures were kept at first in Angerstein's house in Pall Mall (plate 24); then in Montague House, Bloomsbury, and then, together with many others that had by that time been added to them, they were re-hung in the National Gallery which was completed in 1828.[4]

As well as being closely involved with the building of the National Gallery, George IV was also associated with the new British Museum which was started at about the same time. In 1823 he decided to give to the nation the 65,000 volumes of his father's fine library. The Trustees of the British Museum accepted the gift with pleasure, but recognising that Montague House – already storing the Cottonian Library, Sir Hans Sloane's collections and the Harleian manuscripts, and striving to display the Towneley, Elgin and Phigalean Marbles – would not be large enough to house them, they asked Parliament for enough money to build a library 'worthy of the taste and dignity' of the country. Parliament voted the sum of £40,000, and work began on the new building that same year (plate 25). Its architect, Robert Smirke, was forty-three years old at this time, the son of a painter, a quiet practical methodical man who had travelled widely in Greece and Italy; and the influence of Smirke's Grecian travels may be seen in the inexorable process of Ionic columns which screens the massive structure that swallowed the walls of Montague House.[5]

George IV did not live to see the completion of the British Museum. Nor did he ever move into Buckingham Palace, though Nash had rushed

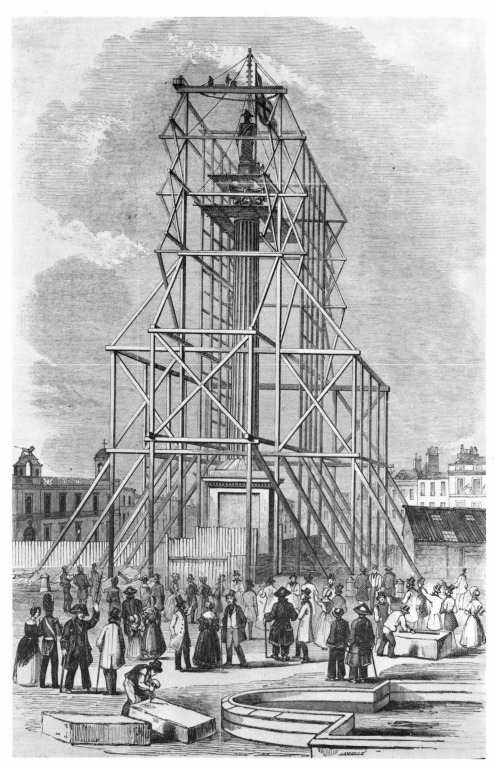

The Nelson Column in Trafalgar Square under construction, 1843.

ahead with the building of it in unseemly haste.

Sir John Soane, Professor of Architecture to the Royal Academy, who had designed so many of London's buildings during the Regency, hoped and believed that he would be given the commission and, disapproving of any suggestions that old Buckingham House should be tampered with, he had prepared drawings for a new palace in Green Park. But the King had made up his mind to move to the site of Buckingham House, protesting that there were 'early associations' which endeared him to the spot. So when Soane was deprived of the commission he had so much wanted and Nash was given it instead, the old house at the end of the Mall began to disappear. Soon far more than the £200,000 voted by Parliament for 'repairs and fitments' had been spent. New stables had been built, gardens laid out, wings pulled down and new ones put up, colonnades erected. Members of the Commons strongly protested. Joseph Hume argued that 'the Crown of England does not require such splendour. Foreign countries might indulge in frippery, but England ought to pride herself on her plainness and simplicity.' People in the country were starving; how could the Chancellor of the Exchequer justify such extravagance? Other Members criticised the style of Nash's new buildings, its 'square towers at the side and wretched inverted egg-cup at the top'. But work went on, and was to continue for the rest of

The new Buckingham Palace Nash built for George IV.

the reign and for the whole of the reign of the King's brother, William IV, who died in 1837.

Yet when Buckingham Palace was finished at a cost of over £700,000, Queen Victoria found it scarcely habitable. Few of the lavatories were ventilated; there were no sinks for the chambermaids on the bedroom floors; the drains were faulty; the bells would not ring; some of the doors would not close; and many of the thousand windows would not open.

Its whole history had been one of miscalculation and misfortune. Nash himself had professed himself wholly dissatisfied with his own work, and was so dismayed by the sight of two wings when they were finished that he had them pulled down again.

After George IV's death Nash had been dismissed, a Committee set up to enquire into his conduct, and another architect, Edward Blore, appointed. Blore gave the palace an entirely new front, which was, in turn, replaced by the present Portland stone façade in 1913.[6]

The original scheme for the western approaches to Buckingham Palace has also not survived. The young architect entrusted with this work was Decimus Burton, the son of James Burton the builder, and a protégé of Nash. His plan was to make a grand sweep from the forecourt of the Palace, through the Marble Arch, which Nash had designed to stand between the two projecting wings of the Palace as its main entrance, up Constitution Hill, through a new Corinthian arch at Hyde Park Corner and then, between the columns of an Ionic screen, into the Park. In 1851 the Marble Arch was moved to the top of Park Lane, and although the Ionic screen still stands beside Apsley House, where Burton placed it, his new arch had to be rebuilt in the 1880s in a different position at the western end of Constitution Hill and its relationship to the screen was thereby lost.[7]

Hyde Park Corner as laid out by Decimus Burton, the gate to Buckingham
Palace on the left and to the Park on the right.

But while Decimus Burton's grand conception cannot be appreciated now, the dramatic approach to the Palace down the Mall from Trafalgar Square, through Admiralty Arch and past the Victoria Memorial, is a not unworthy substitute.[8]

The years that passed between the purchase of Buckingham House and the completion of the Palace saw an astonishing number of additions to the list of London's public buildings, most of them constructed after the Peace of Paris of 1763. There were impressive new buildings at the Bank by Soane, for the University of London by Wilkins, and for King's College by Smirke. Smirke was also responsible for a huge Post Office in St Martin's-le-Grand,[9] an improved Royal Mint,[10] and a vast prison covering eighteen acres, the Millbank Penitentiary.[11] There were numerous new buildings for the growing professions (such as Henry Hakewill's Plowden Buildings for the Middle Temple), for educational institutions (such as the London Institution by William Brooks), for charitable bodies (like W. S. Inman's London Orphan Asylum at Hackney), for hospitals (like St Katherine's Hospital, Regent's Park, St George's Hospital, Knightsbridge and the new Bedlam in Lambeth Road),[12] for London's expanding trade (like the City Custom House),[13] and for the humanitarian organisations (such as Trinity House, built for the Brethren of the Trinity).[14] There were four new bridges across the Thames (all of them since demolished and rebuilt); and there were scores of new and restored churches, many of them the result of the Church Building Act of 1818 which allocated a million pounds for this purpose, much to the gratification of the good Anglican, concerned as he was by the spread of non-comformism.[15]

While churches and chapels were being built, so too were new theatres. Between 1808 and 1809 a new Covent Garden Opera House was built by Smirke;[16] a few years later a new Drury Lane appeared by Benjamin Wyatt;[17] and in 1820–21 Nash rebuilt the Theatre Royal, Haymarket.[18]

This, too, was the great age of club building. The first club to appear was the United Service, founded by General Graham, Lord Lynedoch, in the year of Waterloo. Its first home was in Lower Regent Street in a building designed by Sir Robert Smirke, himself an officer in the Militia. This building, introducing a club-house style that was widely imitated, was followed in 1826 by William Wilkins's University Club in Suffolk Place and in the same year by the Union Club in Trafalgar Square. The next year Crockford's, a gambling club, was opened in St James's Street; the Oriental, a club for men who had served in the East India Company, in Tenterden Street, Hanover Square; and Nash's new premises for the United Service Club, Pall Mall. And it was Pall Mall, a street of Italianate *palazzi*, that was now to become the centre of London's clubland.

Opposite the United Service Club is the Athenaeum, built to the design of Decimus Burton between 1828 and 1830. Next door the handsome premises of the Travellers' Club, founded at a time when the Grand Tour had been virtually halted for twenty years by the Napoleonic Wars, and soon to have a ten years' waiting list. The Italian Renaissance premises of the Travellers' Club were not finished, however, until 1832 when Barry had had the opportunity of making a lengthy tour of Greece and Italy which was responsible for its style and for Barry's future taste.

The club premises to the west of this were all built after the death of George IV; but most of them maintained the Palazzo style – the Reform Club (built, also by Barry, in 1841), the Carlton Club (designed by Sir Robert Smirke in 1835–36 and rebuilt by Sydney Smirke in 1847–54) and on the north side (both recently replaced by modern blocks), the Army and Navy Club (1848–51) and the Junior Carlton Club (1866–69).

The Oxford and Cambridge Club, designed earlier than the others (by Robert and Sydney Smirke in 1835), is, in contrast, in the neo-Greek taste of the Athenaeum, while the huge premises of the Royal Automobile Club built on part of the site of the demolished Carlton Club between 1908 and 1911, might have been brought intact from a French provincial town of the Third Republic.[19]

More massive than any club house was the huge palace, now known as Lancaster House, which·was originally intended for the Duke of York, but which remained unfinished – and unpaid for – when the Duke died in 1827. The shell was sold to the Marquess of Stafford, and it was under his successors, as Dukes of Sutherland, that the house, at length completed, came into its own as a fashionable artistic and social centre. By then Smirke, Benjamin Dean Wyatt, and Charles Barry had all had a hand in its design and decoration and between them they left a peculiarly undistinguished façade.[20] Inside, however, Lancaster House – like Buckingham Palace, Apsley House[21] and Clarence House[22] – paid elegant tribute to the opulent Louis XV style that was from now on to dominate the rooms of the rich and fashionable for over half a century.

While these ornate mansions, with their splendid staircases and spacious galleries, were rising above their neighbours around St James's, terraces of more modest houses continued to spread outwards in the new suburbs.

In Bloomsbury, for example, the Fitzroy estate was rapidly developed in the years of the Regency. Euston Square, named after Colonel Fitzroy's country house in Suffolk, was started north of Gordon Square; building in Fitzroy Square, begun in 1790, was continued until 1828. The Portman Estate grew quickly, too; and further to the north-west the Eyre Estate at

Thomas Cubitt: copy of portrait by H. W. Pickersgill, 1849.

London from the village of Hampstead by John Constable.

St John's Wood was developed on highly original lines, with rows of detached and semi-detached houses instead of terraces (plate 32).

After 1820 the dominant figure in Bloomsbury was a young builder named Thomas Cubitt. Cubitt was responsible for Woburn Place, part of Gordon Square and much of Tavistock Square, for Woburn Walk, Gordon Street, Endsleigh Street and Endsleigh Place. Nor did he confine himself to Bloomsbury. Already before starting work there he had built houses in Highbury, Stoke Newington and Camden Town; and in the 1820s, recognising the new importance given to the Grosvenor Estate by the building of Buckingham Palace, he began to lease the swampy land behind the Palace gardens, to drain it and to raise its level.

Soon Belgrave Square, one of the biggest squares in London – its most handsome houses designed by George Basevi, a clever pupil of Sir John Soane, later to design Thurloe Square and Pelham Place in Kensington – began to assume its still familiar shape; while Eaton Square, where work began in 1827, had soon stretched as far as Hans Town, an estate begun in the 1770s on land leased from Lord Cadogan by Henry Holland and named in honour of Sir Hans Sloane, the physician and collector, whose daughter, Jane, was Cadogan's wife.

In Belgravia – Earl Grosvenor was also Viscount Belgrave – as in Blooms-

138

22. John Nash by Sir Thomas Lawrence.
23. *(overleaf)* George IV going in state down Whitehall, 23 Jan. 1821.

bury, Cubitt's houses, ample and spacious behind their Greco-Roman stucco fronts, were constructed with painstaking care and attention to the smallest detail. Men compared them with the slipshod work behind the graceful fronts of Nash's terraces in Regent's Park; and the name of Cubitt became a synonym for soundness and solidity.

Such praise could not be given to most of the builders of those rows of houses which, as the new century progressed, stretched like ribbons out into the open country to the north and east, and, after the new Thames bridges were built, to the south as well, to Stockwell and Brixton, Kennington, Camberwell and Peckham.

Some satisfactory small estates were developed in the later years of the eighteenth century and the early years of the next: the Bishop of London's estate in Paddington, the New River Company's estate around Myddleton Square, the Lloyd-Baker estate north-east of Gray's Inn, and several on a less ambitious scale in Islington. But the majority of the buildings which straggled along the country roads beyond the more densely built-up areas were ill-designed and worse constructed. Terraces and groups of houses and cottages, factories and workshops, builders' yards and breweries, warehouses, stables and taverns stretched out in a muddled jumble, backing onto expanses of nettle and dockweed, waste land and brick-fields. As the ribbons extended new developments grew up in the open fields they left behind them. Not part of London proper, yet with little distinctive character of their own, they stood for a generation or so isolated and forlorn until swallowed up by the remorselessly expanding city. Somers Town, begun in 1786, on land belonging to Lord Somers was a characteristic example. Camden Town, started in 1791 on fields then owned by Lord Chancellor Camden, Walworth New Town, Agar Town, Bromley New Town and Pentonville were others.

Yet, despite the growth and proliferation of these new communities and the dispiriting built-up roads that led through them, the unspoilt country was still not far away. A merchant with offices in Lombard Street in the heart of the City had scarcely more than a mile's coach drive either north or south to reach open fields and quiet villages. He could build himself a villa with acres of garden at Chiswick, Hammersmith, Paddington or Peckham; he could live in a handsome house in a village street at Hampstead, Highgate, Tottenham or Hackney; or he could build himself a rural retreat, a picturesque Gothic cottage – a miniature version perhaps of the thatched *cottage orné*, Royal Lodge, which Nash had built for George IV at Windsor.

The completion in 1757 of the New Road which, serving as a bypass for the busy Oxford Road, linked Paddington and Islington, the gradual improvement of other main roads and their multiplication by contractors –

24. The National Gallery still hung in Mr Angerstein's house, by F. McKenzie.
25. Work on the British Museum's Lycian Room, 1845: watercolour by G. Scharf.

tempted by the profits to be made out of the tolls collected at turnpike gates – and the disappearance of highwaymen, had all accelerated the development of London's surrounding villages by those whose work entailed a daily journey into the town.

Kensington's expansion in the last years of the eighteenth century and the early years of the next was typical. The two great houses here, Holland House and Nottingham House, had already made Kensington fashionable; but in the reign of Queen Anne, Kensington Square, the first square to be built in the village, was entirely surrounded by fields and gardens. And it was not until the Regency that the real expansion began with the building of Edwardes Square, Trevor Square, Montpelier Place, Pelham Crescent and Earl's Terrace.

By the time these squares had been built Hampstead and Highgate, too, had developed into large and fashionable villages; and, although most of the best building in London took place to the north of the river, Dulwich and Camberwell had also become large and attractive communities with a life and character of their own but with good roads leading from them into the capital.

The most extensive development was along the river itself. Greenwich and Blackheath, Woolwich and Brentford, Chiswick, Richmond, Twickenham and Chelsea, had all become self-sufficient and agreeably populous. Around the Countess of Suffolk's beautiful Marble Hill House[23] and Horace Walpole's charming essay in extravagant eccentricity at Twickenham,[24] around the grace and favour houses in the park of Richmond Palace[25] and Ham House at Petersham,[26] around the house which Sir Hans Sloane had built on the site of Sir Thomas More's demolished mansion at Chelsea,[27] families lived a peaceful country life, close to London yet untouched so far by the inexorably spreading surge of brick and mortar soon to reach their parish boundaries.

A shell-shaped bench from Horace Walpole's Strawberry Hill.

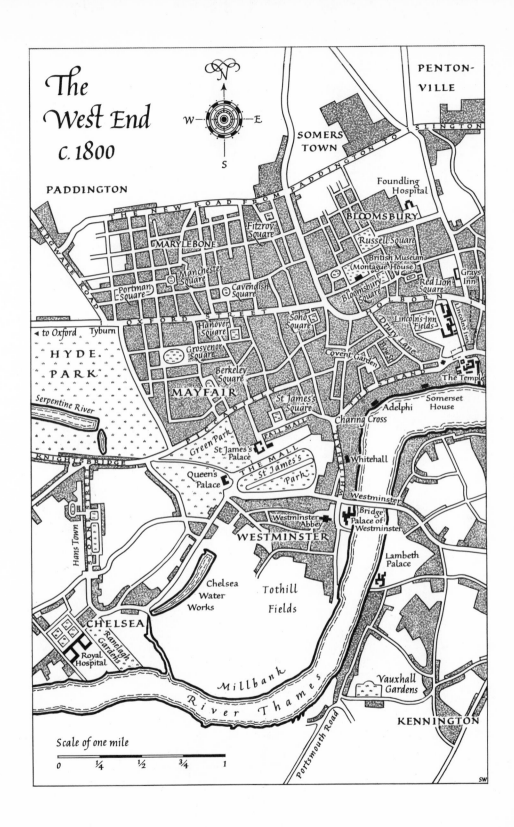

The West End c. 1800

PENTON-VILLE

N
W E
S

SOMERS TOWN

ISLINGTON

PADDINGTON

Foundling Hospital

THE NEW ROAD FROM PADDINGTON TO

Fitzroy Square

BLOOMSBURY

MARYLEBONE

Russell Square

British Museum

Montague House

Grays Inn

Manchester Square

Cavendish Square

Bloomsbury Square

Red Lion Square

Portman Square

HOLBORN

EDGWARE ROAD

OXFORD STREET

Soho Square

Lincoln's Inn Fields

Lincoln's Inn

Hanover Square

Drury Lane

to Oxford   Tyburn

HYDE. PARK

Grosvenor Square

Covent Garden

Bow St.

STRAND

The Temple

Berkeley Square

MAYFAIR

Serpentine River

St James's Square

PICCADILLY

Adelphi

Somerset House

St James's

Charing Cross

PALL MALL

Green Park

St James's Palace

THE MALL

Whitehall

KNIGHTSBRIDGE

Queen's Palace

St James's Park

Westminster Bridge

Hans Town

Westminster Abbey

Palace of Westminster

WESTMINSTER

Lambeth Palace

Chelsea Water Works

Tothill Fields

CHELSEA

Ranelagh Gardens

Royal Hospital

Millbank

Vauxhall Gardens

River Thames

Portsmouth Road

KENNINGTON

Scale of one mile

0   ¼   ½   ¾   1

SW

The London of
Hogarth & Rowlandson
1720–1820

In 1720, six years after the first of the Hanoverian kings arrived in England, William Hogarth – then a young man of twenty-two and yet to make his name – set up as an engraver on his own account. In 1820 George I's great-great-grandson came to the throne, and in that same year Thomas Rowlandson – then at the height of his powers – issued his series of extraordinary plates, *Dr Syntax in Search of Consolation.*

During those hundred years the physical aspect of London had been transformed; but the lives of the people, their pleasures and vices, pastimes and follies, remained much the same throughout the working careers of the two artists who so vividly recorded them.

For most of the eighteenth century the visitor to London would be drawn to the same well-known sights that had entranced visitors for generations, to St Paul's and the Abbey, London Bridge and the Tower, the Royal Exchange and Bedlam, St James's Palace, Tyburn Fair, and 'a marvellous wonder' more recent than these, the Monument, erected to commemorate the Great Fire, a towering Roman doric column, 202 feet high, and 202 feet away from the house in Pudding Lane where the Fire had started.

James Boswell (plate 26) decided to climb the 311 steps of its 'turnpike stair' soon after his arrival in London from Scotland in 1762; but halfway up he grew frightened and would have come down again had he not felt he would despise himself for his timidity. He persevered and got upon the balcony where he found it horrid to be so monstrous a way up in the air, so far above London and all its spires. He dared not look around him despite the rail, and he shuddered as every heavy wagon passed down Gracechurch Street, dreading that the 'shaking of the earth would make the tremendous pile tumble to the foundation'.[1]

Boswell enjoyed less disquieting mornings walking to the Exchange and sauntering into Guildhall, inspecting the 'numerous curiosities' at the British Museum, going to the Tower – where one spring morning he saw the ambassadors from the Republic of Venice land from their barges and proceed in coaches to St James's – or in visiting St Paul's and climbing up to the whispering gallery and on to the leads of the Cupola where the immense prospect

'Night': engraving by William Hogarth, 1738. The scene is near Charing Cross.

of London failed to impress him, for the streets and beauty of the buildings could not be observed on account of the distance. He just saw 'a prodigious group of tiled roofs and narrow lanes'.

Once Boswell was taken to the House of Lords to hear George III make the speech from the throne which opened the new session of Parliament. It was 'a very noble thing,' he thought. 'His Majesty spoke better than any man I ever heard: with dignity, delicacy, and ease. I admired him. I wished much to be acquainted with him.'

Foreign visitors who went to watch the proceedings in Parliament (plate 27) were not always so impressed. A Lutheran pastor from Berlin, Carl Philip Moritz, described in his memoirs Members stumbling clumsily into the House in 1782 'in their greatcoats and with boots and spurs. It is not at all uncommon,' he added, 'to see a member lying stretched out on one of the benches while others are debating. Some crack nuts, others eat oranges . . . There is no end to their going in and out.'

The strange behaviour of Members of Parliament was but one of the oddities of London life which the foreign tourist noticed. What was bound to strike him immediately, if his appearance were at all unusual, was the Londoner's prejudice against him. In many parts of the town he would be stared at, laughed at, shouted at, spat upon, jostled and pushed; and it was difficult enough not to be jostled and pushed even if his foreignness had not been recognised. If he knew Paris, the rough bustle, noise and impatience in the crowded streets would have been familiar; but if he came from some quiet, well-ordered and well-mannered town in the Low Countries, he was amazed by the rough treatment meted out to the unwary pedestrian, and by the continual roar made by the rattle and screech of iron-rimmed wheels on stone, by the shouts of water-carriers, costermongers, sandmen, cherry-girls (plate 28), milkmaids and tinkers, by the songs of ballad-singers, the music of street fiddlers, the bells of barrow boys and women selling ginger-bread, the raucous demands of 'Ring! Ring!' when space was required for the settlement of some quarrel by a fight.

Most of London's new streets were paved; but there were still many thoroughfares, even towards the end of the century, which were little more than tracks, with haphazard jumbles of round stones and cobbles placed outside their front-door steps by individual shopkeepers and householders. As late as 1750 when the only approach to the Houses of Parliament was down King Street or Union Street, both of these streets were in such an appalling condition that their holes and ruts had to be filled with sticks and straw before the King's state coach could make its way to the House of Lords. In a debate in the House on a Bill for paving and cleansing the streets of Westminster one Member protested that 'the filth of some parts of the town and the inequality and ruggedness of others, could not but in the eyes of foreigners disgrace our nation and incline them to imagine us a people not only without delicacy, but without government, a herd of Barbarians or a colony of Hottentots . . . The passenger is everywhere surprised or endangered by unexpected chasms, or offended or obstructed by mountains of filth . . . such as a savage would look upon with amazement.'

Walking the streets without becoming bemired or injured was an acquired skill. It was obviously best to keep as close to the wall as possible; but as Dr Johnson said, there were two sorts of people in London, those who gave the wall and those who took it; and despite the recognised rule that 'every man keeps to the right', there were many who refused to give way. Although some protection was afforded by the rows of posts that marked out the difference between the foot- and carriage-ways, these were little use when a selfish and quarrelsome pedestrian pushed you out of his way into the path of a drayman, a hackney coachman, or, worst of all, a sedan chairman.

Chairmen were supposed to keep to the middle of the road. But they were mostly rough Irishmen and had a reputation for being even more selfish and troublesome than footmen. They seemed to take a delight, so more than one observer recorded, in driving their poles into the backs of slow-moving pedestrians or squeezing them up against the nearest wall: Dean Swift once saw one fat man thus pinioned who 'wisely' retaliated by pushing his elbow through the side window smashing it 'into a thousand pieces'.

Those nimble enough to avoid the angry frustration or spite of the chairmen had other hazards with which to contend. A sudden storm would send piles of filth and garbage flooding down the street, overflowing the kennels,

Streetsweepers: heading from John Gay's *Trivia or the Art of Walking the Streets*, 1716.

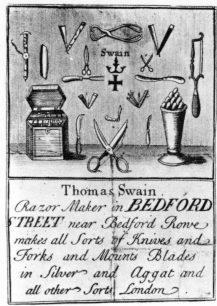

Trade cards of a nightsoil collector and a knife maker.

cascading down steep alleys; while overhead the water-spouts would pour down water on hats or powdered wigs. If there was a wind as well, one would be in danger from falling tiles, or, more likely, from one of the numerous huge sign-boards.

Many of these signs were framed in iron; some of them were thick as paving stones; nearly all of them hung out on long brackets seeming to vie with each other for attention. They were frequently falling down 'to the great danger and injury of the inhabitants'; and one that tumbled into Birde Lane, carrying with it the whole front of the shop, killed four people who happened unluckily to be passing beneath it. Indeed, houses collapsed often enough without the help of sign-boards; one evening in 1740 a house in Shoe Lane suddenly fell into the street killing six of its occupants and two passers-by.

As common as boards in the eighteenth century were huge models, intricately wrought in iron or carved in wood – three sugar loaves for a grocer, three tents for an upholsterer, three hats for a hatter, three golden balls for a goldsmith. But the presence of a particular shop beneath its distinctive sign was never to be guaranteed. Premises were sold or re-let, new owners or tenants came in, yet the signs stayed where they were. Addison claimed he had seen the sign of a goat outside a perfumer's, a king's head above a sword-cutler's, a boot above a cook-shop, and a cobbler living under a roasted pig.

26. James Boswell by Sir Joshua Reynolds.

The models were quite as heavy as sign-boards, some much heavier, and all constituted a constant threat to the limbs of the passers-by who trod the streets beneath them.

Even if he managed to avoid physical injury in the streets – and, after all, he usually did – there were certain hazards which the pedestrian found inevitable. In the City the smoke was often suffocating. It had been bad enough in the previous century when Evelyn had complained of the way in which it fouled his clothes, wrapping the City in 'Clouds of Smoake and Sulphur, so full of stink and Darknesse'. A hundred years later it was far worse. A day spent walking abroad would leave a man covered in soot; and although he could soon get his shoes cleaned by one of the bootblacks – who were to be found with a pot of blacking, a pair of brushes, an old periwig and a three-legged stool at every street corner – keeping the hair and clothes clean was a more difficult matter.

James Boswell, who enjoyed living rough on his Grand Tour in Germany, exulting in not having taken his clothes off for over a week, felt it necessary in London to change his linen every day.

The lady who chose to go out shopping would usually manage to avoid the most unpleasant of London's annoyances. Securely enclosed in her silk-lined leather sedan-chair with the roof and door tightly shut, she would be carried from her own front door to the front door of the shop, and would be followed into it by her footman. In the early part of the eighteenth century the best shops were scattered far and wide over London, for certain trades still congregated in particular districts. The best-known booksellers remained around St Paul's Churchyard, Paternoster Row, Fleet Street and Temple Bar, although good bookshops were beginning to appear in Pall Mall and Piccadilly; the most fashionable milliners were to be found near the Exchange; the smartest linen drapers and silk mercers on Ludgate Hill; the most select goldsmiths in Cranbourne Street; and the most exclusive perfumers in Shire Lane. Many of the less expensive establishments, however, traded in a variety of goods; and it was not unusual for cabinet-makers and upholsterers to deal also in such disparate goods as women's hats, musical instruments, Dutch mats, and coal.

Although each new building development in the western suburbs had its own market, certain metropolitan markets were renowned for their own specialities: Leadenhall Market for beef and herbs, Newgate Market for mutton, St James's Market for veal, Clare Market for pork, Thames Street for cheese, and Covent Garden, of course, for fruit and vegetables.

Prices were rarely fixed anywhere and haggling was still usual, not only in the markets but also in the more fashionable shops. When Messrs Flint and Palmer opened their doors for business at eight o'clock one morning in the middle of the century on London Bridge, having marked all the widely-ranging goods they sold with price-tags, their customers were at first astonished, particularly as the assistants showed themselves unwilling to argue or even to deal with those who hesitated over a purchase. But these assistants, though firm, were always polite; Mr Palmer himself was fair and consistent in his prices; and soon the new method of sale became so popular that the shop was still crowded at eleven o'clock at night. Robert Owen, the Welsh social reformer who worked there as a boy, remembered how he and his companions sometimes did not get to bed, after tidying the unsold goods on the counters and rolling up the lengths of material, until two o'clock in the morning, and then had scarcely enough energy left to pull themselves up the banisters to the attic where they slept.

Most shops were small and dark, their wares stacked behind the counter in piles which reached as high as the ceiling. Some of them were little more than shacks propped up against the sides of houses and serving as kitchen and bedroom for the shopkeeper when his day's work was done. The glass fronts of the better premises were used not so often for the inviting display of goods as to indicate, by a straw hat, a big phial of cordial or a pair of riding boots, what kinds of merchandise were to be found within. In the first half of the century the fronts were little more than enlarged windows – the goods frequently being sold through them – and it was not until the 1750s that the double-bowed front, like the one that can still be seen at Fribourg and Treyer's tobacco and snuff shop in the Haymarket, came into its own. Nor was it until the Regency period that a street was designed purely as a shopping street – such a one is Woburn Walk, Bloomsbury, finished in 1822 and now restored. There were, however, several shopping arcades.

Burlington Arcade was designed by Lord George Cavendish's architect, Samuel Ware, who helped his employer to remodel Burlington House between 1816 and 1819. Although Cavendish's enemies said he had merely wanted to prevent passers-by from throwing rubbish over his garden wall, he himself insisted that the arcade was intended 'for the gratification of the publick and to give employment to industrious females'. Royal Opera Arcade, which stretches from Pall Mall to Charles II Street and was designed by Nash and George Repton as part of the King's Opera House reconstruction, was built at about the same time as Ware's arcade in Piccadilly.

Both Burlington Arcade and Royal Opera Arcade were immediately fashionable as shopping centres, for by the time of their construction most of the best shops had begun to move westwards out of the old City to the new suburbs where the richer people now lived. Here were the smart pastry-cooks' shops with their eating-rooms and showrooms decorated with looking-glasses, chandeliers and damask-covered serving tables; here were the expen-

Billingsgate fishwives by Thomas Rowlandson.
The Covent Garden vegetable market: engraved after Rowlandson.

sive cabinet-makers dealing in carpets, curtains and wall decorations as well as furniture; here, in Grosvenor Square, was, for a time, Josiah Wedgwood's showroom designed exclusively for the patronage of the rich and so successful that it was soon too small for him. Larger premises were offered him in Pall Mall. But no, he decided Pall Mall was by now too far east, 'for you know that my present sett of Customers will not mix with the rest of the World'.

New Bond Street had established its reputation by the 1750s, 'lovely Oxford Street', as a German visitor called it, by the 1780s; and when one of George III's footmen, Charles Fortnum resigned from the royal service in 1788 in order to devote all his time to the grocery business he had started a few years before, Piccadilly was already famous for the elegance of its shops and the high quality of their wares which people from all over the country would come to inspect.

Towards the end of the eighteenth century the huge sign-boards and models, so distinctive a feature of Hogarth's pictures, gradually began to disappear, and before it was over their danger to the public had led to their being declared illegal.

As the picturesque signs disappeared, however, the fire marks of insurance companies came to take their place. These marks, usually of painted or gilded lead, cast in a mould which stamped the company's distinctive design upon them, ensured that the company's fire engines did not waste their water on a rival office's fire. For it was not until 1833 that the London Fire Brigade was established. Before that cooperation between Westminster Fire Office or the Hand in Hand, for example, was unthinkable. Each office had its

Two lead fire insurance companies' marks: the London Assurance of 1720 and the Hand in Hand of 1696.

150

engines kept in sheds as close as possible to the properties for whose safety it was concerned; and on the alarm being given the office's firemen, equipped with iron hats, hatchets, demolition hooks and leather buckets, would trundle them out towards the smoke and flames.

Unpleasant as it often was walking the streets, all visitors agreed that a stroll in one of London's parks provided a delightful experience.

There were four main parks excluding that which became known as Regent's Park – Green Park, Hyde Park, St James's Park and Kensington Gardens. The largest, Hyde Park, was given to the people by the King in 1637 and ever since had been, like St Paul's at an earlier time, a fashionable promenade. It was also in the earlier years of the eighteenth century a fashionable place to take a coach ride; and on most summer evenings, after the theatres had closed, the sand track of 'The Ring', a semi-circular loop in the centre of the Park, was filled with coaches whose passengers greeted each other through the swirling dust. Later it was the carriage road known as Rotten Row, a gravelled *route du roi* made by George II in 1737, and the paths around the Serpentine, a lake formed to the north of it at the suggestion of Queen Caroline, which became the chosen rendezvous of the *beau monde*.

In winter, when the Serpentine was frozen over, ladies and gentlemen skated across it or watched the expert among them trying to win the £50 offered to the first skater who could cover a mile in a minute. In 1826, 'the most daring feat of all times was carried out on the Serpentine', when Mr

Skating on the Serpentine, 1787.

Henry Hunt, of Hunt's Matchless Blacking, drove one of his company's vans and four blood horses across the ice at the broadest part and won a hundred guineas from 'a Noble Lord of Sporting Celebrity'. But it was in the summer that the Serpentine was at its most gay, and never so gay as in July 1814 when a Great Fair was held there to celebrate the peace. There were sword swallowers and military bands, fire-eaters and the 'fattest ladies of forty in the world', cake-houses and apple-stalls. Men sold draught porter and hot mutton pies, women danced in the light of Chinese lanterns, a girl undressed and ran to bathe in the lake where, at eight o'clock, the battle of Trafalgar was re-enacted with guns roaring and the French Squadron sinking in flames to the strains of the National Anthem.

At other times the early morning quiet of the Park was shattered by the crack of pistol shots as two men settled an affair of honour. The Duke of Wellington preferred the seclusion of Battersea, but it was in Hyde Park that John Wilkes was wounded by the egregious Samuel Martin and that Lord Mohun, 'one of the arrantest rakes in the town', and the Duke of Hamilton engaged in that celebrated contest described by Bishop Burnet: 'Fighting with so violent an animosity that, neglecting the rules of art, they seemed to run on one another, as if they tried who should kill first, in which they were both so happily successful that the Lord Mohun was killed outright, and Duke Hamilton died in a few minutes.' When the body of Lord Mohun, who had twice before been tried for murder, was brought home and placed upon a bed, his widow perfunctorily complained that it should not have been placed on the *best* bed as it spoiled the bedclothes. It was in Green Park that Count Alfieri fought his mistress's husband, Lord Ligonier, bravely returning to the Haymarket Theatre with a sword wound in his arm to sit through the last act and later generously to comment, 'My view is that Ligonier did not kill me because he did not want to, and I did not kill him because I did not know how.'

To draw a sword in St James's Park was illegal, and not so many duels were fought here as in the other parks, though it was here that the Earl of Bath fought John, Lord Hervey at three o'clock of a January afternoon in 1731. If not a rendezvous for duellists, though, St James's Park, in the Abbé Prevost's opinion, 'the public walk of London and open to all ranks', was a recognised haunt of whores. The gates were locked at night, but 6,500 people were authorised to possess keys to them and thousands of others had keys unofficially. James Boswell was a frequent visitor here, not only in the afternoon when he liked to watch the soldiers on parade, but also after dark when the gates were unlocked by girls who came in to stroll up and down the paths which, during the day, had been a favourite promenade of the ladies of the Court. He was there one evening in December 1762 with his friend, Andrew Erskine, and was accosted 'by several ladies of the town.

Kensington Palace.

Erskine was very humorous and said some very wild things to them. There was one in a red cloak of a good buxom person and comely face whom I marked as a future piece, in case of exigency'. The following March he was there again and 'picked up a whore . . . a young Shropshire girl, only seventeen, very well-looked . . . Poor being, she has a sad time of it !' He returned the same week and took the first whore he met, 'ugly and lean and her breath smelt of spirits'.

Kensington Gardens were far more respectable, and were not in Boswell's time open to the general public at all. For Kensington House, since its purchase by William III from the Earl of Nottingham in 1689, had been the most private of London's royal palaces. William III had been attracted to it by its site, which he believed would be better for his asthma than Whitehall or St James's; his Queen, Mary, had been attracted by its grounds. The house was enlarged for William by Wren and remodelled in a more opulent style for George I by Vanbrugh and William Kent; while the grounds were transformed by Henry Wise, gardener to Queen Anne.[2] They were opened to the public in the 1790s when the Court moved to Richmond, but only on Sundays and then only to those formally dressed. Sailors, soldiers and liveried servants were all denied entry. It was not until Victoria's reign that this Park was opened all the year round; but by then, in Princess Lieven's view, it had been 'annexed as a middle-class rendezvous. Good society no longer [went] there except to drown itself', as poor Harriet Shelley had done in 1816.

Rigid as the rules of Kensington Gardens had been in the eighteenth century, however, a man was scarcely more safe there from footpads and highwaymen than he was in the other parks where they abounded. George II, himself, was once robbed at Kensington by a highwayman who climbed over the wall and 'with a manner of much deference, deprived the King of his purse, his watch, and his buckles'.

In Hyde Park, although carriages generally passed through it in armed convoy, highway robbery was an almost commonplace occurrence. It was here that Horace Walpole was robbed by the 'Gentleman Highwayman', the Presbyterian Minister's son, James M'Lean, whose pistol exploded in Walpole's face, blackening his skin with powder and shot marks, and leading him to complain that one was 'forced to travel even at noon as if one was going into battle . . . what a shambles this country is grown!'

Walpole's words were no more than the picturesque exaggeration of an undoubted truth. For the first fifty years of the eighteenth century all the main roads leading into London were infested with highwaymen, 'garnis de voleurs à cheval', as a French visitor put it. The Abbé le Blanc recorded that these brigands even went so far as to fix up 'papers at the doors of the rich people about London, expressly forbidding all persons, of what condition or quality soever, to go out of town without ten guineas and a watch about them upon pain of death'. In the 1770s the Prime Minister, the Prince of Wales, the Duke of York, the Lord Mayor, like countless other less distinguished men and women, were all threatened and robbed in the London streets or on the country roads leading into them. The proprietors of pleasure gardens felt compelled to hire companies of Foot Guards to escort their patrons safely back to their homes. People who had spent a day out at Islington took to gathering at the Angel where a mounted patrol guarded them on their return to London; and a bell was rung throughout the night in the village of Kensington so that parties could be collected for the dangerous homeward journey through Knightsbridge and along Piccadilly.

It was not until 1805, when a permanent Horse Patrol came into being, that a visit to one of the outlying villages could be conducted in security. Before that none but the foolhardy travelled alone at night; after that the villages, which had been previously cut off from London by perilous highwayman's country of wood, common and heath, could develop as metropolitan suburbs, providing pleasant places to live for the families of businessmen who could now travel into London each day with impunity.

Sir John Fielding, the 'Blind Beak' of Bow Street.

The establishment of the Horse Patrol was almost entirely due to the determination and energy of two remarkable men, Henry Fielding and his half-brother John.

When Henry Fielding came to Bow Street as a magistrate in 1748 he had no ideas for reform in mind. His career as a dramatist had been ended by the Licensing Act which closed the theatre in Haymarket where his satirical comedies had been performed; his novels were unprofitable; his gifts as a barrister were limited. The reason why he went to Bow Street, after asking a fellow old Etonian to help find him a job, was that he was an extravagant man and he needed to earn some money.

Yet he was determined not to accept bribes and commissions as his predecessors had done, not to sell justice as justice had been sold in the past. He was determined also to form some kind of efficient and permanent police force out of the parish constables of Westminster, most of whom had always looked upon their term of office as an opportunity to put into their own pockets some of the money which lined those of the magistrates.

At the time of Fielding's arrival in Bow Street, Londoners regarded the idea of a professional police force with horror. True to their concept of freedom and to their innate hatred of change, they regarded the police forces of Europe as a fearful threat to individual liberty, as well as an unjustified and exorbitant expense. The very word 'police' – a French word not used in official English until the beginning of the century – was, in its modern sense, unknown. They were content to rely on time-honoured and traditional methods of crime prevention – ferocious punishments for transgressors and payments of rewards to those who brought criminals to justice.

This reliance on the thief-taker as a generously rewarded officer of the law had led inevitably to appalling corruption as well as to the emergence of such underworld leaders as Jonathan Wild as the most successful thief-takers of all. For a man like Wild – who had himself started his criminal career as a whore's bully, brothel-keeper and fence, and had risen to be undisputed master of the early eighteenth-century London underworld – could maintain his hold over his minions, as well as increasing his fortune, by handing over to the courts for punishment all those who disobeyed his commands.

The profession of thief-taker had continued long after Jonathan Wild's execution at Tyburn in 1725, and it was, indeed, on the thief-takers' rewards that Henry Fielding's Bow Street constables had to rely for their remuneration. But 'Mr Fielding's People', as his well-trained constables were called, were honest and trustworthy men. They enforced the law not for profit but for the benefit of society at large. Fired by Fielding's enthusiasm they remained on at Bow Street (plate 29) after their term of office had expired, and were the prototype of the Bow Street Runners.

Soon after Fielding's appointment to the magistracy he was joined at Bow Street by his half-brother, John, whose ears, it was extravagantly claimed, had been so sharpened by his blindness that they could recognise three thousand thieves by their voices. Certainly, there were few thieves in London who did not come to fear and respect the Blind Beak, who strove to make both the Londoner and the Government accept the idea of a paid professional police, and who, by his untiring efforts and the success of the foot and horse patrols he sent out regularly into the streets, did much to make London a safer and rather less violent city.

In view of the reluctant support which was given them, and the slender means at their disposal there was, of course, a limit to what the Fieldings could do; and throughout the eighteenth century London remained a dangerous place. The incidence of armed robbery became less frequent as the century drew to its close, but a reading of contemporary newspapers confirms the belief that the London of the Regency, as the London of Queen Anne, was one of the most lawless cities in Europe. A single issue of the *Public Advertiser* for 12 February 1761 reported the hold-up of the Hampstead caravan at Kentish Town, the dispersal of intending housebreakers at North End, Hampstead, by the embattled inhabitants who fired their shot-guns at them, a robbery on East Sheen Common where there were 'so many thieves that people are afraid of stirring out after dark', yet another highway robbery on the Deptford Road by 'six footpads armed with horse pistols'. A few years later in another single issue of the same paper there were reported robberies at Kew Green, Acton turnpike, Hammersmith, and Blackheath. Nor were the streets in the middle of the town much safer than the outlying roads. Robberies were frequently committed in such central areas as Holborn and Fleet Street, St James's Square and Park Lane, Piccadilly and Grosvenor Square, in all of which the lighting was considered to be worse than in any other capital in the world.

For the greater part of the eighteenth century what light there was came from the lamps hanging above the front gates of the larger houses, or from glass globes, half filled with whale oil and with bits of cotton twist for wick, which were fixed to posts at irregular intervals and suspended from poles sticking out from the walls on either side of the street. Often the globes were almost black with dirt, for the lamplighters employed to look after them, to light them at dusk and extinguish them at midnight, were 'a contingent of greasy clodhopping fellows' with filthy fingers, who seemed forever incapable of filling a lamp without spilling the oil onto the head of anyone who passed under their ladder.

It was not until the Westminster Paving and Lighting Act was passed in 1762 that street lamps cast more than a glimmer into the surrounding darkness; and even then lighting in all but the main thoroughfares was uncertain and spasmodic. Those parts of London not covered by the Act had to await the advent of gas. The only sure way of avoiding the potholes and dirt in the streets was to employ the services of a link-boy who walked along in front of his employer holding up a torch of flaring pitch and tow.

But a link-boy was no protection against the gangs that roamed the streets and hid in alleys watching out for likely victims; according to John Gay, indeed, the link-boy was often enough in league with the robbers:

> *Though thou art tempted by the linkman's call*
> *Yet trust him not along the lonely wall,*
> *In the midway he'll quench the flaming brand,*
> *And share the booty with the pilf'ring band.*

A country visitor to London in 1744 thought the metropolis had become 'really dangerous'. Pickpockets, he told a friend, formerly content with mere filching now made 'no scruple to knock people down with bludgeons in Fleet Street and the Strand, and that at no later hour than eight o'clock at night. In the Piazzas, Covent Garden, they come in large bodies armed with couteaus.'

Forty years later Horace Walpole assured a friend that his neighbours at Twickenham did not feel safe even when they stayed at home; while if they so much as stepped over the threshold of the chandler's shop for a penny-worth of plums, they stood in danger of being murdered. By the end of the century the dangers of walking about in the evening were scarcely less great. In the autumn of 1790, *The Times* – the first edition of which had been pub-

'A peep at the Gas lights in Pall Mall': engraving by Woodward and Rowlandson, 1809.

lished under the name of *The London Daily Universal Register* five years before – reported that the street robbers had become so daring 'that on Monday evening, a few minutes after five o'clock, two ladies were knocked down within a few minutes of each other, and robbed by four men in Coventry Street (one of the most public in London)'.

Nor was it the professional criminals who always provided the worst threat. Swift and Addison have described the savage activities of the Mohocks, a society whose name was derived from the supposedly most ferocious of Red Indian tribes and whose members were dedicated to the ambition of 'doing all possible hurt to their fellow creatures'. They employed their ample leisure in torturing old watchmen, in forcing prostitutes to stand on their heads in tar barrels so that they could prick their legs with their swords, in throwing maidservants through the windows of their employers' houses, or in slitting the noses and slashing the cheeks of anyone foolhardy enough to oppose them. Few Mohocks were ever brought to justice, for, like the Nickers and the Bold Bucks whose activities were more specifically directed against young girls, they were usually rich enough to buy their way out of trouble. Most of those who were hanged at Tyburn came from the teeming, warren-like slums of St Giles and Southwark, Whitechapel and Smithfield.

A hanging day at Tyburn was a public holiday; and the scene around the gallows – with orange-sellers bawling down ballad-sellers, pickpockets jostling their way through the crowds and footmen fighting each other for seats in the grandstand known as Mother Proctor's Pews – took on the aspect of a fair, frequently ending in a riot when the gallant hero of the hour was cut down from the rope and his body sent for dissection at Surgeons' Hall.

The crowds on Tower Hill at the beheading in 1746 of the Scottish rebel Lords Kilmarnock and Balmerino.

Riots, common enough at Tyburn, were of almost weekly occurrence else-where. Footmen, notoriously arrogant and ungovernable, rioted when they were stopped from going to the theatre where numbers of them were to be seen every night, 'lolling over the boxes with their hats on, playing over the airs, taking snuff, laughing aloud, adjusting their cockscombs, or holding dialogues with their brethren from one side of the house to the other'. Soldiers rioted against their Hanover shirts; workmen rioted against the threat of cheap Irish labour; weavers rioted against the importation of Indian calico. There were High Church Riots and Corn Riots, Election Riots and 'No Popery' Riots, above all there were Gin Riots.

For gin was the cheapest of anodynes, the only means that thousands knew of escaping from misery, squalor and hunger. And when the Licensing Act of 1751 threatened to make it less easy to obtain, the populace rose in revolt. For thirty years before that the wildly excessive gin-drinking in London had become an almost permanent orgy, 'the principal cause', so the Westminster justices reported, 'of the increase of the poor and of all the vice and debauchery among the inferior sort of people, as well as of the felonies and other disorders committed about this town'. The number of dram-shops was enormous; in some parts of London it was estimated that by 1743 every eighth house sold spirits over the counter. It was sold in workhouses, prisons, factories, brothels and barbers' shops; it was even sold privately in cellars and garrets as well as in the streets by hawkers. Eight million gallons were drunk each year, and this meant about two pints a week for each man, woman and child in London. The bodies of the incapably drunk could be seen lying where they had fallen, by day as by night, in Bethnal Green and Spital-fields, Westminster Sanctuary and particularly in St Giles's, the slum quarter known as 'the Rookery' which Hogarth chose for the scene of his admonitory picture. In the cellars of such 'gin lanes' as these, rows of bodies sat upon the reeking straw, propped up against the walls. By 1751 the worst years were over, but Henry Fielding still felt compelled to warn that 'should the drinking of this poison be continued in its present height during the next twenty years, there will be by that time few of the common people left to drink it'. Gin was 'the principal sustenance (if it may be so called) of more than a hundred thousand people in the metropolis . . . The intoxicating draught itself dis-qualifies them from any honest means to acquire it, at the same time that it removes sense of fear and shame and emboldens them to commit every wicked and desperate enterprise.'

Fielding's warning was recalled in 1780 when the London mob erupted into the worst riots of the eighteenth century. They were supposedly 'No Popery' riots; but the violent resentments which were aroused by the leader of the Protestant Association, the fanatically anti-Catholic Lord George Gordon, went far beyond religious prejudices. For many Londoners the call

LOWE and his Companions setting Fire to the INN in Aldersgate Street.

LOWE and his Companions Plundering the Houses in Aldersgate Street.

Arson and looting during the Gordon Riots: a popular print.

161

to arms in the name of Protestantism was merely an excuse to wreak havoc, to attack Irish labourers and loot foreign chapels, to settle old scores, and to get drunk for nothing. When Langdale's distillery was broken into and set alight by the rioters, hundreds of people risked their lives by dashing down into the cellars through the raging flames with pails and jugs, bowls and even pig troughs. Soon after their reappearance with blackened faces and burning eyes, carrying their overflowing containers or with untapped casks of gin, the intense heat burst the stills. Fountains of raw spirits came gushing up into the streets to pour down the gutters and over the cobbles, mixing with gallons of rum which flowed from an immense pile of staved-in barrels. Deliriously excited, the people knelt down to gulp up the liquid which burned their throats like acid; but they went on drinking until their faces turned blue, their tongues swelled, and they collapsed. Some of the women had children screaming and struggling in their arms. By the time the Northumberland militia arrived to open fire on the pickpockets rifling the prostrate bodies, Langdale had suffered a loss of £100,000 and at least twenty people had drunk themselves to death. There were also unknown numbers of men and women, overcome by the fumes and flames, burning to death in the cellars and the warehouse.

No one can tell how many people died in the Gordon Riots. Twenty-one are known to have been executed and the Government admitted that 285 rioters had been shot by the troops and 173 wounded. It was subsequently admitted that these numbers were an under-estimate. A contemporary witness calculated that over 700 people lost their lives; and the most recent historian of that terrible week in London's history believes that the true figure was probably not less than 850.

The damage done to property was incalculable. The chapel of the Sardinian Ambassador in Lincoln's Inn Fields was the first to be looted and burned, and here a magnificent reredos was alone valued at £2,500. The rioters then made for the chapel attached to the Bavarian Embassy in Warwick Street, Golden Square; and on subsequent days numerous smaller chapels, many of them in Moorfields and Spitalfields, where there were large Irish colonies, were pulled or burned to the ground. The rioters did not limit themselves to attacking these 'Papishe dens' or to setting fire to the houses and business premises of Roman Catholics. They ransacked and burned the homes of anyone who interfered with them and of those few magistrates who attempted to arrest them – Sir John Fielding's house in Bow Street was virtually demolished. They roared into Bloomsbury Square, raging drunk and ringing a great bell, shouting their intention of roasting alive the Lord Chief Justice and the Archbishop of Canterbury; the Archbishop escaped, but Lord Mansfield's house was plundered, his furniture and all his books tossed out onto a bonfire in the street. They attacked and set alight the prisons

28. London street scene: *The Cherry Barrow* by H. Walton, 1779.

Night watchmen in the Marylebone Watch House: aquatint by Rowlandson, Pugin and Bluck, 1809.

— convicts from Bridewell and New Prison in Clerkenwell, from Newgate, from the King's Bench and the Fleet, from the Clink in Southwark and Surrey Bridewell poured out into the streets. They made an attack on the Bank and on Downing Street.[3]

Yet not until George III threatened to lead the Guards in person could the authorities be stirred to act decisively. At first the Lord Mayor, a former brothel owner, declined to interfere at all. 'I must be cautious what I do lest I bring the mob to my own house,' he told a silk merchant whose premises were under attack. And later he observed, in a nervous voice, half-deferential, half jocular, to a mob who, having demolished one house in Moorfields were turning their attention to another, 'That's pretty well, gentlemen, for one day. I hope you will go to your own homes.' After all, he commented complacently to Lord Beauchamp, who angrily went up to him and told him it was his duty to do something, 'The whole mischief seems to be that the mob have got hold of some people and some furniture they do not like and are burning them and what is the harm in that?'

The watchmen and constables were scarcely more effective. Nathaniel Wraxall remembered how, when the mob were screaming through the streets, when houses were burning on every side and the sky 'looked like blood', an old watchman 'with his lantern in his hand', passed by the wall

29. The Bow Street Office, 1808: engraved by Rowlandson and Pugin.

of St Andrew's Churchyard, 'calling the hour as if in time of profound tranquility'. When troops were at length called out, magistrates could rarely be found to give them any orders, let alone to read the Riot Act.

The Gordon Riots, in fact, made it unmistakably clear that a new system of professional police was essential for London's safety. But as soon as the danger was past, the protests against a police force on the Continental model were renewed; and it was to be several years yet before the old system was reformed.

Despite the undoubted dangers involved in being out in the streets at night, and the explosive violence of the mob, men could and did move about London by themselves without coming to any harm from one year to the next. Dr Johnson, though he carried a big stick which he could wield to good purpose, often did not come home to Gough Square, Fleet Street, till two o'clock in the morning.[4] Nor does James Boswell, from his arrival in London in November 1762 until August 1763 – the period covered by his *London Journal* – record a single instance of his being assaulted or robbed, except by a prostitute who picked a handkerchief out of his pocket in Privy Garden, now known as Whitehall Gardens; and he, although of a nervous disposition, was often to be found in dark alleys such as this toying with girls and walking home alone late at night. He was uneasy when he did so for, as he wrote, 'robberies in the street are now very frequent'; but he never came to harm.

Life in London for a young gentleman of moderate means and no demanding occupation was, in fact, enjoyable and stimulating. Boswell, himself, after settling down comfortably in lodgings in Downing Street for £22 a year, decided that London was 'undoubtedly a place where men and manners may be seen to the greatest advantage . . . the immense crowd and hurry and bustle of business and diversion, the great number of public places of entertainment, the noble churches and the superb buildings of different kinds, agitate, amuse, and elevate the mind.' He would go out, perhaps, for a walk in St James's Park before breakfast, return to his room about ten o'clock to be served with buttered toast or muffins and tea by his landlord's maid, reading while he ate; or, sometimes, he would stay out to have breakfast with a friend.

A quiet day might entail a morning spent in Child's coffee-house in St Paul's Churchyard, reading the newspapers by the fire, or sitting at one of the small tables to talk to the other customers about the matters of the day. A shilling dinner at a chop-house – often the New Church chop-house in the Strand – at three or four o'clock would be followed by tea at six o'clock. Then, after having his hair dressed and powdered by his barber, he would go out to visit a friend. On returning to his lodgings he would sometimes ask the maid to wash his feet in lukewarm water.

On other days Boswell would go for a more expensive and convivial meal than was to be had at a chop-house, to Dolly's Beefsteak House, perhaps, or to a tavern, to the Queen's Head in Holborn, to the Rose in Russell Street, the Star and Garter in Pall Mall, the Mitre in Fleet Street (a house much favoured by Dr Johnson), or to the Shakespeare's Head in Covent Garden where he once took two girls he picked up in the piazza, bought them a bottle of sherry in a private room, sang them a song from *The Beggar's Opera,* and then made love to them 'one after the other, according to their seniority'. On Sundays Boswell often stayed at home and had dinner, of 'good roast beef with a warm apple pie', with his landlord's family in Downing Street.

An unusually full and extravagant day might include breakfast at the Somerset Coffee-house in the Strand, and then a walk with friends, before dinner at the Beefsteak Club. One of his favourite walks was to the Temple, 'a most agreeable place. You quit all the hurry and bustle of the City in Fleet Street and the Strand, and all at once find yourself in a pleasant academical retreat. You see good convenient buildings, handsome walks, you view the silver Thames. You are shaded by venerable trees. Crows are cawing above your head . . . '

Less enjoyable was a visit to Newgate where he saw, among those awaiting execution, 'Captain' Paul Lewis, the Sussex parson's son who had been an artillery officer before becoming a highwayman. Lewis was a 'genteel, spirited young fellow', and Boswell 'really took a great concern for him, and wished to relieve him. He walked firmly and with a good air, with his chains rattling upon him.'

Boswell's visit depressed him all afternoon. Newgate was on his mind 'like a black cloud'; he felt himself dreary at night and asked his barber to read him asleep with David Hume's *History of England;* but the barber made 'very sad work' of his task, and Boswell was more unhappy than ever. The next morning he went to see Paul Lewis hanged and so fulfilled a 'sort of horrid eagerness' to go to Tyburn. He climbed upon a scaffolding and could clearly see 'all the dismal scene'. 'Most terribly shocked and thrown into a very deep melancholy' by the fearful exhibition, Boswell dared not sleep by himself that night, and went to spend the night with his friend, Andrew Erskine.

The Beefsteak Club afforded the mind relief from such gloomy terrors. The Club then met in a room above Covent Garden Theatre with the remains of the gridiron, which had survived the fire in their previous premises, embedded in the plaster of the ceiling. It was an extremely jolly place. The president sat in a chair under a canopy above which was the noble sentiment: 'Beef and Liberty'; and after eating beefsteaks and drinking wine and punch in plenty, the company sang songs. They were a very mixed society in the 1770s. They included John Beard, former manager of Covent Garden, William Havard, the actor, John Wilkes, the outrageously amusing politician, Wilkes's friend Charles Churchill, the truculent parson who had made his name with *The Rosciad,* a violently satirical attack on the leading actors and actresses of his day, and Wilkes's adversary Lord Sandwich, whose dedication to gambling was such that he could not bring himself to leave the table even for a meal but preferred to have a waiter bring him a piece of meat or chicken between two slices of bread, thus adding a new word to the English language.

A dinner at the Beefsteak Club might be followed by a visit to the Cockpit. When Boswell went he was careful to leave behind his watch, purse and pocket-book, to put on his old clothes, fill his pockets with gingerbread, nuts and apples, and to take with him a heavy oak stick. The cocks, armed with silver spurs, fought with 'amazing bitterness and resolution' in a sunken ring beneath the terraces of seats. The uproar of the betting was prodigious, and large sums of money quickly passed from hand to hand; but Boswell was shocked to see the distraction and anxiety of the gamblers, and felt compassion for the poor cocks, who were mangled and torn in a most cruel manner. He looked around and failed to see – as Hogarth evidently also did – 'the smallest relenting sign in any countenance'.

An evening with politer companions might be enjoyed at Northumberland House (plate 21) where Boswell, thanks to the recommendation of his father, Lord Auchinleck, was frequently invited by the Countess. Sometimes there was a small private party; sometimes a more formal rout; but always at some point in the evening the guests sat down to cards for stakes so high they made Boswell shudder.

On his way home he often consoled himself with one of the girls who could be found as easily in the Strand as in St James's Park. Occasionally he picked up a girl elsewhere. Once, when his barber's illness prevented him from going to the rout at Northumberland House, he found a girl at the end of Downing Street and went down a lane with her to a snug place; on another occasion in Whitehall he told a girl that he was a highwayman and asked her if he could have her for nothing, but she refused; one day he enjoyed a girl in the City; later he picked up 'a strong, jolly young damsel' at the bottom of Haymarket and, having a whim to engage her on Westminster Bridge with the Thames rolling below them, he took her by the arm to do so on that 'noble edifice'.

But it was usually in the Strand that Boswell had his adventures. Sometimes he would take a girl to one of the nearby dark courts where he was not always successful, as on one summer night in 1763 when a girl, to whom he had promised the customary sixpence, refused to complete the performance and screamed so loudly that 'a parcel of more whores and soldiers came to her relief'. Sometimes he went to a tavern – as after attending a performance of *Macbeth* at Drury Lane – taking with him a 'monstrous big whore' who displayed to him 'all the parts of her enormous carcase' but could not agree with him as to the terms for his use of them. Or sometimes he went to the girl's room, as after watching the annual race between the watermen who rowed against each other each year from London Bridge to Chelsea.[5] On his return from the race, walking down the Strand, Boswell was tapped on the shoulder 'by a fine fresh lass . . . She was an officer's daughter, and born at Gibraltar.'

The frankness with which Boswell recorded his adventures was unusual, but the adventures themselves were certainly not so. Eighteenth-century London seemed to some foreign visitors a city 'dedicated to venereal pleasures'. The Swiss traveller César de Saussure noticed how many coffee-houses were also 'temples of Venus', advertising their ability to provide more than sustenance by a sign outside depicting a woman's arm and hand holding the coffee-pot. *Henry's List of Covent Garden Ladies* was sold out as soon as each new edition was printed.

Since its early residents had abandoned Covent Garden for the newly built mansions in Hanover, Grosvenor and Cavendish Squares, the area was famous for its bagnios and bawdy-houses, its taverns with upper floors divided into useful cubicles, its coffee-houses such as Tom King's founded by the old Etonian husband of a celebrated procuress.

Tom King's, whose low smoke-filled room was decorated with a big obscene picture of a monk and a nun, did not open until midnight; but from then until dawn it was full of rakes and whores, noblemen who had come from Court and market-women reeking of brandy and tobacco. Here 'the chimney-sweeper, the pick-pocket, and maudlin peer', so a pamphlet of 1761 recorded, 'were often to be seen in the same seat together'.

Not far from Tom King's was the Rose Tavern in Russell Street, where Hogarth set the scene for the third plate of his *Rake's Progress* (plate 31), and where the drunken rake is seen entertaining a party of prostitutes, one of whom has her left hand inside his open shirt while her right hand passes his watch to a companion.

At the other side of the picture is a servant bringing in a large pewter dish and candle. He is one Leathercoat, porter at the Rose, remarkable not only for his universal knowledge of women of the town but also for his remarkable strength. For the price of a drink he lies down in the street and allows a carriage to run over his chest. The house's dancer, or 'posture woman', is seen taking off her stockings in the foreground.

For other tastes there were houses like the one 'near the end of Old Bailey' which is described in a pamphlet inspired by Jonathan Wild and directed against the homosexual City Marshal, Charles Hitchen. To this place, so the writer alleged, Wild was taken by Hitchen who 'was complimented by the company with the title of Madam and Ladyship. [Wild], asking the occasion of these uncommon devoirs, the Marshal said it was a familiar language peculiar to the house. [Wild] was not long there before he was more surprised than at first. The men calling one another 'my dear', and hugging, kissing, and tickling each other . . . and assuming effeminate voices and airs. Some telling others they ought to be whipped for not coming to school more frequently. The Marshal was very merry in this company.' He was also very merry, it seems, at a 'noted house in Holborn, to which such sort of persons used to repair, and dress themselves up in women's apparel, and dance and romp about'.

The cost of a night out in such places as this, or at the Rose was not high. But it was easy enough to spend a fortune in London within a year or two, even without increasing the rate of its dissipation by gambling. There were certain courtesans who charged the immense sum of fifty guineas for their company for a single night; and at certain fashionable taverns – 'court-end taverns' they were called before the term West End came into general use – it was possible to spend more on food and wine in an evening than your first footman could expect to earn in a year.

Boswell's meagre allowance – £25 every six weeks – permitted him few extravagances; and the life he led in London, the meals he ate, the wine he drank and the clothes he wore would have been considered very mean by the rich young men who received callers in their dressing-rooms in Grosvenor Square before beginning their elaborate toilets. These toilets, with the ministrations of valet and barber, might last two hours before the beau was satisfied with his clothes, scent, wig, powdered face, the hang of his sword and the angle of his hat, and would go downstairs to the sedan-chair waiting at the door. Life for such men as this was a perpetual round of coffee-house and chocolate-house, theatre and drawing-room, Park and gaming-room – one morning to Betty's fruit shop in St James's to eat strawberries, the next to a dressing-room levée at Lady Cornewall's, one evening to gamble at White's, the next to drink at Brooks's, one afternoon to the Duke of Cumberland's, the next to Holland House at Kensington.[6]

The sums won and lost at gambling were enormous. The case of Sir John Bland, Member of Parliament for Ludgershall, who squandered his entire vast fortune playing hazard and in one single night lost £32,000, was far from being an exceptional one. Hundreds of men such as Charles James Fox regularly sat up gambling all night, protecting their ruffles with bits of leather and turning their coats inside out for luck – Fox once gambled continuously for twenty-four hours, losing money at the rate of ten pounds a minute.

Foreigners considered, with good reason, that gambling was a kind of national fever, even more virulent in London than it was in Paris. Londoners would not limit their betting to games of chance, to faro, *jeu d'enfer* or blind-hookey, nor to sporting events, horse races, dog fights, cricket matches and political contests. They would bet on anything. At White's, as at most other similar establishments, a betting book was kept in which were recorded wagers as to the duration of wars, the ages at which various male members would die, the numbers of children that their wives would have, whether or not Mr Cavendish would succeed in killing 'the blue bottle fly before he goes to bed'. When a man fell down one day outside White's – according to one of Walpole's stories, perhaps untrue but certainly *ben trovato* – bets were immediately placed as to whether he were dead or not; a sympathetic passer-by suggesting that he should be bled, was immediately shouted down by the gamblers as this, they protested, would affect the fairness of the betting.

Just as men would sit up all night to gamble, so would they sit up all night to drink. Bolingbroke would go to his office in the morning straight from the dining-table with a wet napkin round his head; and according to Sir Gilbert Elliot, 'men of all ages' [drank] 'abominably', Fox 'a great deal', Sheridan 'excessively', Pitt 'as much as either', and Grey 'more than any of them'.

Although the middle-class citizen in London led a much more sober and industrious life than the average aristocrat, his working hours were probably shorter than they are today. He would spend as long as an hour in a coffee-house before going to his office which he often did not reach till after ten,

'Pastimes of Primrose Hill': a summer outing, 1791.

even though it was below his sitting-room. At about four o'clock it was time for dinner; and not until the end of the eighteenth century did any but the most assiduous do much work after that.

On summer evenings there would be trips on the water to Hampton Court to see the great Tudor palace,[7] to Chelsea where Don Saltero's served the best custard-buns in London, or to Smith's Tea Gardens, Vauxhall and Finch's Grotto Garden, St George's Fields.

The pleasure gardens on London's south bank were one of its chief delights, a constant source of traffic jams on the London bridges and, when London Bridge had no rivals, of profitable trade to the Thames watermen. Vauxhall Gardens were still the most popular. They were not expensive: the price of admission remained a shilling until 1790; and they were always crowded, particularly on Saturdays and Sundays, with all classes of society, from the Prince of Wales and his friends, to shop boys, apprentices, prostitutes, pickpockets, and highwaymen looking out for suitable victims to rob on their way home. The grounds were spacious, and lovers could usually discover a quiet place beneath the tall trees in one of the walks away from the bright lights of the globe lamps and the noise of the orchestra; while for those who were hungry or thirsty there was generally a vacant booth where they could enjoy a bottle of wine, a dish of tea or a glass of Vauxhall punch. On special occasions there were fancy dress balls with dancing all through the night.

More expensive and exclusive than Vauxhall was Ranelagh, a pleasure-garden opened in 1742 in Chelsea in the grounds of a villa once the property of the enormously rich Lord Ranelagh (plate 30). The Gardens at Ranelagh were immediately successful and were soon admitted by the bucks and maca-ronies who were their patrons to have 'totally beat Vauxhall'. The Rotonda was a principal attraction, and there was dancing here as well as by the river bank. Like Vauxhall, Ranelagh also provided concerts and 'genteel' walks, as well as spectacles on the lake where young men gaily dressed endeavoured to knock each other into the water by means of long punt-poles. The entrance fee of half a crown included coffee and punch.

Ranelagh, however, declined in favour towards the end of the century, and closed its gates for the last time in 1804. By then Cuper's Gardens had also closed down, suppressed because of the 'profligacy of the company by whom it was frequented'. Many other south bank gardens were forced to follow its example. The owner of the Temple of Flora, in Westminster Bridge Road, was sent to prison in 1796 for keeping a disorderly house.

But if the pleasure gardens declined in repute and popularity towards the end of the century, many other amusements were found to take their place. There were ridottos and festinos, masquerades at James Wyatt's Pantheon, 'a new winter Ranelagh on the Oxford Road' (plate 19), and routs at Almack's assembly rooms. William Almack, a Yorkshireman who

30. Ranelagh Grove at the entry to Lord Ranelagh's House, by Francis Hayman (detail).
31. *(overleaf)* An orgy at the Rose Tavern, Covent Garden: from Hogarth's *Rake's Progress*.

The *beau monde* at Almack's Assembly Rooms, 1821.

seems to have started life as a valet and later became a coffee-house keeper, had opened his celebrated rooms in Pall Mall in the 1760s as a rival establishment to Mrs Cornelys's in Soho Square which soon, in consequence, fell from favour. Almack provided gaming-rooms, dancing-rooms and supper-rooms. Rigid rules of behaviour were imposed upon the guests. Even the Duke of Wellington could not, in later years, gain admittance wearing trousers instead of the knee-breeches which the rules ordained. Tickets were not transferable; they were obtained through the payment of an annual subscription of ten guineas, though the rooms were open only once a week.

For those who could not afford Almack's prices there were 'cock and hen' clubs (where men and women met to drink and sing songs), 'cutter clubs' (formed by apprentices who enjoyed themselves on the river and in riverside taverns), political and debating clubs (such as 'The House of Lords' whose meetings, attended mostly by the 'more dissolute sort of barristers, attorneys and tradesmen', were held at the Three Herrings in Bell Yard), and the Robin Hood Society whose members (artisans and tradesmen) met for debates at the Robin Hood tavern, Butcher Row.

Then there were the continuing fairs, Bartholomew, Southwark and May Fair; the puppet shows produced by Robert Powell, the dwarf, in the Little Piazza, Covent Garden; the waxworks at Mr Goldsmith's, in Green Court, Old Jewry – or in the second half of the century at Mrs Salmon's in Fleet Street. And the numerous freak shows everywhere: the famous posture-maker, at the Duke of Marlborough's Head in Fleet Street, a man who – so it was advertised at the beginning of the century – could twist his hip bone up to his shoulder blade; the 'wonderful tall Essex woman' at the Rummer in Three King's Court, Fleet Street, who – so was claimed towards its end – was 'seven feet high and proportionable to her height, though not nineteen

32. Lord's Cricket Ground and the new villas of St John's Wood: lithograph of *c.* 1830.
33. Skating in Regent's Park: aquatint issued as a fashion plate for the winter of 1838–39.

years of age. To be seen at any hour from eleven in the morning till eight at night. Any family may see her at their own residences by giving timely notice.' There were 'Young Colossuses', and 'Wonderful Giants', 'Tall Saxon Women', 'Corsican Fairies'; and as the *Daily Advertiser* announced on 4 June 1778, the 'Ethiopian Savage. This astonishing Animal is of a different species from any ever seen in Europe, and seems to be a link between the Rational and Brute Creation, as he is a striking resemblance of the Human Species, and is allowed to be the greatest Curiosity ever exhibited in England . . . Also the Orang Outang, or real Wild Man of the Woods . . . a Calf with eight legs, two tails, two heads, and only one body; a very remarkable foreign Cat, and an extraordinary exploit done by a wild mouse . . . Offered to public Inspection, at a commodious Room, opposite the New Inn, Surrey side of Westminster Bridge at 1s. each person.'

Then, to match the display of freaks, there were the displays of violence. There was cock-fighting at the New Red Lion Cockpit at Clerkenwell as well as at the Royal Cockpit, Birdcage Walk. There was bear-baiting at the Bear Garden, Hockley-in-the-Hole, where bulls also were baited, some of them advertised as mad and 'dressed up with fireworks', others with cats and dogs tied to their tails: any person who brought a dog was admitted gratis. At Mr Broughton's amphitheatre in Oxford Road an occasional tiger

'The Humours and Diversions of Southwark Fair': engraving of 1833, presumed to be after Hogarth.

was to be seen: the first on display here, 'one of the fiercest and swiftest of savage beasts, being eight feet in length', was baited to death in December 1747. At Mr Stokes's Amphitheatre in Islington Road prize-fights were staged between savage and powerful female boxers: the most famous of these Amazons being 'Bruising Peg' who, in the summer of 1768, in the Spa Fields near Islington, 'beat her antagonist in a terrible manner'.

For those who preferred less savage sports, there were shooting and archery competitions, regattas on the river, football matches in St George's Fields and games of rounders in Lamb's Conduit Fields, bowling alleys and billiard-rooms everywhere. Towards the end of the century cricket, too, became a popular sport in London, though it was a game much older than that. A primitive form of it had been played in the thirteenth century, and it had soon become so popular that it was later declared illegal since it interfered with archery practice. A London club, which played matches on the Artillery Ground at Finsbury, was formed about 1700; but it was not until about 1780 when the Finsbury players moved to White Conduit Fields, Islington, and formed the White Conduit Cricket Club, that the game assumed the nature of a national summer sport. One of the founders of the White Conduit Cricket Club was the Earl of Winchilsea; and it was for the Earl and his friends that Thomas Lord, a Yorkshireman of Scottish descent, superintended the ground on which the Club played. The club changed its title to the Marylebone Cricket Club in 1767, and its ground, having moved from Islington to a field near Marylebone, eventually settled in 1814 in St John's Wood, where Lord's remains as the most famous cricket ground in the world (plate 32).[8]

In these early days of cricket, the players wore neither gloves nor pads, nor were they obliged to wear any formal clothes. White top hats with black bands were preferred, but a player wearing a black cap and a red striped shirt would not be disallowed. Thousands of Londoners came to watch the games, more often to bet on them than to admire the style of the performance, to cheer and hoot, to send their dogs chasing the ball along the boundary fence, and to admire the fresh beauty of the lusty girls whom most clubs then fielded in their teams.

Before the Marylebone Cricket Club had settled down at Lord's, a new sport had caught the fancy of the Londoners. This was ballooning. Balloons occupy everyone, Walpole told Sir Horace Mann; 'France gave us the *ton*, and as yet we have not come up to our model.' They soon did so. Blanchard's balloon ascent was made in France in 1783; and within a year the secretary to the Neapolitan Embassy in London, accompanied by a dog, a cat and a pigeon, ascended from the Artillery Ground in Finsbury in the presence of the Prince of Wales. The next year two men ascended from a field in Chelsea,

Mr Lunardi's balloon ascent, 13 May 1785.   David Garrick as King Lear, 1779.

and from then on scarcely a month passed without a balloon putting up from Green Park or Vauxhall Gardens, to the delight of the London crowds.

One of the Londoner's most unfailing sources of entertainment throughout the century was the theatre.

There were crowds of people outside the playhouse long before the doors were opened, for the only way to be sure of a seat in the pit or galleries was to get inside and sit on it – or to have a servant sit on it – before the play began. When Garrick played *King Lear* at Drury Lane in 1763 the pit was already full at four, even though the performance did not start till half past six. Queues were unknown and would have been uncontrollable even if attempted, so that there was invariably a painful scramble at the entrance. Once inside, the audiences were almost as unruly as they had been in Shakespeare's day, roaring their approval or condemnation at the end of each scene, shouting at the actors during its performance if they did not care for it, throwing orange peel and insults about with indiscriminate abandon. The orchestra were protected from the audience by a row of tall sharp spikes, and the musicians often had cause to be grateful for their protection.

The seats were hard benches, usually without backs, which added to the

'The Laughing Audience': engraving by Hogarth, 1733.

danger of tumult; and the lights were candles in sconces or chandeliers – there were candles also on the stage until Garrick introduced side lights in 1765 – and this increased the danger of fire. The price of the seats was reduced after the end of the third act of the main piece; and when an attempt was made to change this custom in 1763 the audience reacted in a characteristic way by breaking out into riot, smashing the benches and wrecking the chandeliers.

It had come to be expected that the main piece would be preceded by First, Second and Third Music and followed by a farce or a pantomime. Indeed, at Sadler's Wells playhouse, the various productions sometimes lasted for almost four hours and included – as well as two short comedies, two operettas, a ballet and a pantomime – displays by a strong man, a rope-walker and an acrobat. To sustain the audience through this theatrical marathon, meals of chops, pasties and wine, were served on shelves fixed to the backs of the benches.

Few people, of course, sat through the whole performance. It was well recognised by the management of the Drury Lane and Haymarket theatres, in fact, that the audience would always include many men who had come merely to make assignations, and to see what girls were offering themselves in the saloons. In Hogarth's 'The Laughing Audience' the gentlemen in the boxes are far more interested in the pretty orange-girls than in the play which so amuses the spectators in the pit.

For those who preferred the tragedy and comedy of life to the dramatics of the theatre, London provided a continuous display of the grotesque, the shocking, the pathetic and the ludicrous.

There was, for instance, the sadly absurd ritual of a London funeral. Notice of the death would be advertised by means of a black-edged card on which was stamped a variety of admonitory symbols from skulls and cross-bones to hour-glasses and old men with scythes. The house of death was shuttered and curtained, its door knocker wrapped round with flannel, and on its front door step, pale of face and black of garb, stood a professional mute enacting the agonies of despair at sixpence an hour, Sundays extra. Inside the house in a room hung with black cloth, the deceased lay in his coffin, his features enlivened by paint and powder, surrounded by tall candles; while those who came to pay their respects would be handed black gloves with which to hold the quarts of ale and claret that accompanied the mourning feast.

If some funerals were strange affairs, many of those clandestine marriages conducted in the area of the Fleet Prison – before they were made illegal by the 1754 Marriage Act – were even stranger. At first the ceremonies, performed by parsons incarcerated as debtors, took place in the prison chapel; but later – since the numbers of weddings grew so large and since the reverend debtors were allowed to wander outside the prison during the day – the ceremonies took place in taverns and brandy shops, indeed, anywhere that a sign depicting a male and female hand joined together was displayed above the legend: 'Marriages Performed Within'. The fee was slight – enough to pay for the parson's brandy and tobacco – the marriage was registered in a note-book or forgotten as circumstances required, the details recorded were real or fictitious as fancy dictated. Fleet Marriages were popular with all classes, quite as convenient for men like the Hon. Henry Fox who married Lady Georgiana Lennox by the 'Rules of the Fleet' in 1744, as for those such as Alexander Bunts, mariner of Deptford, and his bride Martha Norwood; according to an account of this marriage by the keeper of the tavern where it took place, both were 'very wicked and abusive and Raised a mobb at ye corner of Eastland's, beate my daughter Kitty, swore violently that if the Parson or I evver dare to come out they would have our hart's blood, and a woman whoe was with them whoes name I could not learn swore many times she would come and bring her Giant whoe would break every bone in our skins, or if we dare come to Deptford wee should not be suffered to [go] alive away. Bunt's wife it was whogh Beat the child . . . Bunts struck me.'

The curiosities and marvels of London, its riches, squalor, exuberance and conceit seemed to many visitors to have resulted in a depressingly morbid amalgam of physical tumescence and spiritual atrophy. Soon after the horses of their stage-coach clattered to a halt at the Bull and Mouth in Piccadilly, at the Golden Cross at Charing Cross or in the yards of the Bell or the George at Southwark,[9] their delight in the wonders of the capital would be tinged with alarm at its glaring faults.

To William Cobbett, the Kensington farmer, the London of the Regency was 'the Great Wen'; to Samuel Bamford, the Lancashire weaver, it was the 'Great Babylon'. The *beau monde* were selfish, ostentatious and vulgar, the men corseted and overdressed, the women flamboyantly overblown. The poor, huddled into squalid tenements which most rich men preferred not to think about, were forced from discontent and deprivation into crime. Even the fine new buildings, which neither Cobbett nor Bamford deigned to notice in their writings, were roundly condemned by other critics who saw in the ill-assorted medley of Greek and Roman, Gothic, Egyptian and oriental styles, a sad decline from the classic grace and simplicity of the earlier masters. Prince Pückler-Muskau described Nash's architecture as 'monstrous'; Maria Edgeworth was 'properly surprised by the new town that has been built in Regent's Park – and indignant at plaister statues and horrid useless *domes* and pediments crowded with mock sculpture figures which damp and smoke must destroy in a season or two'.

The charges were understandable. There was much in Nash's work that did reflect the grandiose, extravagant, showy, profusely exuberant and cheerfully superficial spirit of his time. Although London was a magnet for provincial talent, it was a magnet, too, for the frivolous and flippant, the venal and the villainous. And whether or not a wen, it was undeniably expanding at an alarming rate and in a regrettable manner.

By the time of George IV's coronation in 1821 its population had risen to more than a million, a considerable part of the increase being due to the continuing immigration of foreigners – Germans, Frenchmen, Danes and Swedes – as well as to the inflow of Irishmen and Scotsmen, of country people hoping to find work and better wages in the city, and of Negroes. The majority of these foreign immigrants joined their fellow-countrymen in ever increasingly cramped quarters in their own particular parts of the town – the French, for instance, in certain streets in Soho, in Carnaby Street, as well as in Moorfields and Spitalfields; the Negroes, of whom there may have been

St George's Turnpike (now Circus) at Southwark: engraving of 1809.

as many as 10,000 in the 1770s – mainly freed, escaped or abandoned slaves – crowded in ghettoes along the river front east of the Tower.

It was here that London revealed itself as the commercial centre of the greatest power in the world. Its trade had increased fivefold in the eighteenth century, and, within the first five years of the nineteenth, four huge new docks were built, the West India Dock, the London Dock, the Surrey Dock, and the East India Dock. 'What a Capital lies here in buildings, wares and vessels,' exclaimed Prince Pückler-Muskau after a visit to these new docks, more impressive even than Barclay and Perkins' Brewery where the machinery was worked by '*steam-engines*'. At West India Dock the Prince inspected the brick warehouses and marvelled at their immensity. Goods worth £20,000,000 were stored in them, and 2,000 workers toiled amidst the cranes and winches, hoists and pulleys. He was amazed at the amount of work they did, just as he was amazed by the riches that passed through the port, by the fortunes made by the merchant and the financier, the landowner and the speculator, by the reverence for wealth which was one of the most significant aspects of the new age dawning.

12 'Confused Treasures of Iron and Wildernesses of Bricks' 1834–1886

In 1834 – the year in which King William IV arbitrarily dismissed Lord Melbourne's administration and Joseph Aloysius Hansom introduced his 'Patent Safety Cab' to a curious public – work began on the London and Birmingham Railway under the direction of Robert Stephenson.

The success of the Liverpool and Manchester Railway, opened four years before, had provoked that 'railway mania' which was soon to sweep across the country, inducing Parliament to sanction hundreds of thousands of miles of rail before Victoria had been three years a queen, making some men millionaires, devouring the fortunes of others, and altering the appearance and character of London for ever. 'What a gulf between now and then,' says one of Thackeray's characters. '*Then* was the old world . . . But your railroad starts a new era . . . We who lived before railways and survive out of the ancient world, are like Father Noah and his family out of the Ark.'

The London and Birmingham Railway cut through the northern suburbs, past its depot at Camden Town to its terminus in Euston Square where, as a fitting tribute to the solidity of Stephenson's enterprise, an enormous Doric arch designed by Philip Hardwick was erected at the entrance to this the first of London's main terminal stations.

Euston Station, *c.* 1838: a train at the departure platform, and the arrival platform.

'Over London—By Rail': engraving by Gustave Doré, 1872.

Euston was opened in 1838; but by then the London and Birmingham was not the only railway in London. A line from London to Greenwich had been in use for two years, and the London and Blackwall Railway's tracks already stretched to a terminus in Fenchurch Street. These were followed by lines to Croydon, Southampton, Hastings and Dover. Within the next few years several more terminal stations had followed Euston, most of them with large hotels adjoining.

Vast areas of London were transformed by this revolution in transportation. As early as 1844, when a London terminus for the Great Western Railway had been built in Bishop's Road, Paddington (plate 40), a foreign visitor noticed how a 'completely new and continually interesting district' had been called into life by its construction there. The same sort of development took place around the other main line stations as soon as they were constructed; and to make way for the tracks which led to them, rows of houses, streets and squares were demolished, scores of thousands of their inhabitants displaced. Twenty thousand people were obliged to abandon their homes by the building of the London and Birmingham Railway, most of them, unwilling to move far away, crowding into already overpopulated areas nearby, pouring in their hundreds into houses abandoned by the middle-classes who took advantage of the railway to move even further out from London's centre.

Excavations for the building of the *Scotsman*'s engine house in Camden Town, 1839.

The railway companies had a legal responsibility towards the people whose homes they destroyed; but it was not always observed, and the new houses which were provided were frequently offered to tenants at rents they could not afford. Nine hundred houses were demolished by the North London Railway Company for the laying of two miles of track; and it was found beyond the Company's means to rehouse their occupants adequately.

In *Dombey & Son,* Dickens describes the metamorphosis of Camden Town, how houses were knocked down, streets broken through and stopped, deep trenches dug into the ground with enormous piles of soil thrown high above them, undermined buildings shored up. 'Here, a chaos of carts, overthrown and jumbled together, lay topsy-turvy at the bottom of a steep, unnatural hill; there, confused treasures of iron soaked and rusted in something that had accidentally become a pond. Everywhere were bridges that led nowhere; thoroughfares that were wholly impassable; Babel towers of chimneys, wanting half their height; temporary wooden houses and ragged tenements, and fragments of unfinished walls and arches, and piles of scaffolding, and wildernesses of bricks, and giant forms of cranes, and tripods straddling above nothing.'

After Camden Town it was the turn of Barnsbury, of Praed Street and Charing Cross, of Pimlico, Southwark and the City. Acre upon acre of land was covered with iron rails, platforms, shunting yards and engine sheds, repair shops and ticket offices, refreshment rooms and coal bunkers. Curve after glass curve, the roofs of the new stations caracoled across the tracks. At Paddington, Isambard Kingdom Brunel, with help from Matthew Digby Wyatt and Owen Jones, enclosed the terminal of the Great Western with a vaulting expanse of wrought iron and glass, providing a suitably impressive adjunct for what was then the biggest and most expensive hotel in England. At King's Cross, Lewis Cubitt, younger brother of the builder, designed a complex of arcades, arched roofs, Venetian windows and a 120 ft. high clock tower to serve the patrons of the Great Northern, for whose additional convenience the adjoining hotel was opened in 1854. The Italianate structures of Blackfriars and Broad Street stations, Langley's additions to the white brick bays and pedimented front of Fenchurch Street, the quirkish buildings for the South Eastern Railway in Cannon Street, the extensive edifice put up for the London, Chatham and Dover Railway on the Grosvenor Estate beside the Grosvenor Hotel and named after the Queen, John Hawkshaw's Charing Cross Station and E. M. Barry's richly ornamented hotel in front of it, Sir George Gilbert Scott's vast hotel and station which towered in all their Gothic fancy and splendour over St Pancras, were all built between 1863 and 1886.[1]

The coming of the railways not only transformed the appearance of London; it altered its whole shape and character. The rich had always been able to live outside the city centre and drive up each morning in their carriages, even though their coachmen were finding it more and more difficult to guide the horses through the congested traffic. The poor, on the other hand, had been constrained to live within walking distance of their work – walking distance being interpreted more generously than it is today: a four-mile tramp to work in the morning, and back again at night was not in the least uncommon. Horse-drawn omnibuses had made their appearance in London in 1829, but the fares demanded were far more than most clerical workers and nearly all manual ones could regularly afford. There was no such thing as a 2d fare before 1846: the cost of a ticket from the Yorkshire Stingo, near Paddington, to the Bank of England was a shilling; and from the Angel, Islington, to the Bank, sixpence.

Railway fares, on the other hand, were comparatively cheap, and trains were fast. As the suburban lines spread, so it later became possible for men to live at increasing distances from their work; and as new suburbs developed for the new railway-travelling public in such places as Norwood and High-gate, Sydenham, Walworth and Camberwell, so the decline of the City as a place of residence became almost complete.

London had already been growing fast before the railways came. In the first thirty years of the nineteenth century its population rose from 865,000 to one and a half million. 90,000 people crossed London Bridge every day in 1837. After the railways had made it possible for London to expand still further outwards, this increase in population was accelerated; almost half a million more people were to be counted living in and around the capital every ten years after 1841. Already by 1845 the congestion of traffic in the streets had become so serious that a Royal Commission was appointed to examine proposals for its relief. Central London was becoming chocked with its thousands of pedestrians, its carriages and carts, gigs, tilburies, phaetons, dogcarts, landaus and victorias, hansom cabs, broughams and growlers, its twenty thousand equestrians, the unnumbered animals bumping into each other on their way to Smithfield, the scores of horse-drawn omni-buses.

One of the most astonishing proposals for the relief of this congestion was put to the Royal Commission by Charles Pearson, the enterprising and en-thusiastic Surveyor to the City of London. Pearson suggested that, since there was no longer any room for people to move about comfortably in London at street level, they should be transported beneath it. Objections to such a quixotic idea were immediate and numerous: the houses above the lines would collapse into the tunnels; digging holes in the ground for such a purpose must surely be against the laws of God; the Duke of Wellington's fear that

The first underground steam train: the inaugural trip on the first section of the Metropolitan Line from Edgware Road on 24 May 1862, before it was opened in 1863; the passengers included Gladstone and his wife.

one day a French army would arrive in London by train without anyone knowing it had landed, was widely shared. But Pearson persisted; and having persuaded several rich men in the City that the underground railway would prove immensely profitable, he had his way at last. It had been a long struggle, though, and by 1863 – when the North Metropolitan Railway Company on its opening day carried thirty thousand passengers in open trucks underground between Paddington and the City – Charles Pearson was dead.

Although thousands of poor families displaced by the building of the railways, and the simultaneous construction of new roads, were reluctant to move far from their former homes, the office worker and clerk, the skilled craftsman and Civil Servant, the schoolmaster and book-keeper joined the swelling exodus to those new housing estates which speculative builders were putting up in that haphazard and uncontrolled way that had long since determined the sprawling pattern of London's growth. Communities developed around the new outlying railway stations, at first no more than rows of villas, perhaps, but soon small towns with a life – if only a temporary life – of their own. In their outward appearances most of these new suburbs were sadly dispiriting. The houses were standardised and cheaply built, depressingly monotonous in shape and tone, arranged in rows of terraces or cramped semi-detached pairs in neatly measured order. 'It is impossible,' said Disraeli, complaining of this dreary repetitious mediocrity, 'to conceive of anything more tame, more insipid, more uniform. Pancras is like Marylebone, Marylebone is like Paddington.' Tulse Hill he could have added was like Camberwell, Nine Elms like New Cross.

This development of Victorian suburbs did little, however, to allay the overcrowding in the slums of central London and the East End. In such districts as Shoreditch and St Giles's, Hackney and Bethnal Green, Lambeth, Bermondsey, Battersea and Whitefriars, in the rookeries of Whetstone Park and Hatton Garden where once great houses had stood, the squalor and congestion were appalling. Men and women intent upon reform worked hard to alleviate the suffering, but the numerous and unwieldy official organisations through which they had to work as often succeeded in thwarting their endeavours as in encouraging them. Outside the City, London was administered by over three hundred bodies, including seventy-eight parish vestries with indeterminate and ill-defined powers. There were Paving Boards and Sewage Commissioners, Boards of Surveyors and Committees of Health; but their individual and combined efforts were peculiarly unrewarding. St Pancras, for instance, had sixteen Paving Boards acting under twenty-nine Acts of Parliament: the bad paving in the parish was notorious. Even after central authorities like the Metropolitan Board of Works were created, the troubles experienced and obstructions encountered by such enlightened reformers as Lord Shaftesbury, Baroness Burdett-Coutts, Octavia Hill and the American merchant George Peabody, were daunting to all but the most patient and persevering spirit. Nor can it be said that the new 'model' blocks of flats and ranges of artisans' dwellings that occasionally resulted from this determined private philanthropy were much more cheerful than the slums they replaced. Usually constructed of a dark stock brick, which smoke and soot made darker still, with iron balcony railings, steep stone stairs and dismal asphalt courtyards, these Buildings seemed to some of their inhabitants more like prisons than houses. Somewhat less dreary were the model dwellings of Prince Albert's Society for Improving the Condition of the Labouring Classes whose first premises were erected at Bagnigge Wells. Yet even they were heavily pervaded with the atmosphere of the workhouse.

At least they had better sanitation; and that was a great deal. For London's drainage system and water supply outside the City, had become, by the middle of the nineteenth century, not merely scandalously inadequate but a constant threat to health and life. Cholera was almost as common as once the plague had been.

In the first place, the water supply was both inadequate and impure. Thousands of people collected their meagre and tainted supplies as their

34. Mlle Rachel's farewell benefit at Her Majesty's Theatre, June 1841, by E. Lami.
35. Evening prayers in an upper-class home: lithograph after E. Lami, 1829.
36. (overleaf) Contrasts in transport—aquatints of the driver of 1832 and the driver of 1852.

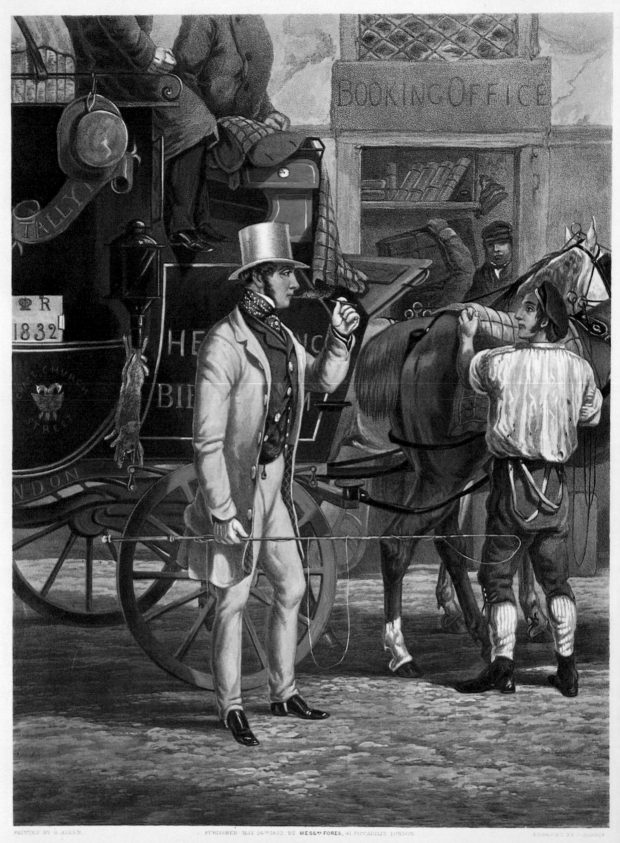

PAINTED BY H. ALKEN.   PUBLISHED MAY 26TH 1832, BY MESSRS FORES, 41 PICCADILLY LONDON   ENGRAVED BY J. HARRIS

THE DRIVER OF 1832.

1st CLASS   2nd CLASS

THE DRIVER OF 1852.

PUBLISHED MAY 24th 1852, BY MESSrs FORES, 41, PICCADILLY, LONDON.   ENGRAVED BY J. HARRIS.

A public bath house: engraving by Doré.

ancestors had done for centuries, filling their bowls and fish kettles from the public standpipes in the streets, one pipe commonly serving for as many as sixteen houses and being turned on for only a few minutes once a week. Those who paid for a piped supply from one or other of the nine water companies were only sure of obtaining it for about eight or nine hours a week. Most of London's water still came from the Thames, polluted though it was by outfall from the sewers, including the now subterranean Fleet, by stable dung, rotten sprats, guano, and by quantities of rubbish and offal thrown into it even at this late period from slaughter-houses, knackers' yards, tanneries and tar works. The colour of the river was a greeny black, its consistency so thick that each time the tide went down a greasy, foul-smelling scum was deposited over the mud. In the hot dry summer of 1858 it was impossible to cross Westminster Bridge without a handkerchief pressed closely over nose and mouth, impossible to take a trip on a river steamer without feeling sick, impossible to breathe in the House of Commons until the windows had been covered with curtains soaked in chloride of lime.

A few years before this, in 1849, the disgraceful state of London's drainage system – if so noisome a collection of leaking pipes, uncovered cess-pits, stinking gullies, rotting privies and gas-filled sewers could be called a system at all – combined with the disgusting state of its 218 acres of shallow and overcrowded burial grounds, and with the pall of smoke-filled, disease-spreading fog that hovered in the streets, produced a most fearful outbreak of cholera which at the height of its virulence killed four hundred people a day. Most of these victims were in the slums where the foulest, most appalling conditions were to be found, where in the rookery of St Giles's nearly three thousand people were crammed into less than a hundred houses and were almost suffocated by their own sewage.

Although London's drainage system had been much improved by the end of the century, for the very poor the squalid conditions imposed by overcrowding remained as before and in some parts of the capital, according to Lord Shaftesbury, were actually aggravated. In a single nine-bedroomed house in Spitalfields, for example, as late as the 1880s, there were sixty-three people living with only nine beds between them. A Royal Commission on Housing reported on privies being shared by numerous households and overflowing for months on end; in some parts of London they were actually 'used as sleeping places by the houseless poor'.

'That great foul city of London,' John Ruskin cried out in anguish in the 1860s, ' – rattling, growling, smoking, stinking – ghastly heep of fermenting brickwork, pouring out poison at every pore . . . '

It was not only the poor who suffered – although they, of course, suffered by far the worse. In the smartest and most expensive districts there were houses with defective drains which threatened the health of their inhabitants long after the campaign fought by the persistent and outspoken Edwin Chadwick had helped to reform the more outrageous of the abuses elsewhere. Belgrave and Eaton Squares, Hyde Park Gardens, Cavendish, Bryanston, Manchester and Portman Squares all stood over sewers which, in the words of an official report, abounded 'in the foulest deposits, in many cases stopping up the house drains and emitting the most disgusting effluvium'. Some of these sewers were so old that it was considered impossible to make any attempt to flush them for the removal of 'their most loathsome deposit', for that would 'have brought them down altogether'.

Typhus was a common disease amongst the upper-classes, even amongst the Royal Family. Queen Victoria's apartments at Buckingham Palace were ventilated through the common sewer; and in many other large houses swarms of rats came up from the sewers every night in their nocturnal search for food. Reports of children in well-to-do households being attacked in their nursery cots at night were not uncommon.

In the second half of the nineteenth century, the seemingly intractable problem of London's slums was to some extent alleviated by the replanning of London undertaken by the Metropolitan Board of Works, whose wide new roads, sorely needed for generations, cut through acres of slum buildings and swept them away. The pattern had been set in the 1830s and 1840s by the construction of the approaches to the new London Bridge which entailed demolition costs of one and a half million pounds, by the re-organisation of Trafalgar Square which swept away the tangled slums known as Porridge Island around St Martin-in-the-Fields, by the remodelling of Liverpool Street, the rebuilding of Hungerford Market, the construction of Hungerford Bridge, and by the driving of New Oxford Street through part of the notorious rookery of St Giles's. Enormous as the sums spent on these endeavours were, however, they were little enough when compared with those afterwards spent by the Metropolitan Board of Works. For the Board was responsible not only for an extensive new main drainage system and the construction of the Victoria, Albert and Chelsea Embankments, but also for a complex of roads that were the pride of Victorian London: Victoria Street in Westminster and Queen Victoria Street in the City, Northumberland Avenue, Southwark Street, Charing Cross Road, and Shaftesbury Avenue.

Victoria Street cut through acres of slum west of the Abbey towards Victoria Station; Queen Victoria Street was the long eastern extension of a route that led from the Bank to Blackfriars Bridge and was then continued along the river by Victoria Embankment to the Houses of Parliament by Westminster Bridge; Northumberland Avenue, cutting through what had once been the gardens of Northumberland House, linked Charing Cross with Victoria Embankment by Hungerford Bridge; Southwark Street linked the approaches to London Bridge with Blackfriars Road; Charing Cross Road provided a new route northwards from Trafalgar Square; and Shaftesbury Avenue was an easier way of reaching Piccadilly from Holborn.

By the time the last of these two thoroughfares had been completed towards

Old London Bridge and its replacement under construction, 1828.

the end of the 1880's, London, with a population already approaching five millions, had extended to a size which would have been unthinkable even a hundred years before. 'Alexander's armies were great makers of conquests,' wrote Wilkie Collins in *Hide and Seek*, 'but the modern guerrilla regiments of the hod, the trowel and the brick-kiln, are the greatest conquerors of all, for they hold the longest the soil that they have once possessed . . . with the conqueror's device inscribed on it – *This ground to be let on building leases.*'

The thin lines of houses stretching out from the swollen centre had disappeared in a mass of building that covered the open spaces between them; the new communities which had grown up around the suburban railway stations had been enveloped by the spreading town as had the older country villages; the separate industrial centres along the river front were separate no more. Only here and there had a patch of common – once, perhaps, part of the shared land of a medieval community – or a public park, the sooty successor of an Elizabethan manor garden, managed to escape the builder's spade.

In the north the solid blocks of buildings had reached Hampstead, Highgate, Stroud Green and Stamford Hill, strongholds of the middle-class; in the west there was no open country now between Bayswater and Shepherd's Bush, or between Knightsbridge and Fulham; Bayswater and Notting Hill

Sectional view of the Thames Embankment at Charing Cross, showing the Metropolitan Railway and the low level sewer, 1867.

had been early and densely built up, Hyde Park Gardens in 1836, Leinster Square, Princes Square and Lancaster Gate in the 1850s. To the south, beyond the solid arc of buildings from Wandsworth and Clapham and through Camberwell to Deptford, new lines of buildings were stretching out to Tooting, Dulwich and Brockley; the East End was expanding past Bethnal Green and Poplar to Mile End and Canning Town.

Inside this vast array of brick and stone, tile and slate, glass and iron, new public buildings had arisen on an unprecedented scale. Ragged schools and board schools, hospitals and prisons, mechanics' institutes, and warehouses, music-halls and gin-palaces, museums and lecture rooms, hotels and barracks, banks and insurance offices, churches and chapels, all appeared with so surprising a speed that every street was scarcely recognisable from one decade to the next. A huge new Post Office headquarters was built in St Martin-le-Grand in 1873, the Wool Exchange in Coleman Street in 1874, Knightsbridge Barracks in 1879, the City of London School in 1882, St Paul's School and Brompton Oratory in 1884,[2] an enlarged Stock Exchange in 1885,[3] the Guildhall School of Music and the Guildhall Art Gallery in 1886, G. E. Street's law courts in the Strand between 1874 and 1882;[4] a big new addition to the Admiralty begun in 1894, and an even larger War Office designed in 1898, added to the number of government buildings

George Gilbert Scott's palazzo for the Foreign Office.

between Charing Cross and Parliament Square, a part of Westminster already loaded with the massive weight of the Treasury completed in 1847, and George Gilbert Scott's cinquecento palazzo, the Foreign Office, finished in 1873.[5]

Down by the river, east of the Tower, a series of docks were built to replace or supplement those built during the Regency and no longer adequate: the Royal Victoria Dock in 1855, Millwall Dock in 1868, the South-West India Dock in 1870, the Royal Albert Dock in 1880, the Tilbury docks in 1886. The Blackwell Tunnel was opened in 1897, three years after Tower Bridge first raised its twin, thousand-ton bascules which have never since failed to swing upwards to allow ships to pass upstream between the Tower and Pickle Herring Stairs.

In 1834 the Palace of Westminster – that is to say the conglomeration of buildings, including the two Houses of Parliament, which had grown up around Westminster Hall on the site of the Saxon royal palace – was burned to the ground. Two workmen, anxious to get home, had overstoked a stove with wooden tallies for which the Clerk of the Works could find no other use. It was decided that the new building should be 'either Gothic or Elizabethan' and ninety-seven designs – only six of them Elizabethan – were submitted in the competition held the following year.

The drawings submitted by Charles Barry were chosen, though Barry, who had designed the Travellers' Club a few years before, would himself have preferred to work in an Italian style. But he had enlisted the help of the twenty-three-year-old Augustus Pugin, a passionate not to say fanatical devotee of Gothicism, whose beautiful, minutely detailed drawings were, it seems, what caught the imagination of the committee and largely determined their decision.

The collaboration was a rewarding one: Barry was a cautious, solid and matter-of-fact man whose character was ideally suited to dealing with obtuse committees and whose gift for planning ensured that, despite its picturesque appearance, the building was a practical one. Pugin was volatile, nervous, inclined to hysteria – he died insane at forty – a man whose agile imagination and inventive enthusiasm bestowed on Barry's massive form its colourful, intricate ornamentation.

Work began in 1840. Seven years later the House of Lords was finished, and 'nothing,' in Nathaniel Hawthorne's opinion, 'could be more magnificent and gravely gorgeous'. Five years after that the rest of the building was ready; the clock tower, known as Big Ben, was completed in 1858, the pinnacled Victoria Tower in 1860.

While the Palace of Westminster was nearing completion, another extraordinary masterpiece was rising in all its strange grandeur in Hyde Park – the Crystal Palace, a monumental structure of 4,000 tons of iron and 400 tons of glass, nearly two thousand feet long and over four hundred feet wide, the work of the Bedfordshire gardener who was to become Sir Joseph Paxton.

The Crystal Palace was designed to house the Great Exhibition of 1851, the exhibition which Prince Albert had proposed to a meeting of the Society of Arts two years before. At first a brick building had been preferred, but the lowest estimate submitted for its cost was £120,000, a figure which provided the numerous opponents of the Exhibition with fresh grounds for disapproval, so that when Paxton's drawing – modelled on the conservatory he had built for the Duke of Devonshire at Chatsworth – appeared in the *Illustrated London News*, the Exhibition Committee fell upon it eagerly and obtained a satisfactory tender of £80,000 for its construction.

By the end of 1850 well over two thousand workmen were engaged upon it, erecting its cast iron girders and wrought-iron trusses, its 30 miles of guttering, 200 miles of wooden sash bars and 900,000 square feet of glass.

But when it was finished, and had demonstrated its capacity to remain in one piece by surviving the vibrations set up by squads of soldiers jumping and stamping inside it and by quantities of round shot being rumbled over

A contemporary photograph of some of the sculpture exhibits at the Great Exhibition.

its wooden slatted floors; even when the right to print the catalogue had been sold for £3,200, and Messrs Schweppe had secured the refreshment contract for £5,500, there were still many who insisted that the scheme was folly, that it could not but fail to lose money, that no good could possibly come of it since it was the brainchild of that Prince Albert. The number of foreigners, it was said, and provincial people arriving in London to see it would inevitably lead to 'confusion, disorder and demoralization, if not actual revolution . . . famine and pestilence'. The Treasury was unhelpful, Parliament dismissive.

Nevertheless, in May the Exhibition opened. Season tickets were three guineas for gentlemen, two guineas for ladies; no one without season tickets would be admitted to the opening ceremony at which the Queen, Prince Albert, the Prince of Wales, the Archbishop of Canterbury and the Duke of Wellington would be among those present (plate 37). On the second day the entrance would be £1; on the fourth, 5s; thereafter from 5s. to 1s. depending upon the day of the week.

From the beginning the Exhibition was an astonishing success. Over six million people came to London to see it from all over the country and all over the world. Members of royal houses, and their uniformed suites, came from Germany; eight hundred agricultural labourers 'in their peasants' attire' came from Surrey and Sussex conducted by the clergy of their parishes; and whoever they were and from wherever they came, the visitors were all wonderfully impressed by the 19,000 exhibits arranged beneath the light blue framework and the glittering glass, the tall elm trees of the Park which the builders had not cut down but left to spread their leaves between the galleries.

The profits of the Exhibition were considerable. With these profits a long stretch of land was bought between Kensington Gardens and Cromwell Road on which were later built a number of museums, concert halls, headquarters of learned societies, colleges and schools, that paid an overdue tribute to Prince Albert's earnest faith, enthusiasm and enterprise.

The first of these cultural institutions to appear was an ugly utilitarian purple brick and terracotta building put up by Sir William Cubitt in 1856 as an art gallery and museum in Cromwell Road and afterwards partly replaced and partly absorbed by the Victoria and Albert Museum.[7] North of it, in 1867 – on the site of Gore House where Lady Blessington had held court with Count D'Orsay – was begun the Royal Albert Hall, a huge circular red brick building with a dome of glass and iron, reminiscent of an opera house at Dresden which had been designed by a German political refugee whose work Albert had greatly admired.[8] Standing facing the Albert Hall, and those numerous institutions which his vision had inspired, is the Prince's more personal memorial.

A state concert in the Albert Hall, 1873, lit by lime-light.

It was started in 1864, not finished until twelve years later, and described in 1882 as 'beyond question the finest monumental structure in Europe'. Certainly its designer, Sir George Gilbert Scott, who spent £120,000 on it, regarded it as his 'most prominent work'. His idea, he wrote, 'was to erect a kind of ciborium to protect a statue of the Prince . . . its special characteristic was that this ciborium was designed in some degree on the principles of the ancient shrines . . . These shrines are models of imaginary buildings such as had never in reality been erected; and my idea was to realise one of these imaginary structures with its precious metal, its inlayings, its enamels . . . '

A work of intricate craftsmanship in white Italian marble, bronze, wrought iron, granite, agate, onyx, jasper, cornelian and crystal, it has been variously condemned as grossly vulgar, impossibly sentimental and crudely eclectic. More temperately, though no less dismissively, a critic described it ten years after its designers' death, as 'an uncomfortable feat of engineering'. Now, a hundred years after its inception, its peculiar virtues are beginning to be admitted along with its High Victorian arrogance.

Beneath its Gothic gabled canopy and pinnacle is the fourteen-foot high wistfully contemplative figure of Prince Albert wearing the collar of a Knight of the Garter and the garter itself above the bulging calf of his bronze left leg. In his right hand he holds a book. Is it the Bible? awestruck children have

The Oxford Music Hall.

196

felt compelled to ask, looking up from the steps beneath. But no; it is the catalogue of the 1851 Exhibition, which was held close by the statue across the road to the east.

The huge glass conservatory in which the Exhibition was held was later moved across the river to Sydenham. Renamed Crystal Palace it was burned down in 1936, only its strange plaster prehistoric animals now surviving in Crystal Palace Park. But for eighty years it was the central feature of a new pleasure ground, a concert hall, theatre, menagerie, exhibition room, restaurant, and a favourite resort of the families of the middle-class and of the solid, skilled and comfortable workman.

Although it was not until the end of the nineteenth century that Charles Booth could suggest that the respectable and fully employed working-man's family in London ate meat and vegetables every day, never went hungry and had sufficient money left over for a Sunday outing, even in the 1850s there were thousands of skilled artisans who were able to share some of the comforts and a good deal of the security of the middle-class.

Masons and carpenters, workers in the metal and transport industries and in the clothing trade, watchmakers in Clerkenwell, makers of printing machinery in Southwark, of furniture in Oxford Street, railway engineers in Nine Elms and Kentish Town, workers in the chemical factories in Silvertown and Wandsworth, in the breweries on Bankside, and in the powder-mills at Isleworth and Enfield, fishermen and boat builders from Barking, compositors from Wandsworth, craftsmen in the china industries at Lambeth, silk workers from Bethnal Green, could all be found enjoying the air in the grounds of the Crystal Palace or walking there from the railway station.

Most of these men had to work long hours; few in the 1850s worked less than twelve hours a day, though by the 1890s they were more likely to be working nine. But they made the most of what spare time they had. The clerical worker in the City commonly worked even longer hours than these, for in few offices was there any regularly observed custom that the working day ended at a particular time, even though most offices were supposed to close at six o'clock: the clerk went home when his work was done, and not before. There was no early closing on Saturdays until 1863; nor were there any Bank Holidays. Yet the office worker and shop assistant, too, contrived to find time for pleasure.

They found time to go fishing at Richmond, or pigeon-flying at Battersea, to watch cricket at Islington or the Thames Regatta at Hammersmith, to go to the Flower Show at Chiswick, the Zoos at Walworth Manor House and in Regent's Park (plate 39).[9] They could take a cheap train ticket to places which their grandparents could never have hoped to see, or a steamboat down the river to Greenwich Fair.

In the evenings they might feel able to afford a meal out in a small chop-house where they could buy a plate of liver and bacon for tenpence (potatoes and bread 2d. extra), gooseberry pie for fivepence and a pint of stout for $4\frac{1}{2}$d. They could spend the night and have breakfast at Anderton's Hotel in Fleet Street for no more than two shillings. They might go out to a theatre (a ticket in the gallery at Drury Lane could be had for 1s.), to a tea-garden, a music-hall (plate 43), the Panorama in Leicester Square, the Cosmorama in Regent Street, to Madame Tussaud's or to that metropolitan institution which the young Charles Dickens so much loved, Astley's in Westminster Bridge Road, home of melodrama, fireworks, acrobats, clowns and dancing horses.

Such diverse pleasures could also be enjoyed at Cremorne (plate 38), the successor, in King's Road, Chelsea, of the eighteenth-century pleasure gardens. Cremorne House, once the home of Lady Huntingdon, had been

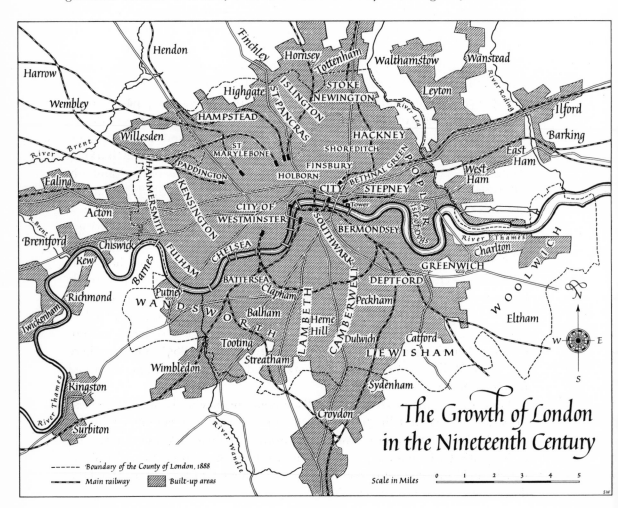

The Growth of London
in the Nineteenth Century

------ Boundary of the County of London, 1888
—·— Main railway   ▨ Built-up areas

Scale in Miles   0 1 2 3 4 5

bought by a Prussian baron of dubious repute who had opened the grounds for *fêtes champêtres,* dancing and balloon ascents. In 1849 it had come into the hands of a former headwaiter at the Albion who bought additional land, built a pagoda and two theatres, and entertained his patrons with all the delights of the fairground, with processions and tournaments, river pageants, and a dance floor capable of accommodating two thousand couples at once. For many other thousands of less fortunate Londoners, however, there could be no such pleasures at all.

Goodred's Royal Saloon, Piccadilly, 1833.

Mayhew's London 1840–1887

A doctor giving evidence before a parliamentary committee in the 1840s described conditions in a London match factory. There were nearly two hundred people employed in the factory, most of them children under thirteen years of age, some of them under ten. The work was repetitive, hard, boring, disagreeable and dangerous. The fumes of the sulphur were foul and noxious, and induced fits of violent coughing. The children, 'not looking well nor cheerful', had to take their meals in the evil-smelling workroom. They were paid about five shillings a week, which because not all children could stand up to the conditions of work, was about twice as much as the usual wages of children in London.

The worst horrors of the Industrial Revolution were to be found not so often in London as in the new towns of the north where children were kicked and beaten with leather belts for falling asleep at their benches, their screams unheard above the roar of the machinery, where boys in nail factories were

A match factory of 1870.

Match seller, 1905.

drawn up feet first to the ceiling for not doing their work well, and girls, naked to the waist, pulled coal carts through the mines with chains tied round their waists like animals. But the exploitation and cruel treatment of children in London was distressing enough. When exhaustion made it impossible for them to keep awake any longer, they were hit on the head at their work, or made to take pinches of snuff, were dipped into tanks of cold water, or shaken by the shoulders until their teeth rattled.

They had to work, for even the few shillings they could bring to their families at the end of the week might mean all the difference between cold and warmth, between hunger and enough to eat. Many of them worked at home, stitching gloves, perhaps, even at the age of three, pinned to their mothers' knees so that they did not fall over if they dropped off to sleep, often kept up until midnight. Many others went out to work, small boys, even as late as the 1860s, as climbing-boys for chimney-sweeps, their flesh hardened by rubbing with the strongest brine. The masters of these climbing-boys stood over their charges with a cane, forcing them to bear a few more rubs, or offering them a halfpenny if they would but lie still; and when the boys came back from work, their elbows and knees covered in blood, they were made to stand close to a hot fire and were rubbed with brine again.

In the middle of the century only about half the children in London

Chimneysweep and boy, 1877.

between five and fifteen were at school. In the streets children abounded who had but the sketchiest knowledge about anything that did not concern their day to day existence. Even after the Government began to face up to its responsibilities in the 1870s, education for the poor remained extremely haphazard. The mothers of most of those London children who did go to school felt obliged to go out to try to find work to make up the loss in the family income, leaving the children too young for the schoolroom drugged with large doses of 'Godfrey's Cordial' and other dangerous preparations of opium and treacle.

It was a fortunate boy who could, after a rudimentary education, get himself apprenticed to a decent and well-organised trade such as the building trade, the largest group of workers in London, numbering over 60,000 in 1851. Most boys found themselves in work far less desirable than this. To be sure there were apprenticeships to be had in other skilled trades, in the breweries, for example, with firms such as Whitbread's of Finsbury or Barclay and Perkins of Southwark, in marine engineering, with firms like Green's of Blackwall or Fairbairn's of Millwall which built the huge iron steamer, the ill-fated *Great Eastern,* between 1853 and 1858. There were also increasing numbers of vacancies in the newly developing industries. The great gas works in Horseferry Lane and Brick Lane, the expanding workshops of the London Gas-light and Coke Company which had already laid well over a hundred miles of gas-mains in the early 1820s, the sprawling sheds and lines and depots of the railways, all took in growing numbers of apprentices. Yet throughout the Victorian age the majority of London children were forced into work which was neither skilled nor profitable, and entailed far longer hours than the sixty-four a week in summer and fifty-two in winter which were standard in the well organised building trade. Few of those who entered domestic service – and there were 121,000 general domestic servants alone in London in 1851 – could expect to work for less than eighty hours a week for about ½d. an hour and their keep.

Poor as this remuneration was, there were plenty of casual workers in London who had to be content with less. Multitudes of the ragged vagrants and casuals who pass through the pages of Henry Mayhew's monumental study, *London Labour and the London Poor,* existed close to the verge of starvation.

The most numerous group in Mayhew's gallery were the costermongers. He estimated in the middle of the century that the numbers of these men, dealing in fish, fruit and vegetables alone, were no less than 30,000 and were growing year by year. There were as many as four hundred public houses that relied mainly on their custom for their trade. These costermongers daily attended one or other of the markets to buy their goods which they then sold either from a stall or from a barrow, a cart, or a tray slung round their necks. They were a rough, quarrelsome, illiterate and vital set of men, much given to fighting, drinking and gambling, to tattooing their arms and throwing bricks at policemen. Anxious to keep the secrets of their trade from the police and potential rivals they spoke to each other in an esoteric language, incomprehensible to the uninitiated, which involved the use of a considerable cryptic vocabulary and an ability to pronounce words backwards. Few of them could read or write, few troubled to marry the women they lived with, most – although not above cheating their customers – were honest amongst themselves and kind to their children and donkeys, nearly all were Chartists, hardly any had ever been inside a church.

They were fond of dancing at 'twopenny-hops', jigging and jumping and leaping at clog-hornpipes and polkas, flash-jigs and pipe-dances. They were regular visitors to the theatres and penny concerts, to dog fights, above all to the tap-room; and everywhere they went they gambled. They betted on skittles and fights, on shove-halfpenny and three-up, on pigeon races and on card games, all-fives, cribbage and put. They sat for hours, full of beer and shrouded in tobacco, thumbing their torn and filthy cards from which the symbols had almost been effaced, muttering to each other in that curious language of theirs, breaking off now and again to watch a boxing match – all self-respecting landlords provided gloves – to have another drink, or to listen to one of their more literate companions recounting the latest episode in Reynolds's 'Mysteries of the Court'.

Their children began work with them at a very early age, usually before they were seven, watching the cart and the donkey, mastering the tricks of the trade and the markets – how to swell oranges, boil prunes and bake filberts – learning to shout their wares: 'Ni-ew mackerel, six a shilling! . . . All large and alive-O, new sprats, O, 1d. a plate! . . . Penny a bunch turnips!'

When they were about fourteen the boys started in business on their own and with a woman of their own, settling the arrangement by giving the girl a silk neckerchief which was usually taken back after a time either as a gambling pledge or as a scarf for themselves. All costermongers were inordinately proud of their silk neckerchieves – King's Men they called them – and, indeed, of all their clothes. The men wore long cord waistcoats with huge and numerous pockets and shining brass buttons, seamed trousers fitting tightly at the knee and billowing out over highly polished boots, and a worsted skull-cap or a cloth cap pulled very much down on one side of a head covered with ringlets at the front and with long hair, 'Newgate-Knocker style', hanging down over the ears.

Costermongers were but one kind of the innumerable hawkers who made a living, or at least some sort of subsistence, in the London streets. There were sellers of cooked food and sellers of drink, piemen and muffinmen, spice and rhubarb girls and hot eel boys, mice exhibitors and snake swallowers, penny-gaff clowns and stilt-vaulters, crossing-sweepers and scavengers, street mechanics and flagstone artists, reciters and penny profile cutters, rag and bottle men, dog finders, packmen and cheap johns, running patterers and chaunters, old men with trays of cough drops and hot elder wine, old women with pickled whelks and cress, boys with oranges and nuts, girls with boiled puddings, Irish cats'-meat dealers, Italian organ boys, Jewish clothes-men, French singing women, Dutch buy-a-broom girls, Highland bagpipe players, Ethiopian serenaders and Sicilian salamanders.

Thousands lived by what they could pick up on the streets, along the water-front and in the sewers. In the early morning they could be seen moving about with bags on their shoulders looking for bits of wood and coal, cigar ends, rags, bones, and dogs' dung which was known as 'pure' because the Bermondsey tanners used it for purifying leather.

The bone-pickers and rag-gatherers went out armed with a spiked stick which they prodded into piles of dust and rubbish in back streets, picking up anything they could sell and placing it in their greasy bags, making their breakfast on any bits of bread they came across or on the meat they found sticking to the bones. They covered about twenty-five miles each day in the course of their searches, taking eight or nine hours to do so, and selling what they had collected, to some such dealer as the unsavoury Krook in *Bleak House,* for an average of sixpence a day. In the evening they went to sleep in a lodging-house or, perhaps, on a pile of sacks in a deserted tenement between St Katherine's Docks and Rosemary Lane.

Cat's meat seller in Greenwich, 1885.

Sewer scavenger: engraving from Mayhew's *London Labour and the London Poor*.

The 'pure'-finders were rather better paid, as a bucketful could be sold for as much as 1s. 2d., and many of the more active collectors could be sure of taking home between 5s. and 6s. a week. This, though, was a poor wage when compared with the sums earned by those who scavenged in the sewers. For these men, London's 'toshers', taking one week with another, thought themselves unfortunate if they did not make £2 a week. 'Toshers', in fact, were almost an elite among scavengers. They entered the sewers on the river's fore-shore, and came out on occasions laden with copper and silver coins, bits of iron, ropes and bones, even plated spoons and ladles, silver-handled knives and pieces of jewellery. They were not begrudged their fortune, though, for the work was extremely dangerous. Most of the sewers were incalculably old and ramshackle and the brickwork constantly threatened to collapse. There was also the constant danger of drowning as the tide often rushed in without warning at the speed of a mountain torrent, and there was an ever-present possibility of being suffocated or poisoned by the foul vapours in the branch sewers where a man had to crouch to move along. Since no one knew the sewers' extent there were many tales of 'toshers' having lost their way and died of exhaustion and hunger in them. As they were full of un-expected and perilous quagmires there were many tales, too, of 'toshers' having been sucked down into the mud, struggling vainly to extricate themselves by means of the seven-foot-long pole they carried with them always; and as the sewers swarmed with rats there were even more terrible stories of the scavengers being overpowered by them and of their skeletons being discovered a few days later picked clean of skin and flesh.

It was certainly true that many 'toshers' were attacked by rats, and there were few of them who did not bear scars on their hands and even on their faces. Only the foolhardy worked in the sewers alone.

Despite the dangers of the 'toshers'' life and the supposedly poisonous qualities of the air in which they worked, they were a cheerful and healthy group, carrying on their work until they were seventy or eighty years old, well fed and well satisfied with their lot.

Far less fortunate were the 'mud-larks' who scavenged on the river-front at low tide. Most 'mud-larks' were very old or very young or badly crippled, as none but the weak would undertake such hard and filthy work for so poor a return. Even the bone-pickers earned twice as much as they did: a 'mud-lark' considered himself lucky if he could sell all that he found in a day for a halfpenny.

They went down into the mud by the banks of the Thames carrying old hats or rusty kettles, poking about for pieces of coal or copper nails, their clothes a collection of old rags stiff as boards, their feet bare and in danger of being cut on fragments of buried glass. It was the greatest pleasure they knew in the winter to stand in the hot water that ran down from the steam factories and warm their frozen feet. Some of them were only six years old. Henry Mayhew talked to one who was nine. His father was dead; his mother went out washing for a shilling a day when she could find such work to do, which was not often. It was very cold standing in the mud. He had once had a pair of shoes, but that was a long time since. He had been mud-larking for three years, ever since he could remember and supposed he would always be a mud-lark for that was all he knew how to do. He had been to a school once but had forgotten it. He had been there for a month. He could not read or write and did not think he could learn now even if he tried ever so much. He had heard of Jesus Christ but could not recall just what he was. His mother did not take him to church because they had no clothes. His mother came from Aberdeen. He did not know where Aberdeen was. He knew that this was London. England was in London somewhere, but he did not know just where. All the money he got he gave to his mother. She bought bread with it. When he couldn't get any money they lived as best they could.

The little water-cress girls lived a life scarcely less terrible than the boy 'mud-larks'. At seven or eight years old they would get up before dawn to go down to Farringdon Market to haggle with the saleswomen. In the cold weather they shivered in their cotton dresses and threadbare shawls as they tied up the bunches, and their fingers ached as they washed the leaves at the pump. They walked the streets crying, 'Water-Creases, four bunches a penny, Water-Creases!' and on an average day they would make 3d or 4d. One of them, aged eight, said, 'I used to go to school, but I wasn't there long. I've forgot all about it now, it's such a long time ago; and mother took me away because the master whacked me. He hit me across the face with his cane . . . The creases is so bad now. They're so cold, people won't buy 'em; for when I goes up to them they say, "They'll freeze our bellies" . . . We never goes home to breakfast till we've sold out; but if it's very late, then I buys a penn'orth of pudden, which is very nice with gravy. I don't know hardly any of the people, as goes to Farringdon, to talk to; they never speaks to me, so I don't speak to them. We children never play down there, 'cos we're thinking of our living. No; people never pities me in the street – excepting one gentleman, and he says, says he, "What do you do out so soon in the morning?" but he gave me nothink – he only walked away . . . No, I never see any children crying, it's no use . . .

'I always give mother my money, she's so very good to me. She don't often beat me. She's very poor and goes out cleaning rooms sometimes. I ain't got no father, he's a father-in-law. No; mother ain't married again – he's a father-in-law. He grinds scissors, and he's very good to me. No; I don't mean by that that he says kind things to me. He never hardly speaks. When I get home, after selling creases, I puts the room to rights. I clean the chairs, though there's only two to clean, and scrubs the floor . . .

'I don't have no dinner. Mother gives me two slices of bread-and-butter and a cup of tea for breakfast, and then I go to tea, and has the same. We has meat of a Sunday, and, of course, I should like to have it every day. Mother has just the same to eat as we has, but she takes more tea – three cups, sometimes . . .

'Sometimes we has a game of "honeypots" with the girls in the court, but not often . . . I knows a good many games but I don't play at 'em, 'cos going out with creases tires me. On a Friday night, too, I goes to a Jew's house till eleven o'clock on a Saturday night. All I has to do is snuff the candles and poke the fire. You see they keep their Sabbath then, and they won't touch anything; so they gives me my wittals and 1½d., and I does it for 'em . . . All the money I earns I puts in a club and draws it out to buy clothes with. It's better than spending it in sweet-stuff, for them as has a living to earn. Besides it's like a child to care for sugar-sticks, and not like one who's got a living and wittals to earn. I'm past eight, I am. I don't know anything about what I earn during the year, I only know how many pennies goes to a shilling, and two ha'pence goes to a penny, and four fardens goes to a penny. I knows, too, how many fardens goes to tuppence – eight. That's as much as I wants to know for the markets.'

Compared with some London children this one was content. At least

Boy selling fusees (Bryant and May's Alpine Vesuvians) in Greenwich, 1884.

she had a home and had found work to do. Hundreds of others had neither home nor work. One such was a boy of thirteen whose clothes were so scant and torn that most of his chest was bare and what he had wrapped round his legs for trousers covered only one of his legs. On one foot he wore an old shoe tied round his instep with a piece of ribbon, on the other a woman's old boot. His face was swollen with the cold. His father died when he was three days old; his mother had gone out begging and was dead too. He had sixpence in his pocket when she died, but he couldn't help crying to think he'd lost his mother, and he cried about it still. He'd gone out begging on his own: 'I begged, but sometimes wouldn't get a farthing in a day; often walking about the streets all night. I am very weak – starving to death. I never stole anything. A boy wanted me to go with him to pick a gentleman's pocket, but I wouldn't. The boy asked me to do it to get into prison. He was starving about the streets like me. I never slept in a bed since I've been in London. I generally slept under the dry arches in West Street, where they're building houses – I mean the arches for the cellars. I begged chiefly from the Jews about Petticoat Lane for they all give away bread that their children leave – pieces of crust and such-like.'

Children who could rely on help or encouragement from adults usually found some sort of work to pay for more than crusts of bread – even if it were only selling nuts and oranges at the doors of theatres at night, sweeping crossings, hanging round cab-stands in the hope of payment for holding a horse or opening a door, hawking fuzees – 'Buy a fuzee to light your cigar, your honour, sir. A row of lights for a ½d.' But the competition in such pursuits was intense; and for those in which a better living might be had either some skill or capital was necessary.

There was a ready market for goldfish in the streets, but the fish had first to be bought from a dealer in Kingsland Road or Billingsgate; birds' nests, snakes and frogs also sold well, but experience was required to find them. One young man sold twenty nests a week at 2d. or 3d. apiece, snakes for five shillings a pound – either for their skins or to a gentleman in Theobald's Road who dissected them. He sold good frogs, too, for a shilling a dozen to the French hotel in Leicester Square, and in the streets as well – 'many people swallows young frogs, they're reckoned very good things to clean the inside' – but it was hard and skilled work collecting his wares and he had few rivals.

There was good money, too, in dredging the river for corpses since the rewards were often high; but you had to have a boat and tackle. You could decide to be an itinerant tin-smith, but you had to have pots and pans; you could think of becoming a hurdy-gurdy woman, but you had to have the instrument to churn out its fearful noise. You could make a reasonable living tumbling in Waterloo Place after the Opera, or in the Haymarket where the

38. Cremorne Gardens in 1864, by Phoebus Levin.

39. The Zoo, Regent's Park, in 1835: colour lithograph after George Scharf.

Coalseller, Greenwich, 1885.

street girls were – they did not part with money themselves, but they told their gentlemen to – but you had to be able to do it well and not everyone could learn. You might decide to become a rat-catcher, for the demand for rats by 'sporting gentlemen' who attended such establishments as the King's Head, Compton Street, Soho, to watch them being killed by dogs, was enormous. But long experience was required to catch a rat without getting yourself bitten to the bone. Many men made a good income out of dealing in coal, for there were thousands who could not afford to buy more than a few lumps at a time, and a ton or so bought from a merchant and stored in a back room would soon bring in a handsome profit. But then, you had to have the money for the merchant.

Although the poorer families used little coal, over three and a half million tons of it were burned in London in a year; and this provided regular work both for the chimney-sweeps, who could in winter make as much as £1 a week, and for the dustmen, who were paid 8d. a load by the dust-contractors and could usually manage to cart away to the dust-yards at least two, and perhaps three, loads a day.

The dustmen walked down the street in their hooded caps with the leather flaps hanging down behind their necks, leading a horse and box-cart, crying 'Dust oy-eh! Dust oy-eh!', stopping outside the houses where there was dust

to collect, filling their buckets from the dust-bins, emptying the loads into the cart, then trundling the refuse away to the dust-yard where, amidst pigs rooting about for bits of offal and hens picking at cabbage leaves, men, women and children would be hard at work on the mountainous heaps of rubbish with iron sieves to separate the 'brieze' from the 'soil' – the 'brieze' or coarse cindery dust being despatched to the brickfields, the finer 'soil' being sold as manure. Broken bricks, old boots, kettles, rags, bones and oyster shells all found their appropriate market to the great profit of the dust-contractors.

The labourers on the heaps stood up to their waists in dust, the women in black bonnets, their dirty cotton dresses tucked up behind them, banging their sieves against their leather aprons. At the larger dust-yards – one of the biggest stood on the banks of the Regent's Canal in the middle of the century – there were usually well over a hundred people at work.

Although little or no skill was required to work for a dust-contractor, a dustman frequently earned more in a week than many a skilled worker could. A chairmaker, for example, would work from six o'clock in the morning until nine or ten at night, stopping for a ten-minute breakfast at eight o'clock, twenty minutes for dinner and eight minutes for tea, eating in the room where he worked. He worked the same hours every Saturday and for forty Sundays in the year. Including the time spent carting his finished articles to the purchaser, a chairmaker might well work a hundred hours a week year in, year out.

The thousands of men who worked in the London Dock were no more fortunate. The Dock area now covered an area of over ninety acres in the parishes of St George, Shadwell and Wapping. In this turmoil, and surrounded by a ferment of smells, three thousand casual labourers of all sorts and nationalities had a daily struggle to find work. When the gates opened in the morning they streamed in towards the calling foremen, shouting, jumping, scuffling, waving their arms, in a frantic attempt to gain their notice and a hard days' work for half-a-crown pay. There was never enough work for all of them; some came every day for weeks on end never to be called, relying upon those who were called for enough food to keep them alive until their turn came. The work that most of them did was to supply motive power for the huge wheels which operated the cranes, six to eight of them inside each wheel walking up the battens like convicts on a treadmill. Others unloaded the cargoes, or carried bales of goods across the quays.

Lumpers (men who unloaded timber), ballast-heavers (those who shovelled ballast into the holds of ships), and coal-backers (those who carried coal on their backs from the ships to the wagons), were usually in the employment of contractors. The contractor undertook to do the work for a fixed sum and arranged to pay his men in a public-house of which he was often enough the

'Iron Billy', a famous horse bus driver, and his conductor, 1873.

proprietor. Wages were commonly not paid until the men had got through two or three pints of beer, and many a time they were incapably drunk by the time what money they had not spent was handed over to them. Coal-backing was dangerously hard work and few men were still capable of undertaking it after twenty years. A boy who started at fifteen, would be old at thirty-five; many were forced to give the work up earlier than that through bursting blood vessels or ruptures. There was never a shortage of men willing to do this work, though. The pay was relatively good and enabled a man to drink heavily, as most coal-backers did, one at least of them drinking sixteen glasses of beer with a measure of gin in each of them regularly before breakfast each morning.

It was one of the most common complaints of the omnibus drivers and conductors that they never had time to go to a public house, or indeed to any other place of entertainment, or if they did have time they were too tired to enjoy it. 'A 'bus driver never has time to look out for a wife,' complained one of them. 'Every horse in our stables has one day's rest in every four; but it's no rest for the driver. It's hard work is mine; for I never have any rest but a few minutes, except every other Sunday, and then only two hours.' 'I never get to a public place,' a conductor confirmed. 'I've asked for a day's holiday and been refused . . . I'm quite ignorant of what's going on in the world, my time's so taken up. We only know what's going on from hearing people talk in the 'bus. I never care to read the paper now, though I used to like it. If I have two minutes to spare, I'd rather take a nap than anything else. I've fallen asleep on my step as the bus was going on, and almost fallen off.'

During the second half of the nineteenth century, the lodgings in which most of such overworked and underpaid workers lived were appalling. An omnibus driver or conductor, earning a more regular wage than most, might live in relative comfort in Battersea or Clapham in a couple of rooms with clean floors and windows, picture post-cards and prints of Jack Sheppard and Dick Turpin stuck on the walls, a few pieces of crockery, a tin tray and a piece of looking-glass on the mantelpiece, a cloth on the table and a sheet on the bed. But most of the London poor lived in conditions far worse than this, many of them crowded into rooms with ceilings the colour of old leather, with broken windows stuffed with paper and furniture broken beyond repair, rotting floorboards covered perhaps with three or four old mats tied together to form a carpet, sleeping five in a bed or on a flock mattress (crawling with bugs) on the floor. Thousands, tens of thousands, perhaps, slept in cheap lodging-houses down by the docks, around Drury Lane, St Giles's, Ratcliffe Highway, Rosemary Lane and Thrald Street, Whitechapel. The charge was twopence a night for a bundle of rags on a bunk and the use of a kitchen where there was a fire on which residents could cook their meals. Most nights in winter the kitchens of the lodging-houses were crowded with a ragged assortment of labourers, pickpockets, Billingsgate porters, beggars and sailors, drunkards and vagrants, in a weird array of clothes and rags, shiny with age and grease, some barefooted, some in women's boots with the toes cut off so that they could force their feet into them. They sat at tables round the walls drying the ends of cigars they had picked up in the streets, or crowded round the fire toasting herrings or bits of meat which one of their number had stolen from a butcher's stall. For a penny reduction in the fee a man could sleep on the floor of the kitchen and many did so, women as well as men, girls and boys, most of them having taken the precaution of getting drunk if they could afford it for there was no sleep otherwise to be had.

Those who could not face a lodging-house could usually find room to sleep with a family who needed the extra penny to pay the rent. There were hundreds of such sub-tenants in the courts off Rosemary Lane and Drury Lane where ten people would sleep in a single small room, where neighbours who lived opposite each other could carry on a conversation from their windows almost within touching distance, where women sat knitting on the pavement, men squatted in the road playing cards and marking their scores on the stones with chalk. Their sons leant against the walls smoking pipes, and their daughters having washed their petticoats, hung them out to dry on the poles which stretched across the narrow streets like tie-bars.

In areas such as these a man earning a regular fifteen shillings a week was comparatively well off, able to spend about sixpence on tobacco, a shilling on gin, and half-a-crown on beer in addition to the two shillings a week he might have to pay in rent and the eight shillings or so on food. His main foods were bread, potatoes, soup, herrings, pickles and onions, sausages and plum pudding. He would hope to have meat on Sundays, boiled beef perhaps or bacon with liver, or even a piece of roast lamb; and when times were good he might treat himself to a breakfast of coffee and bread and butter with pickled whelks at a street coffee-stall, to pea-soup with hot eels, sheeps' trotters, boiled meat pudding and fruit pie for a midday meal, and in the evening to meat pie with hot cabbage, baked potatoes and plenty of pepper, in a tap-room. Purl, a concoction of hot beer laced with gin, spiced with ginger and sweetened with sugar, was considered an excellent accompaniment to any meal in winter.

Those who did not eat at home were well provided for with cook-shops,

A slum street, 1911.

eating-rooms and street-stands. There were numerous coffee-stalls to be found everywhere in the mornings, protected from the wind by sheets thrown over clothes horses. There were also about five hundred stands where on a cold morning a labourer could buy hot pea soup and hot eels, and almost as many stalls which specialised in pickled whelks and onions. The baked-potato man, the ham-sandwich-seller, the man with ginger-beer fountains, chestnut stoves or trays of sugar-sticks, were regularly stationed at most street corners and outside every theatre.

Food for taking home was still sold in the open street markets; and on a Saturday night streets where these were held – Leather Lane and Whitecross Street, Tottenham Court Road, the Brill and the New Cut, Lambeth – were as crowded as a fair. On the stalls the goods for sale were lit up by oil lamps or candles stuck inside turnips or sieves. It was not only food that was sold in these Saturday night street markets. Clothes were sold here and floor mats, old shoes and tea trays, crockery and shirts, saucepans and handker-chiefs; and the shouts of the dealers selling them were deafening – 'Who'll buy a bonnet for fourpence?' 'Pick 'em out cheap here!' 'Three pair for a halfpenny! Bootlaces!' 'Come and look at 'em!' 'Penny a lot! Old shoes!' 'Eight a penny, stunning pears!' 'Chestnuts, all 'ot, a penny a score!' 'Ho! Ho! Hi-i-i! What d'you think of this 'ere? A penny a bunch! Hurrah for free trade. Here's your turnips!' 'Mussels a penny a quart!' 'Ni-ew macherel, six a shilling!' 'Buy a pair of live soles! 3 pair for sixpence!' 'Cod alive, 2d. a pound!' 'All new nuts! A penny a half pint!' 'Hot spiced gingerbread. Buy my gingerbread! Smo-o-oking hot. If *one*'ll warm you, *wha-at'll* a *pound* do? – *Wha-a-a-t'll* a *pound* do?' Around the market stalls were shops lit by rows of glittering gas lights, the boy assistants standing in the doorways by the counter which let down onto the kerb, describing in loud, hoarse voices the glories of the bargains to be found within.

The noisiest market was Billingsgate. Here salesmen and hucksters tried to shout each other down as they stood in their white aprons on top of their tables and competed for their customers' attention, crying, 'Ye-o-o! Ye-o-o! Turbot! Turbot! All alive turbot! . . . Here you are, governor, had-had-had-had-haddick! All fresh and good . . . Oy! Oy! Oy! Now's your time! Fine grizzling sprats! All large and no small! . . . Hullo! Hullo! Hullo! Here! Fine cock crabs, all alive O! . . . Now or never, five brill and one turbot – have that lot for a pound!' Between four and seven o'clock on a Friday morning the approaches to Billingsgate were crammed with fish-mongers' carts and costermongers' barrows, and in the square wooden building where the sales were held their owners in ragged, greasy, fish-smelling trousers and canvas jackets argued, shouted, cursed and laughed amidst the piles of shining wet fish, brown baskets and herring scales.

Porters pushed their way through the crowd with huge black oyster bags on their shoulders; sailors wandered about in striped guernseys and red worsted caps; women with cods' tails dangling from their aprons elbowed their way past each other; boys eagerly offered their services in the carrying of loads of fish out into the streets; girls begged the auctioneers' customers to buy their baskets; and the customers themselves walked from table to table, asking, 'What's the price, master?', picking up a sole from a shiny pile to smell it and then letting it slither back onto the table, kicking a crawling lobster back into its heap, peering into herring barrels and sackfuls of whelks, turning over the smelts on their marble slabs.

Less noisy and rather more sweet smelling was Covent Garden, its roadways littered with squashed oranges, broken walnut shells, haybands, and slimy cabbage leaves. It was crowded with costers in their corduroy waistcoats, greengrocers in blue aprons, countrymen in smocks, porters who struggled about with teeth clenched and neck muscles taut in their efforts to support and balance the high piles of baskets on their heads, Irish apple-women, sitting on the rings of rope which the porters used between their heads and the bottom baskets, smoking pipes and greeting every passer-by with a 'Fine eating apples! Have a basket, your honour?' Beside the railings of St Paul's Church were piles of baskets for sale, larks and linnets in cages offered at two pence a head, and bunches of coloured grass; while at the pump, boys who had spent the night sleeping in the hampers washed themselves, and here, later on, the flower-girls would water their bunches of violets.

Apart from the fruit, flower and vegetable market at Covent Garden, the cress market at Farringdon, the fish market at Billingsgate and the meat market at Smithfield, there were several other London markets which specialised in particular merchandise. Houndsditch Market, run by Jews, was the place to go for cheap oranges, lemons and nuts. Petticoat Lane and Rosemary Lane, Holywell Street and Monmouth Street, were the centres of the old-clothes trade. As well as at Smithfield meat could be bought in the markets at Newgate, Leadenhall and Whitechapel. For that jumble of nautical items and miscellaneous junk to be found in marine-stores, the intending purchaser could confidently be directed to Ratcliffe Highway, and the purlieus of Covent Garden and the King's Bench Prison.[1]

The wares on sale in these marine-stores were displayed inside the shops as well as on tables and trays in the street. They comprised an astonishing collection of buttons, keys, compasses, canvas boots, tins, bottles, boxes, trays, razors, knives, steel-pens, sealing-wax, satin waistcoats, prints, umbrellas, china ornaments, spurs and candlesticks, most of them second-hand and all of them dusty. A rather less variegated and far dirtier collection of goods could be found in the rag-and-bottle shops to which the scavengers who picked up these articles in the streets sold them. The smell in all such shops was nauseating, their floors thick with grease and dust, their filthy

41. Holborn in 1861, by Arthur Boyd Houghton (detail).
42. (overleaf) London street scene with posters, by John Parry, 1835.

windows obscured by piles of the oddments which the scavengers had brought them. Their fronts were usually painted a vivid colour so that the old, illiterate and often feeble-minded scavengers would have no difficulty in locating them; and their proprietors were sometimes almost as well off as the dust-contractors whose fortunes were also made from the refuse of the crowded city.

There was either a rag-and-bottle shop or a marine-store in nearly every street in the poorest parts of London. There was also a chandler's shop where, in a dark cramped room, the poor people of the neighbourhood would buy their meagre supplies of cheese, bread, tea, coal and cow-heels. Most small shops of this nature were entirely run and staffed by the owners and their families; but a few of the larger ones kept a shop-boy or two who lived on the premises, rose at six o'clock or earlier and arranged the stock before breakfast.

The working day of the shop-boy was longer than all but the most hard-worked of labourers. Gaslight had lengthened shop hours so that the doors of most shops stayed open until ten o'clock at night – until midnight on Saturdays – and even after that the shop-boy could not go immediately to bed for there was all the clearing up to do. In the last decade of the century many shop assistants could still complain with truth that they never had an opportunity of putting on their hat and coat except on Sundays; and then they were frequently too tired to enjoy themselves.

For those who had the time and energy, however, Victorian London provided a marvellous range of pleasures and pastimes for the poor. The streets themselves were always full of diversions for all those with but a few pennies to spend (plates 41 and 42). There were innumerable sellers of food and drink, men who dispersed steaming hot baked potatoes from brightly painted potato-cans, ginger-beer ($\frac{1}{2}$d. a glass) from mahogany fountains with glittering brass handles, treacle rock, almond toffee, halfpenny lollipops and peppermint sticks, ice-cream (which first became popular in the 1850s), hot meat pies (which had never been other than popular), and glasses of milk. There were cow-cellars and cow-houses in nearly all the inner suburbs – there were still seven hundred licensed cow-houses in the 1880s before 'railway milk' from country farms at last pushed them out of business – and the milk sellers bought skimmed milk at $1\frac{1}{2}$d. a quart from the London dairymen, watered it down, and then sold it, usually sweetened with sugar at a halfpenny a pint. More nourishing than this sweet and water milk was rice-milk, the sticky result of boiling rice in the 'skin' and then strongly sweetening it with syrup.

The sellers of rice-milk, and more often the sellers of pies, had to be prepared to toss their customers for the price of their wares. If the pieman won the toss his losing customer had to give him a penny without receiving a pie in exchange; if the pieman lost he had to hand over the pie without charge. 'If it wasn't for tossing we shouldn't sell any,' one pieman said. 'Very few people buy without tossing, and the boys in particular. Gentlemen out on the spree at the late public houses will toss when they don't want the pies, and when they win they will amuse themselves by throwing the pies at one another, or at me.'

In addition to the street-sellers of food and drink, there were sellers of pamphlets, books, and sealed packets of 'secret papers', supposedly pornographic. The books and pamphlets were invariably scandalous, sensational, horrifying or erotic, containing descriptions of duels between ladies of fashion, accounts of savage murders, the biographies of criminals and hangmen, the reports of jealous quarrels at Windsor or Buckingham Palace, or 'The Diabolical Practices of a Doctor on his Patients when in a State of Mesmerism'. Then there were the numerous street entertainers, the conjurors in Jermyn Street, the fire-eaters in Gray's Inn Lane, the Punch and Judy men in Leicester Square, Oxford Street and Tottenham Court Road, the Fantoccini men who manipulated dancing dolls and comic skeletons, and the exhibitors of mechanical figures, telescopes (a penny a peep), and peepshows, which an enterprising boy might be allowed to see for a bottle if he had no money,

Baked potato seller.

though bottles could not be sold for more than threepence a dozen. Even if he had neither bottles nor money, a boy could usually manage to watch the performance of an acrobat or strong man, juggler or knife swallower, clown or tightrope dancer, dancing dog or gymnastic monkey, and then run away before the collection began.

One of the most popular of all pastimes among the poor was the rat-match at which bets were placed on dogs fancied to kill a greater number of rats in a given time than any of their rivals. There were about forty taverns in London where these rat-killings took place in a special pit in which as many as five hundred rats were slaughtered in a night.

The champion rat-killer was one 'Billy' whose great feat it was to have killed five hundred rats in five and a half minutes. Most terriers, however, could not manage to destroy the rats at anything like that pace, and fifteen a minute was considered highly skilful.

The pit was a small arena with a white-painted floor, about six feet in diameter, surrounded by a wooden wall. The rats were tossed into it from a rusty iron cage by a man whose experience allowed him to thrust his arm into the struggling mass and grab hold of the 'varmints' by their tails. When a sufficient number of rats were in the ring, the order would come to chuck in a dog, and the dog, straining at his leash and frothing at the mouth in his anxiety to get at the throats of the foul-smelling rats in the pit, would be released to fly at them. A stop-watch recorded the minutes allowed for each match and when the time was up the dead and bleeding rats would be picked up and flung into a pile in the corner, and the next contest would begin.

A pleasure less gruesome than the rat-match was the theatre. Many men whose income was less than £2 a week spent three or even four evenings a week at the theatre, taking their wives with them, and cheering or condemning the performance with lusty partiality. Their favourite theatres were those on the south bank of the river, the Surrey, the Victoria or the Bower Saloon, also the Garrick, the Pavilion and the City of London. Their favourite performances were those with plenty of violence in them, with rowdy songs and strongly melodramatic plots.

In the gallery of the Coburg, which held two thousand people, the noise before the show began was tremendous. Young men in their shirt sleeves jumped on each others' shoulders to get a better view, or threw orange peel and nutshells at the heads of the women in front. Others, arriving late, clambered on top of the bodies clustered round the door and rolled down towards the iron railing in front where they forced a space for themselves on the crowded bench. Insults were tossed freely about, fierce arguments erupted and fights were common. Yet at the rising of the curtain the hubbub subsided with shouts for silence and order.

Throughout the performance the spectators munched at the pig-trotters and ham sandwiches which were sold in the intervals, cracked nuts, sucked oranges, drank porter, greeted complaints that the people behind could not see with threats to throw them over the railings, wiped the sweat from their faces with crumpled-up playbills, shouted at the actors to speak up, encouraged them with cries of 'Bravo, Vincent. Go to it, my tulip!', and insisted, each time a favourite tune was played, on singing their words to it or clapping out its rhythm.

For those who could not afford a visit to a theatre, there were the 'penny gaffs', the upper floors of shops which had been turned into places of entertainment where disreputable performers danced and sang to the accompaniment of a noisy band. The audiences at these performances were mostly women and young girls and boys; the boys lighting their pipes at the gas jets which sputtered on each side of the makeshift proscenium or tickling the girls in the seats in front of them; the girls, some of them only eight years of age, laughing and shouting, clapping their hands, waving the shabby feathers in their bonnets backwards and forwards in time to the music. The performance consisted of obscene songs and suggestive dances; and when it was over groups of prostitutes, bare-headed and in Adelaide boots, crowded round the canvas curtain at the entrance in the hope of finding a customer.

'The celebrated dog Billy killing 100 Rats at the Westminster Pit', 1822.

There were an estimated 80,000 professional prostitutes in London in the 1860s, as well as uncounted thousands of amateurs known as 'dolly mops', and of women, kept by those who could afford the luxury, in apartments in such respectable enclaves as St John's Wood, Brompton and Regent's Park. Most of them were young; many were under thirteen.

There were also nearly three thousand brothels, the most squalid of them in Lambeth, Whitechapel, Shadwell, Spitalfields, Wapping, Ratcliffe Highway and the Waterloo Road. The worst of all were down by the Docks where, in certain courts off Bluegate Fields, every room in every house was given over to prostitution, where the smell of opium lay sweet and heavy in the air and the only items of furniture to be found in many of the hovels were damp palliasses and broken bedsteads.

At the other end of the scale were the expensive and well-appointed brothels in King's Place, St James's, Oxenden Street, Curzon Street and James Street, Haymarket. The girls in some of these establishments were completely at the mercy of the bawds who rarely allowed them out of the house and then they were closely followed by a 'watcher'. They had few clothes of their own and were given little money.

The prostitutes who worked in the parks, however, although the cheapest to be found outside the East End – apart from those 'faded and miserable wretches' who offered themselves for a few coppers in dark and dirty courts off Leicester Square and Cranbourne Passage – considered themselves unfortunate if they did not earn two or three pounds a week, and many earned five or six. The French girls, most of whom lived in lodgings in Queen Street off Regent Street and charged their customers a guinea each, made on average twice as much as this. Even these were paltry sums when compared with the income of the girls who wandered about outside the clubs in Pall Mall or frequented the more fashionable night-houses in the Haymarket area, a district where 'in certain streets at night', Dostoievsky said, 'the prostitutes gather in their thousands', a district, so a writer in *Household Words* confirmed, 'absolutely hideous at night with its sparring snobs, and flashing satins, and sporting gents, and painted cheeks, and bawdy-sparkling eyes, and bad tobacco and hoarse horse laughs, and loud indecency'.

Among the smartest of these night-houses in the area were Mott's, Rose Burton's, Jack Percival's and Kate Hamilton's. Kate Hamilton, an immensely fat and ugly woman who sat throughout the evening in a low-cut dress sipping champagne and wobbling like a jelly whenever she laughed, refused to admit any girls who were not attractive and well-dressed, likely to appeal to the rich gentlemen who patronised her establishment. These were the girls who could be found in the daytime in the Burlington Arcade ready at a given signal to dart into a nearby shop whose upper floors had rooms furnished to their taste and for their purpose.

As popular as Kate Hamilton's with expensive prostitutes were the Argyll Rooms, on the site of the future Trocadero Restuarant in Shaftesbury Avenue. Several of these prostitutes lived in lodgings in Windmill Street nearby, where an upper floor apartment cost up to four pounds a week, but was considered worth so extravagant a rent because of its proximity to a meeting-place of so many rich men. Many others lived in comfortably furnished apartments in Soho, and in Pimlico and Chelsea. For men who preferred not to accompany girls to their own apartments, there were several houses of accommodation in Oxenden Street, Panton Street, James Street and in several of the streets off the Strand which was a favourite haunt of street-walkers as it had been in Boswell's time. There were also certain coffee-houses in the Covent Garden area which let rooms to prostitutes for an hour or so in the afternoons and evenings; and others, more disreputable, in the courts around Leicester Square where the blinds were drawn, gas lamps burned dimly inside, and notices over the door announced: 'Beds are to be had within'.

Many if not most of London's prostitutes had their bullies, or as they called them themselves 'fancy men', who, in addition to the money they took from the girls, made a living from petty crime as pickpockets, area-sneaks, dog stealers and burglars. Numerous as they were, they constituted but a very small part of the tens of thousand of those Londoners who lived wholly or partly by crime. Few of them had known any other sort of life. Neglected or orphaned when young, they had wandered about the city dirty, barefoot and in rags begging and stealing, returning at night either to a family which was in part supported by their crimes or to a cheap lodging-house whose inmates were nearly all past or potential convicts. The atmosphere and company in many cheap lodging-houses were, in fact, little different from those in prison.

The most infamous of these lodging-houses were in the criminal slum communities in Lambeth, Southwark, Spitalfields and Seven Dials. Acres of land in Spitalfields, between Union Street and Thrall Street, were given over entirely to the custom of criminals. In Seven Dials whole courts were inhabited by gangs of thieves or coiners and protected by ferocious guard dogs from the attentions of strangers or authority. Holes were cut through walls and ceilings, into cellars and out of roofs so that a criminal in danger of arrest by the police might soon escape from his pursuers in the labyrinthine maze of secret apertures, manholes, and tunnels, concealed passages and hidden exits.

The pressing problem of crime in London had been much relieved by Robert Peel's Metropolitan Police Act of 1829 which provided for a new force of

Slums of St Bartholomew and the Great Cloth Fair, *c.* 1875.

paid policemen under the direction of two justices, or as they were afterwards called, Commissioners. The Commissioners' Office was at 4 Whitehall Place which backed onto a courtyard known as Scotland Yard, being part of the site formerly occupied by the London palace of the kings of Scotland.[2]

Peel's Act had been a long time coming. A London and Westminster Police Bill, which had been introduced five years after the Gordon Riots had so convincingly demonstrated the need for one, had been so strongly opposed it had had to be abandoned. Nor, for all the success of the Thames River Police which was formed in 1800, had any comparable organisation been established until even the most die-hard obstructionist had been forced to modify his views by the soaring crime rate.

The River Police owed its inception to Patrick Colquhoun, a Scottish businessman with a variety of strongly-held views on social reform which had led him to become a magistrate. In a celebrated work, *A Treatise on the Police of the Metropolis,* Colquhoun had demonstrated how urgent was the problem with which London was confronted. Well over 100,000 people in the capital, he maintained, supported themselves by 'pursuits either criminal, illegal or immoral'; two million pounds were lost each year by theft, and professional thieves had become so numerous that it was 'much to be feared that no existing power will be able to keep them within bounds'.

Colquhoun's treatise had had little immediate effect. But its sound sense had persuaded the West India Merchants to ask him for his advice on the prevention of crime in the docks where the Merchants' losses, through gangs of professional river pirates, corrupt officials and dishonest workers, were enormous. So, on Colquhoun's recommendations, a river police had been established and, once its success was proved, it had been adopted by the Government.

The Government had needed more persuasion, however, before they would agree to apply the organisation of the River Police to the metropolis as a whole. The terror caused by the savage murders of two families in Ratcliffe Highway within a week in December 1811 – a terror equalled only by the Jack the Ripper murders of 1888 – and the widespread concern occasioned in 1820 by the Cato Street Conspirators, who planned to assassinate the entire cabinet and attack the Mansion House and the Bank, had led to renewed demands for a more efficient police, but had been followed by a lapse into complacency once the dangers were past. It was not until after some soldiers mutinied during the riots occasioned by the return of George IV's foolish and ill-used Queen to England that steps had at last been taken by the appointment of Peel to the Home Office.

Three months after the formation of Peel's new force, Wellington was able to write and congratulate him on 'the entire success of the Police in London'. At first the men, clothed in tail coats and top hats and armed

44. The rush hour by the Royal Exchange in 1898, by Fritz Werner.

Parade at Sydenham Police Station, *c.* 1864.

only with a short wooden baton, were resented, poorly paid, and frequently assaulted. Handbills against them were handed out in the streets in their thousands; but soon no one could deny that houses were less frequently robbed and the streets were quieter at night. And when a force of five hundred policemen showed their ability to disperse an angry and crowded illicit meeting of the National Political Union in Cold Bath Fields in 1833, without causing serious injury to anyone – although they were violently provoked, three of them being stabbed and one of them killed – the tide of resentment against them began to turn. Parishes outside the Metropolitan District asked to be taken into it; and large provincial towns, where the ancient parochial system still prevailed, had to ask for police officers trained in London to come to their help to deal with the criminals driven out of London by the Metropolitan Police whose efficiency increased every year.

Although the ever-rising crime rate in London was halted by the Metropolitan Police, the criminal code remained almost as savage as it had been in the eighteenth century. Executions, though less in number, were still carried out in public, despite the protests of such influential voices as that of Charles Dickens who, after witnessing the hanging of Mr and Mrs George Mannings on the top of Horsemonger Lane gaol in 1849, wrote to *The Times* to protest against the wickedness of the spectacle, the 'indescribably frightful' conduct of the people. As late as 1864, at the public execution of a man who had murdered a bank clerk in a railway carriage, *The Times* reported that 'robbery and violence, loud laughing, oaths, fighting, obscene conduct and still more filthy language reigned round the gallows, far and

45. St Paul's and the modern City: a detail from
    London 1967 by David Thomas.

near'. The spectators comprised the most 'incorrigible dregs' of London – 'sharpers, thieves, gamblers, betting men, the outsiders of the boxing ring . . . the rakings of cheap singing halls and billiard rooms'. It was not until 1868 that a private Member's bill, introduced by J. T. Hibbert, Member of Parliament for Oldham, provided for the future carrying out of executions within prison walls.

By then the condition of those incarcerated inside those walls had at last improved. The fearful squalor and cruelty described by John Howard in the eighteenth century, and condemned by Elizabeth Fry and Thomas Fowell Buxton at the beginning of the nineteenth, had largely disappeared. But the process of change in the London prisons had not been an easy one.

The huge penitentiary at Millbank, which since its construction in 1813–1816 had cast its gloomy shadow across the north bank of the Thames opposite Lambeth Butts, was well-designed – on lines suggested by Jeremy Bentham's Panopticon – and comparatively sanitary; but life inside was appallingly monotonous and lonely. Only during the second half of their sentences were the prisoners allowed to leave their separate cells to work in association with their fellow inmates.

If life at Millbank was lonely, though, life in Pentonville, a penitentiary completed in 1842 on a radiating plan copied from that of the famous Eastern Penitentiary at Philadelphia, was far more so. The prisoners were made to observe perfect order and perfect silence, to wear masks of brown cloth so that no one should recognise them. Breakfast consisted of ten ounces of bread and three-quarters of a pint of cocoa; dinner was half a pint of soup (or four ounces of meat), five ounces of bread and one pound of potatoes; supper was a pint of gruel and five ounces of bread. Work began at six o'clock in the morning and continued until seven at night, with breaks for silent meals, silent exercise, and the daily service in the chapel where each prisoner had his own pigeon-hole of a pew so that although his head was visible to the warders on duty, he was hidden from the view of his neighbours.

The 520 cells, with their shaded gas-burner, stool, table, hammock, mattress and blankets, were not uncomfortable; but the denial to the prisoners, who were deprived even of their names, of all human contact and communication, drove many of them mad and many others to suicide.

Punishments for attempting to communicate with each other – the water closets were later removed because the prisoners could make contact with each other by tapping the pipes – were frequent and severe. The refractory cells were completely dark and convicts could be confined in them for up to three weeks on end. But the most dreadful punishment was to be denied the privilege of work, though this was as repetitive and monotonous as in other London prisons, if not actually as degrading and exhausting as work on the treadmill, a common form of labour in many of them.

In Cold Bath Fields Prison both men and women worked on the treadmill, a frame of iron steps around a revolving cylinder, for six hours every day. Each treadmill was in its own separate compartment, not attached to any form of machinery, so that at the end of the day the prisoner had achieved nothing except the climbing of 8,640 feet.

In London's other overcrowded prisons life was no more to be preferred than life in Cold Bath Fields and Pentonville. In Newgate – which remained a prison until 1880; in Holloway Prison – a castellated medieval-Gothic institution, built to the north of Pentonville in 1849–51; in Wormwood Scrubs – built in 1874; and in Brixton Prison – which was greatly extended in 1898 – the work the prisoners did, when work was found for them to do, was sometimes painful, often useless and always grindingly repetitive.

The treadmill and other prisoners exercising in the Vagrants' Prison, Coldbath Fields.

The QUEEN

THE LADY'S NEWSPAPER

No. 3361.—Vol. CXXIX.   Saturday, May 27th, 1911.   PRICE SIXPENCE.

Registered at G.P.O. as a Newspaper.   Offices: WINDSOR HOUSE, BREAM'S BUILDINGS, LONDON, E.C.   Postage One Halfpenny.

14 *Edwardian Contrasts 1884–1914*

Early one morning in February 1884, Edward, Prince of Wales, wearing the clothes of a workman and accompanied by two companions and a police escort, set off in a four-wheeler to inspect what he described as the 'worst and poorest' slums in Holborn and Clerkenwell. He was horrified by the poverty and squalor and misery to which he was introduced, the background to so many thousands of Londoners' lives. Finding a shivering, half-starved woman, and her three ragged, torpid children, lying on a heap of rags in a room bereft of furniture, he took a handful of gold coins from his pocket and would have handed them over to her had not his friend, Lord Carrington, warned him that such display of wealth might lead to his being attacked by the woman's neighbours. Lord Carrington was relieved when he and the Prince arrived safely back in Pall Mall in time for luncheon at Marlborough House.

The life which the Prince enjoyed at Marlborough House – modernised for him before his marriage as a London home at a cost of £60,000 – was so remote from life in Clerkenwell that Disraeli's talk of the Privileged and the People forming two nations was still scarcely less than the truth. Marlborough House was at once the centre and the apex of fashionable society, a house big enough for all the members of that society to be entertained there at a single ball. Using it as his comfortable base, the Prince, with energetic gusto and voracious appetite, drove out with his friends to restaurants, clubs, theatres and parties, to Cremorne Gardens and Evans's Music Hall.

Throughout his life, he and the society whose fashions and habits he did so much to form, enjoyed themselves and indulged themselves with all the exuberance that their leisure and riches permitted, riding in the morning, paying calls in the afternoon, dancing and gambling in the evening. It was a carefree life, even though governed by unalterable rules and conventions. In Edwardian London's Season – which began after Easter and ended with the races at Ascot in late June – a well brought up young lady would rarely go out without her maid, or ride side-saddle down Rotten Row without a mounted groom; a gentleman on paying a call would never fail to take his

'The height of the London Season at the Savoy Restaurant', 1911.

hat, stick and gloves into the drawing-room.

With income-tax at sixpence in the pound, the rich had no difficulty in maintaining town houses on as lavish a scale as their grandfathers had done. Most of Piccadilly's mansions remained in private hands until the First World War. Devonshire House, Stratton House, Bath House, Gloucester House, Apsley House, the Rothschilds' five-storeyed mansion at 148, all still retained their former grandeur with troops of liveried servants inside their walls and coachmen in top boots awaiting their masters' summons in the stables behind.

Piccadilly itself, indeed, by the time of King Edward's death in 1910, had taken on that rich, grandiose, resplendent, rather vulgar and pompous appearance which delighted the royal gourmet's eye. Little of its earlier character remained: its new nature seemed epitomised by the plump fishes, crabs, lobsters and oysters that wound their aimless .way round the Art-Nouveau base of Alfred Gilbert's beautiful Eros in Piccadilly Circus as though disdaining to notice – over the way in Coventry Street – the shiny, opulent façade of Scott's restaurant behind whose brass-knobbed mahogany doors so many of their fellows were daily consumed.[1]

St James's Church in Piccadilly was a small and lonely monument to the seventeenth-century taste; and although a few eighteenth-century buildings – such as St James's Club at 106 and the Naval and Military at 94, once the town houses of Lords Coventry and Egremont – still displayed their former elegance, many others had been refaced with richer, grander fronts: the graceful lines of Burlington House had disappeared beneath the heavy Italianate overlays of its subsequent remodellers.

Opposite Burlington House, on the south side of Piccadilly, were new banks and shops, new restaurants with splendid fronts, the palatial offices of prosperous insurance companies. In 1906 appeared the Ritz Hotel, magnificent in Norwegian granite on an iron frame, its name picked out in electric lights beneath its Parisian roof; in 1908 the Ritz was followed by the vast Edwardian baroque edifice of Norman Shaw's Piccadilly Hotel.

Elsewhere in the West End, the character of the streets was altering as drastically as Piccadilly's was. Numerous eighteenth-century houses were being given the facial treatment, both outside and inside, that Edwardian taste demanded – at 3 Grafton Street, for example, (now the showroom of Helena Rubinstein) the wealth of Mrs Arthur James was displayed in the spectacular alterations to the house designed originally by Sir Robert Taylor in the 1750s; scores of Georgian, Regency and Victorian buildings were making way for new theatres – the Duke of York's, the New Theatre, the Scala, the Palladium, the Gaiety, Her Majesty's, the London Pavilion, the Palace, the Apollo, Wyndham's, the Hippodrome, the Strand, the Aldwych, the Globe, the Queen's and the Coliseum, were all built within the last ten years of his mother's reign or within the nine years of Edward's own; hundreds of other old buildings were pulled down to make room for new shops, grandiose emporiums with lavish displays of plate-glass and brass-encrusted, mahogany doors. The terracotta walls of Harrod's began to rise in Brompton Road in 1901, and were soon followed by a rash of other stores in Oxford Street, either wildly baroque as at Waring & Gillow's (1906) or alarmingly colossal such as the immense edifice which was started in 1909 by the Wisconsin merchant, Harry Gordon Selfridge.

By the time Selfridge's was finished, Regent Street had been completely rebuilt, the loop of Aldwych had been cut through a maze of streets north of the Strand opposite Somerset House and filled with rows of monumental buildings, and Kingsway had thrust its way north to Holborn.

These new Edwardian streets did little, however, to lessen the problem of London's congested traffic which was becoming worse than it had ever been (plate 44). As well as horse-drawn vehicles and bicycles, motor-cars were becoming more and more common; motor taxis made their appearance in 1903; motor omnibuses began to compete with the horse-drawn buses which, nevertheless, continued to operate on certain routes until 1911; electrical trams – the successors of horse trams, traction trams and compressed air trams – came into service in 1903 and within the next few years miles of new track were laid, in the streets and across the bridges, along the embankments and underground, linking Waterloo Bridge with Islington. The Northern and City lines came into use in 1904, the Bakerloo Line in 1906.

Horse bus, 1890, in St John's Wood.

By 1900 the population of the County of London had already risen to four and a half millions, but of these less than thirty thousand now lived in the City. The great majority of Londoners who worked there or in the West End returned at night to the suburbs.

In the early years of the new century family life in these suburbs had altered little in the past fifty years. In the houses of the well-to-do middle-class the day still began with a family breakfast, at which the attendance of servants, as a point of 'consideration', was dispensed with; hot dishes were laid out on the dark, solid, mahogany sideboard under silver lids, the boiled eggs under a china cover shaped like a hen. The day still ended with family prayers to which the children, who had seen little of their parents throughout the day, were ushered by their governesses and nurses, and at which the presence of all the household servants was also required.

Very different was the warmly affectionate, sheltered, shared family life in a lower middle-class suburb such as Battersea where Richard Church celebrated his tenth birthday in 1903. His father was a mail-sorter in the South-West District Post-Office next door to Westminster Cathedral, then being built; his mother a teacher at a London Board School in Battersea Park Road. Their joint income was about £250 a year. Their elder son attended the Polytechnic Secondary School to which he had won a scholarship; their

A tandem bicycle, 1884.

A suburban house in Kew of c. 1890.

younger boy went to the Surrey Lane Higher Grade School. Their house, mortgaged to the Temperance Permanent Building Society – to whose offices on Ludgate Hill, Richard and his brother took the payments each quarter – had been bought for £375 from a rubicund man who worked on the *News of the World* and smoked cigars on weekdays as well as on Sundays (a sure sign of prosperity).

Behind the house was a concrete backyard and a bicycle shed where Mr Church stored his treasured tandem; in front of it was a gas lamp – lit at night by a lamp-lighter always followed by a gang of excited children who danced around him and shouted with pleasure when he pushed his flickering brass-topped pole inside the lantern and made the flame pop up – a gas lamp so much more friendly and reassuring than the electric arc lamps that already hissed and spluttered in Battersea Park Road.

Inside the house the doors between the front and back parlours were always open; the arch above them, as also the two fireplaces, were hung with plush, tasselled curtains. The rooms were littered with furniture, photographs, ornaments, stands and bookshelves on which were red-bound copies of *Welcome*, the *Boys' Own Paper* and the *Family Journal*, and loose copies of *Cycling*, *Titbits*, *Chatterbox*, and the *Daily Chronicle*.

The outside of the house was neat and tidy, as were most of the hundreds of other houses in the nearby streets, where lace curtains, crisp and white, were draped inside the shining windows, front door steps were scrubbed and reddled, front paths neatly marked with lines of bottle-ends or metal caps from bottles. The neighbours, mostly skilled artisans, minor Civil Servants, ex-soldiers and ill-paid clerks, included some families, rough, brutal and improvident, who would never go to the Congregational Chapel, who made their money run to bitter beer and pickles in the local public house but would never enter the Creighton restaurant near Clapham Junction for fried plaice and bottled stout.

In the social hierarchy of Edwardian suburban London, well below the august respectability of St John's Wood and Hampstead, but rather above the never completely integrated riverside and marshy quarter of Battersea, stood Holloway, where George and Weedon Grossmith provided a home for the imperishable Pooters.

'The Laurels', 12 Brickfield Terrace, Holloway, contained six rooms and a basement. There was a little garden in front, and a slightly larger one at the back running down to the railway. A flight of ten steps led up to the porticoed front door; a stucco balustrade protected the house from the street; heavy facings surrounded the windows; an out-of-scale parapet, projecting several feet above the level of the flat roof, gave the front façade a false impression of height. The upper panels of the front door – only opened on special occasions – were filled with frosted glass; lace curtains and a half-closed blind in the drawing-room window concealed its occupants from view; the back of Mrs Pooter's dressing-table looking-glass was all that could be seen in her bedroom window above. The house was lit by gas, and in the small bathroom a geyser noisily supplied hot water. Although a telephone exchange had been opened in Lombard Street (with ten subscribers) in 1879, there was no telephone at 'The Laurels'; indeed there were very few in Holloway at all until after the First World War. In the kitchen – as in most such kitchens – there was a maid.

The stair-carpet was not quite wide enough to meet the chocolate-brown paint of the steps on either side of it; the green rep of the front-drawing-room chairs and sofa was covered with chintz; in the hall hung a pair of stags' heads made of plaster of Paris and coloured brown; on other walls were enlarged and tinted photographs, decorated, when parties were given in the house, with Liberty Silk bows. The mantelpiece of the back drawing-room (which served also as the dining-room) was surmounted with two china vases, a calendar, some fans, and an ornamental clock under a glass dome.

Carrying his umbrella, Mr Pooter went up to the City each morning, the journey by omnibus taking him half an hour. On his return, after his meat-tea, he usually stayed at home, reading the newspaper or *Exchange and Mart*, doing odd jobs about the house, listening to his wife playing the cottage piano (bought on the three years' system). Occasionally his friend Cummings (a keen tricyclist and an avid reader of *Bicycle News*) would come in for a game of dominoes or bezique, or a smoke in the breakfast-parlour with a glass or two of whisky (price, 36s. for a dozen bottles); sometimes Mrs Cummings and other friends would call and then Mrs Cummings would sing a song, *The Garden of Sleep* or *No, Sir,* or they would play consequences or more noisy games like 'Monkeys and Cutlets', or listen to Mr Fosselton of the local amateur dramatic society, the Holloway Comedians, doing his celebrated imitations of the ageing Henry Irving. Once a year, or so, there would be a party and then a hired waiter would hand round champagne.

Occasionally Mr Pooter and his wife went out, to a reception at the Mansion House, to the East Acton Volunteer Ball, to meat-tea (on a Sunday) with Mrs James of Sutton, to the Lyceum theatre or the Tank theatre, Islington, or to shop at Peter Robinson's and the Holloway *Bon Marché*. In the summer they spent a week at Broadstairs. On 5 November they went over to the Cummingses to watch the fireworks. On Christmas Day they visited Mrs Pooter's mother, catching the 10.20 a.m. train from Paddington.

After the First World War, London suburban life, of which George and Weedon Grossmith gave so exact an account, was altered for ever. Also transformed were the suburbs in which such families as the Pooters lived.

New underground railways linked them with the City while new arterial roads cut through them, creating sprawls of new houses, factory estates and shopping centres, eating into the countryside to such an extent that the growth of London in the first half of the twentieth century was to be greater by far than its growth over the previous two thousand years.

'From Euston to Clapham Common the transformation is complete': railway poster, 1924.

HERTFORDSHIRE

ESSEX

MIDDLESEX

KENT

SURREY

0   5   10   15
scale in miles

N
W   E
S

The Small Stigma of a Gigantic Sunflower
The growth of London from the Middle Ages until Today

SW

238

15 *The Growth of Modern London 1914–1968*

While the aspect of London's suburbs was drastically changed after the First World War, so too was its centre. The lordly Edwardian amplitude of Piccadilly slowly dissolved as new shapes appeared, sometimes disruptive, often incongruous. First came two banks – Curtis Green's Barclay's Bank in 1921, and Sir Edwin Lutyens's Midland Bank in 1922 – then Devonshire House, a vast commercial block of eight storeys, began to materialise in 1924 and was followed in 1926 by a new neo-Georgian store for Fortnum and Mason. The next year a third new bank arose in the street, the Westminster, and a big new hotel, the Park Lane. Two years later yet another commercial block, Stratton House, was completed, and Beresford Pite provided a new front for Burlington Arcade. In 1935 Joseph Emberton gave Piccadilly its first good building in the modern, progressive manner, the store designed for Simpson's; the next year a second, though less successful, modern design took shape in the hotel known as Athenaeum Court; Nuffield House, the third huge block of offices, showrooms and shops to be built in Piccadilly within fifteen years, was completed shortly before the outbreak of the Second World War.

In these years between the two world wars the development in other parts of London rivalled that in Piccadilly. Modern newspaper offices – like those of the *Daily Telegraph*, modernistic neo-Greek (1928) and the *Daily Express* (1931), black glass and chromium – went up in Fleet Street; luxury hotels – the Dorchester and Grosvenor House, both begun in 1930 – replaced the private houses which had once stood on their sites in Park Lane; neo-Edwardian office blocks – Furness House built in 1922, Stone House in 1927, Hasilwood House in 1928, Royal Mail House and Cunard House in 1930 – were erected in Leadenhall Street and Bishopsgate; department stores – Liberty's and Dickins and Jones – went up in Regent Street; in 1931 Broadcasting House appeared in Portland Place and the Saville Theatre in Shaftesbury Avenue; cinemas, blocks of flats, shops, and banks were put up everywhere.

After the Second World War the face of London was changed far more rapidly and far more drastically than ever before (plate 45). The bombs of the Luftwaffe and the sledge-hammers of demolition contractors laid bare acre upon acre of land on which huge structures of glass and concrete have risen and continued to rise. Many old buildings damaged by bombing have been restored; many others, including twenty of the City's churches and eighteen of its livery halls, have gone for ever. The monolithic offices of the English Electric Company stand upon the site of the charming Edwardian Gaiety Theatre; the St James's Theatre of 1836 has disappeared beneath the concrete of St James's House, the late Victorian Carlton Hotel beneath the nineteen floors of New Zealand House; Parnell and Smith's imposing Army and Navy Club has been replaced by the recently completed building which looks across the south-west corner of St James's Square to the modern block where once stood David Brandon's palatial Junior Carlton Club; the thirty-odd floors of the Hilton Hotel soar above a widened Park Lane; the windows at the summit of the Post Office Tower peer down over five hundred feet upon the roofs of Marylebone; on both banks of the river, in the City, West End and suburbs, along Victoria Street and Millbank, in Mayfair and Clerkenwell, St Giles's Circus and Earl's Court, the offices and flats of modern London, some thrilling and beautiful, others drably depressing, surge towards the sky.

But although many old buildings that might have been spared have been destroyed, although many new ones that should have been at once exciting and harmonious are both dull and incongruous, the London that greets the modern eye still retains its incomparable attraction and exercises its haunting spell.

Around it a sprawling conurbation now extends across Middlesex and into Buckinghamshire, Hertfordshire, Surrey, Essex and Kent. Administered since 1965 by the Greater London Council it contains a population of more than eight million people, almost twice as much as the population of the entire country in 1633, the year that Pepys was born.

The area covered by the medieval city is now lost in the crowded centre of London's map, like the small stigma of a gigantic sunflower. Yet the giant continues to grow; the problems of its growth and congestion increase; its aspect continually changes.

But London is in essence immutable; for all its faults it remains to those who have learned to love it uniquely emotive, uniquely seductive, uniquely beautiful; it still appears now, as it did when a marvelling visitor saw it for the first time in the year that St Paul's was finished, 'the country's finest jewel, a city full of wonders and sweet delights'.

*Notes and Guide
Sources
Index*

Notes and Guide

CHAPTER 1 *(Pages 1–5)*

1. Fragments of London's ROMAN WALL, and its medieval additions, can still be seen in various parts of the City. The most easily accessible are (i) adjoining Tower Hill to the east of Trinity Square, (ii) in the public garden next to St Alphege, London Wall, and (iii) in the south-east corner of the churchyard of St Giles, Cripplegate in Fore Street. There is a well-preserved stretch of the wall in the basement of the Toc H club at 40 Trinity Square which will be shown to visitors by previous application to the Warden, but not at week-ends or after 6 in the evening. Visitors to the General Post Office (see note 9, p. 260) can inspect one of the wall's bastions beneath the loading-yard.

2. Several pieces of marble statuary from this Mithraic temple were discovered in 1954 when the foundations for the huge office block of Bucklersbury House were being dug in Walbrook. They include

Head of Mithras.

marble heads of Mithras himself and of Serapis, god of the Underworld. They can be seen, together with several other RELICS OF ROMAN LONDON, in the Guildhall Museum, at present housed in the court of the Royal Exchange (Threadneedle Street and Cornhill, see note 2, p. 249). A Mithraic relief of the second century is among the large number of Roman exhibits on display in Room 2 of the London Museum at Kensington Palace (see note 2, p. 263). The remains of the temple have been rebuilt in the forecourt of Temple Court behind Bucklersbury House at 11 Queen Victoria Street.

Other Roman relics are preserved in the British Museum, Great Russell Street (see note 5, p. 259). These include the bronze helmet of a legionary who served in Londinium, and the reconstructed tomb of Julius Classicianus, the procurator who saved the British from the fury of the Roman army's revenge after Boadicea's revolt.

In its existing form, the ROMAN BATH at 5 Strand Lane, which is open to the public on weekdays between 10 and 12.30, is not Roman at all. It was either built or very extensively repaired in the early seventeenth century.

The remains of two Roman tessellated pavements and part of the wall of a Roman house may be seen in the undercroft of All Hallows Barking by the Tower (see next note.)

CHAPTER 2 *(Pages 7–21)*

1. The original Saxon church of ALL HALLOWS, BARKING BY THE TOWER (Great Tower Street), was built in about 675. The Barking refers to the Abbey in Essex to which it originally belonged. As well as the Saxon wall of its crypt, it contains a Saxon

arch (the oldest arch in the City of London) behind the screen in the lower part of the Tower, and pieces of two Saxon crosses. The church was rebuilt in the later Middle Ages and restored in the 1950s after being badly damaged by bombing in 1940. From the brick tower, built during the Commonwealth in 1658 – the only surviving ecclesiastical building of that period in London – Samuel Pepys, 'afeared to stay there long', watched the Great Fire raging. The church is open, as the majority of London churches are, for most of the day.

2. The eleventh-century structure of WESTMINSTER ABBEY – apart from the western part of the nave – was rebuilt by Henry III's architect, Henry of Rheims, in the middle of the thirteenth century. It is perhaps the finest example of the Early English style in existence, though the multitudinous array of effigies, tombs, statues, memorials – there are great works here by Rysbrack, Roubiliac, Guelfi and Westmacott, amongst scores of others – distract the eye from its impressive grandeur. The nave was rebuilt by Henry Yevele – the King's master mason who also designed the nave of Canterbury Cathedral – between 1376 and 1388. Henry V's chantry was added in 1441 and Henry VII's huge and magnificent chapel was finished in 1519. The west towers are eighteenth-century additions by Wren and his pupil, Nicholas Hawksmoor. On Sundays, when

Westminster Abbey.

only the naves and transept are open, services are held at 8, 10.30, 11.30, 3, and 6.30; on weekdays there are services at 8, 10 and 5 (Saturdays at 3). The Chapter House and the Chamber of the Pyx are open in summer from 10.30 to 6.30 and in winter from 10.30 to 4. The Ambulatory and Choir Chapels (to see which tickets are needed and a charge is made) are open on Mondays, Wednesdays and Thursdays from 9.45 to 4, on Tuesdays and Fridays from 10.45 to 4, on Saturdays from 9.45 to 2.15 and from 3.45 to 5.

The Museum in the Norman undercroft, which houses a remarkable collection of funeral effigies, is open from 10.30 to 4.0 in winter and from 10.30 to 4.30 in summer.

The Abbey is open for services only on Ash Wednesday, Good Friday and Christmas Day.

The little chapel of ST MARGARET'S WESTMINSTER which lies in the shadow of the Abbey opposite Westminster Hall, was founded in the twelfth century but its present form is of the same period as Henry VII's chapel. Refaced in Portland stone in 1735, it was restored in 1878.

3. The TOWER OF LONDON ceased to be a royal palace when Cromwell pulled the royal quarters down, although Charles II observed the ancient custom of spending the night before his coronation there, the last monarch to do so. It had ceased to be a fortress centuries before the moat was drained in the 1840s and the mock medieval outer walls were built. The royal zoo was moved to Regent's Park in 1834, only the ravens remaining – to be allowed half a crown a week for horseflesh. It had already become a museum when, in the seventeenth century, Christopher Wren replaced its Norman slits with wider windows and its corner turrets were capped by cupolas; and so it remains a museum, as it remains a garrison, armoury and jewel house.

Around the original Norman tower a cluster of later buildings has developed over the centuries, medieval bastions, gatehouses and lodgings, half-timbered sheds and stores, Tudor towers and chapels – the chapel of St Peter ad Vincula was rebuilt after a fire in 1512 – seventeenth-century houses, eighteenth-century guard rooms, nineteenth-century walls. Inside those walls princes have been murdered, spies shot, and traitors tortured on the rack. Archbishops, chancellors and queens, kings of Scotland and of France, rebels, regicides and heretics, Sir Thomas More and Charles of Orléans, Guy Fawkes and Rudolf Hess have been imprisoned here. Anne Boleyn and Lady Jane Grey have walked out to execution on Tower Green; Lord Lovat to the more public scaffold on Tower Hill. The Tower is open on weekdays from 10 to 5 from May to September, from 10 to 4.30 from the middle of March to April and from 10 to 4 from October to the middle of March; and on Sundays from 2 to 5 from May to October. It is closed on Good Friday, Christmas Day, and Boxing Day.

The permission of the Governor is required for admission to the seven-hundred-years-old ceremony of locking the gates which takes place at ten o'clock each night.

4. The fourteenth-century reconstruction of WESTMINSTER HALL was carried out under the direction of Henry Yevele. The hammer-beam roof, which springs to a height of ninety-two feet in the centre, has the widest unsupported span in the country. The Hall has been described, by the Royal Commission on Historical Monuments, as 'probably the finest timber-roofed building in Europe'.

It is open at the same time as the Houses of Parliament (see note 6, p. 266), also on weekdays (except Good Friday and Christmas Day) from 10 until one hour before the House of Commons meets, and when the House is not sitting, on weekdays from 10 to 4 and on Saturdays from 10 to 5. It is closed on Good Fridays and Christmas Day.

5. The present church of ST BARTHOLOMEW-THE-GREAT, West Smithfield, is, in effect, the choir of the large Norman Augustinian priory. The canopied tomb of its founder on the north side of the sanctuary bears his effigy. William Hogarth was baptized in the fifteenth-century font in 1697; and in 1725 Benjamin Franklin worked in the Lady Chapel which was then a printing office.

The CHAPEL OF ST JOHN in the Tower was built about forty years before St Bartholomew's and is scarcely less fine an example of Norman ecclesiastical architecture. Its windows have been widened, but otherwise its appearance has changed little in nine hundred years. Aspirants to the Order of the Bath (after the Order of the Garter the oldest order of chivalry in England) kept their vigil here throughout the night before their investiture, after having been ritually washed in tubs outside and after having eaten dinner with the king.

6. The TEMPLE CHURCH was finished in 1185. Only four other medieval round churches survive in England. The church, extended between 1220 and 1240 and restored in 1841, was badly damaged by bombing in 1941, but has been carefully restored.

CHAPTER 3 *(Pages 23–33)*

1. Fire destroyed most of CROSBY HALL in the seventeenth century but the great hall survived and, in 1910, was transferred from Bishopsgate to Danvers Street, Chelsea, where it may still be seen. It contains a copy of Holbein's painting of the family of Sir Thomas More who lived in the mansion for a short time after Sir John Crosby's death.

Visitors are admitted from Monday to Friday from 10 to 12 and from 2 to 5, and on Saturdays and Sundays from 2 to 5.

2. The entrance porch and crypt of the GUILDHALL (in Guildhall Yard off Gresham Street) are almost all that remain of the medieval structure, which was rebuilt about 1411, partly at the expense of Richard Whittington. The Great Hall, restored after the Great Fire and again after the Second World War, is, however, fifteenth-century in character. The late eighteenth-century Gothic south front is by George Dance, the younger.

The Guildhall Crypt.

The Guildhall – centre of the City's government and rendezvous of its élite on ceremonial occasions – contains an Art Gallery, which owns a large collection of nineteenth-century British paintings and often houses a loan exhibition. There is also a library which, in addition to its 135,000 books, contains a unique collection of London documents, prints and maps, the purchase deed of a house in Blackfriars marked with Shakespeare's signature and various folios of his plays.

The figures of the giants Gog and Magog replace the two early eighteenth-century wooden figures destroyed in the War, themselves supposedly replacements of the medieval effigies which were paraded round the streets in honour of the two legendary giants – descendants of the wicked daughters of Diocletian – who were brought captive to London to serve as porters at the gate of the royal palace after their brothers had all been slain by Brutus the Trojan.

The Great Hall and Crypt of Guildhall are open on weekdays from 10 to 5 and on Sundays and Bank Holidays in May to September from 2 to 5. The Art Gallery is also open on weekdays from 10 to 5, and the Library from 9.30 to 5, though both are closed on Bank Holidays.

3. All these halls of the City Livery Companies have since been rebuilt, some of them three or even four times. Most of them can still be seen by previous application to the respective Clerks. GOLDSMITH'S HALL, Foster Lane, built in 1835 to the Italianate designs of Philip Hardwick is the most interesting of those mentioned in the text and has the finest interior. Other halls well worth visiting are APOTHECARIES' HALL, Blackfriars' Lane, part seventeenth century and extended in 1786; and SKINNERS' HALL, Dowgate, also of the seventeenth and eighteenth centuries. FISHMONGERS' HALL, King William Street, the first of the Halls to catch fire in 1666 and the first again in 1940, has been well restored and contains, in addition to several fine paintings by Romney and Samuel Scott, the dagger with which the Lord Mayor, a Prime Warden of the Company, was armed when he and John Standish stabbed the rebel, Wat Tyler, in the Peasants' Revolt of 1381. The fifteenth-century court room of VINTNERS' HALL, Upper Thames Street, has escaped both fire and bombs; while the court room of STATIONERS' HALL, off Ludgate Hill, though badly damaged in the War has now been restored. The handsome east front is by Robert Mylne. The Stationers may be seen in the crypt of St Paul's on Ash Wednesday, distributing cakes and ale in accordance with ancient custom.

4. The Norman priory-church, burned down in 1206, was rebuilt soon afterwards. Although the nave was reconstructed in the 1890s, SOUTHWARK CATHEDRAL still contains much of the original thirteenth-century fabric, and can be described as the most outstanding Gothic building in London, after Westminster Abbey. Several Elizabethan playwrights and actors from the theatres of nearby Bankside are buried here, and John Harvard, founder of Harvard University, was baptized here in 1608.

Southwark Cathedral.

5. The original LAMBETH PALACE lay closer to the water and was approached from the river steps. The thirteenth-century crypt is the oldest part of the present palace which is an attractive medley of fifteenth-century ragstone, Tudor brickwork, seventeenth-century and Regency neo-Gothic and modern restoration. The valuable library is open every weekday to readers upon application to the Librarian, and the interior of the Palace and its fine collection of archiepiscopal portraits upon application to the Chaplain.

6. The Savoy Palace was badly damaged during the Peasants' Revolt when it was inhabited by Edward III's son John of Gaunt, Duke of Lancaster, whose estates were annexed to the crown by Henry IV. Henry VII rebuilt the Palace as a hospital. On the site of the hospital, Richard D'Oyly Carte, who had already built the Savoy Theatre nearby, built the Savoy Hotel in 1899.

The QUEEN'S CHAPEL OF THE SAVOY, the private chapel of the ruling monarch as Duke of Lancaster, is the chapel of Henry VII's hospital, the only part of it to survive, though most of the present structure is an 1864 reconstruction by Sydney Smirke. It is open on Mondays to Fridays from 10 to 4 in summer, from 10 to 3 in winter, and on Saturdays from 10 to 1. Except in August and September there are services on Sundays at 11.15.

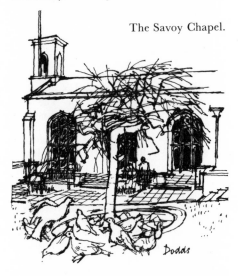

The Savoy Chapel.

Dodds

7. Walks in the courts, yards, lanes and gardens of the TEMPLE, LINCOLN'S INN and GRAY'S INN, are among the most pleasant and quiet in London. The architecture is delightfully varied, from the Tudor brickwork (1518) of the Gatehouse, Lincoln's Inn, to the classical grace of Sir Robert Taylor's Stone Buildings (1774–80), from Roger North's Middle Temple Gateway (1684) to the early nineteenth-century Raymond Buildings in Gray's Inn where at the age of sixteen Charles Dickens was employed as an office-boy by Messrs Ellis and Blackmore. The Hall, Chapel and Library of Gray's Inn may usually be visited on written application to the Under-Treasurer;

Middle Temple Hall and Inner Temple Hall are open from Monday to Friday from 10 to 12, and from 3 to 4.30; on Saturdays, from 10 to 4.30. To visit the Halls, Library and Chapel of Lincoln's Inn visitors may apply at the Porter's Lodge in Chancery Lane, except between 12.30 and 2.

CHAPTER 4 *(Pages 35–53)*

1. The CHARTERHOUSE, Charterhouse Square, an English offshoot of the Grande Chartreuse near Grenoble, was founded by one of Edward III's knights, Sir Walter de Manny, in 1371. Its monks resisted the demands of the Crown at the Reformation, and its Prior was executed and quartered, one of his quarters being hung on the priory gate. After the death of Lord North the Tudor mansion passed into the hands of John Dudley, Duke of Northumberland (who was beheaded in 1553) and then into the possession of the Howard family who sold it in 1611 to Thomas Sutton, a rich colliery-owner. Sutton established a hospital and a school for forty poor boys. Forty old pensioners are still maintained here; but the school, by then one of England's most famous, was moved to Godalming in 1872.

The Charterhouse was badly damaged in the War, but has been sympathetically restored. The Great Hall is early Elizabethan, the Great Chamber of about 1571. Parties will be shown round on Saturdays by previous arrangement with the Registrar.

2. Gresham's ROYAL EXCHANGE, Threadneedle Street and Cornhill, was destroyed in the Great Fire, and its successor, designed by Edward Jerman, one of the City Surveyors – who designed many of the City Livery Companies' Halls – was also burned in 1838. The present classical building, incorporating the surviving sixteenth-century Turkish honestone paving of the central court and bearing on the campanile the huge grasshopper of the Gresham crest, was finished, to the designs of Sir William Tite, in 1844. It houses the GUILDHALL MUSEUM's extensive and varied collection of London antiquities. Both the Royal Exchange and the Guildhall Museum are open on weekdays, (except Bank Holidays) from 10 to 5.

3. The Gatehouse of ST JAMES'S PALACE, at the bottom of St James's Street, is the most imposing part of the original Tudor

palace. It was built when Henry VIII was married to Anne Boleyn and carries their initials on the side doors of the gateway. The State Apartments are not open to the public who may, however, walk in Friary Court where, from the balcony, the official proclamation of a new sovereign is still made by the Heralds, and where the Guard is changed at 10.30 each morning when the Queen is not in residence at Buckingham Palace.

The CHAPEL ROYAL, in Ambassador's Court (where the public are also permitted to walk), was built in about 1532 and, although much altered now, has its original painted ceiling, a splendid work ascribed by some to Holbein. Those who would like to attend a morning service here may do so at 8.30 and 11.15 from the second Sunday in October until Palm Sunday and on Christmas Day, and at 11.30 on 6 January when to celebrate the Feast of the Epiphany royal gifts of gold, frankincense and myrrh are offered.

4. The present building on the site, the early nineteenth-century offices at 14 New Bridge Street, contains the original court room of BRIDEWELL.

5. Very few examples of Elizabethan domestic exteriors survive in London. STAPLE INN, 338 High Holborn, is the best. Founded in the fourteenth century as a hostel for wool staplers, it later became an inn of chancery in 1545 and was rebuilt in the 1580's. The façade was last restored in 1950 after being damaged by a flying bomb.

CHAPTER 5 *(Pages 55–65)*

1. Most of these seventeenth-century houses in Lincoln's Inn Fields have disappeared. LINDSEY HOUSE, however, at 59–60, was built in the late 1630's and, according to Colen Campbell, was by Inigo Jones himself. The seventeenth-century brickwork has been overlaid by stucco, but the essential character remains. The house on its right is a copy of it, built a hundred years later.

2. The royal palace of Placentia, a favourite palace of Henry VIII and his children, was replaced by Wren's beautiful Greenwich Hospital – now the ROYAL NAVAL COLLEGE – at the end of the seventeenth-century. The QUEEN'S HOUSE, begun

for James I's Queen in 1617 and finished for her daughter-in-law, Henrietta Maria, in 1635, survives as the central portion of the National Maritime Museum.

The Painted Hall of the Royal Naval College, which occupied Hogarth's father-in-law, Sir James Thornhill, over a period of nineteen years, may be seen in the afternoons from 2 to 5 on weekdays (except Thursdays) and on Sundays from May to September. The Chapel is also open on weekday afternoons (except Thursdays) and on Sundays for Matins at 11.

The NATIONAL MARITIME MUSEUM – there are some fine portraits and seascapes here as well as a remarkable collection of naval instruments, uniforms, ships' models, state barges and other maritime oddments – is open on weekdays from 10 to 6 and on Sundays from 2.30 to 6 – closed on Christmas Eve, Christmas Day and Good Friday.

3. The QUEEN'S CHAPEL, Marlborough Road, St James's, which was started by Inigo Jones for Charles I's intended bride, the Infanta Maria of Spain, was finished for his Queen, Henrietta Maria. It was redecorated and refurnished thirty-five years later for Henrietta Maria's successor, Queen Catherine of Braganza. The 8.30 and 11.15 Sunday morning services here may be attended from Easter Day to the end of July. On weekdays it is included in the tours of Marlborough House (see note 3, p. 252).

4. Inigo Jones's early masterpiece, the BANQUETING HOUSE, Whitehall, which was started in 1619 and finished in 1622, was the first wholly Palladian building to appear in London. Although originally only the orders and balustrade were of Portland stone – the rest being of brown Oxfordshire and dun-coloured Northamptonshire stones – the front was refaced with Portland stone in 1829 by Sir John Soane. The windows, too, were changed from mullion-and-transom to sash.

It was for the nine allegorical ceiling paintings that Rubens received his knighthood from Charles I. Until recently the home of the Royal United Service Institution, it is now used by the Government for official receptions. It is open (except on Good Friday, Christmas Day and Boxing Day) on weekdays from 10 to 5, and on Sundays from 2 to 5.

5. ST PAUL'S, COVENT GARDEN, was burned down in 1790, but was rebuilt by Thomas Hardwick to Inigo Jones's original

design. The church is entered from the west end and not from what appears to be the main entrance beneath the portico. Although most of the gravestones have been removed, there are believed to have been more famous people buried here than in any other church in England, except St Paul's and Westminster Abbey.

St Paul's, Covent Garden.

6. Although the design of this church in Covent Garden remains recognisable and distinct, nothing survives of the square's vaulted walks or houses. BEDFORD CHAMBERS, built by the 9th Duke of Bedford in 1880 on the northern side of Covent Garden, provides, however, a tolerable imitation of their former appearance.

CHAPTER 6 (Pages 67–79)

1. Among the most interesting of Wren's City churches which escaped destruction in 1940 or have since been restored are ST BRIDE'S, FLEET STREET, with a delightfully fanciful five-tiered spire; ST MARGARET'S, LOTHBURY, its splendid and beautifully furnished interior containing work attributed to Grinling Gibbons, Michael Rysbrack and Hubert Le Sueur; ST MARTIN'S, LUDGATE, a characteristic Wren church with a most handsome front; ST MARY'S ALDERMARY, an early Gothic revival; ST STEPHEN'S WALBROOK, an ambitious essay in baroque; the small and simple ST BENET'S, Upper Thames Street and

ST MARY'S ABCHURCH, Abchurch Lane; ST MARY-LE-BOW, Cheapside; ST ANDREW'S, Holborn Viaduct; ST ANDREW'S BY THE WARDROBE, Wardrobe Terrace; ST EDMUND THE KING, Lombard Street; ST JAMES'S GARLICKHYTHE and ST MAGNUS THE MARTYR, both in Upper Thames Street; ST MARY AT HILL, Lovat Lane; ST PETER-UPON-CORN-HILL, and ST VEDAST'S, Foster Lane. A well-restored Wren church beyond the City's boundary is ST CLEMENT DANES. Built in 1680–82 its spire was added by Gibbs in 1719 and was the only part of the church to escape when the rest was gutted in 1941. The famous bells, though, were thrown to the ground and cracked. The stones of ST MARY'S ALDERMANBURY which was rebuilt by Wren in 1680–87, restored in 1863 and bombed out in 1940, have now been transported to the United States of America and rebuilt to form part of the Churchill quadrangle at Westminster College, Fulton, Missouri.

Among the most unspoiled of Wren's other buildings outside the City is his delightful ROYAL HOSPITAL, Royal Hospital Road, Chelsea. Founded by Charles II as an asylum for old or disabled soldiers, its pensioners still wear uniforms adapted from those in use at the time of Marlborough, dark blue greatcoats in winter, scarlet frock-coats in summer. The red brick building, with its two projecting

St Stephen's Walbrook.

wings and big pillared portico, was finished in 1691 and, although work has since been done here by Robert Adam and Sir John Soane, it remains, clearly and most pleasingly, Wren's work.

The Museum and Grounds, Chapel and Great Hall of the Hospital are open on weekdays from 10 to 12 and from 2 to dusk; on Sundays, in the afternoons only. The Council Chamber is open on Saturdays in the summer from 2 to 4, and on Sundays from 11.45 to 12.15 and 2 to 4 (all the year).

2. Except when services are held (on Sundays at 8, 10.30, 11.30, 3.15, 6.30; on Mondays, Tuesdays, Thursdays and Saturdays at 8, 10 and 4; and on Wednesdays and Fridays at 8, 10, 12.30 and 4) visitors are free to wander round ST PAUL'S CATHEDRAL on any day between 7.45 and 7 from April to September and between 7.45 and 5 from October to March.

Charges are made to see the Library, the Whispering, Stone and Golden Galleries, the Ball, and the Crypt. The Crypt contains the graves of numerous sailors, soldiers and artists, including those of Wellington, Nelson, Turner and Reynolds – St Paul's attracting the remains of such men as, traditionally, Westminster Abbey has attracted those of kings and queens, statesmen and writers. The Whispering Gallery is the best place from which to see both the floor of the Cathedral and Thornhill's paintings in the dome. The Stone Gallery, 233 steps above the south aisle, the Golden Gallery, higher still, and the Ball at the very top of the lantern and 627 steps from the floor, offer unique views over London.

CHAPTER 7 *(Pages 81–93)*

1. It was Wren's contention that ST JAMES'S PICCADILLY was his best design for a parish church. It was badly damaged in the War, but has now been restored. The exterior is plain; the inside – which contains some marvellously exuberant wood carving by Grinling Gibbons and an organ constructed by Renatus Harris in 1685 for Whitehall Palace – is beautifully light and spacious.

2. SCHOMBERG HOUSE, 80–82, Pall Mall was built in 1698 and, although its inside has been made into offices, externally it has been restored to its original appearance. In this house, a rare example of the late seventeenth-century London house of individual design, Gainsborough spent the last four years of his life.

3. Designed by Wren and built in 1709–11, MARLBOROUGH HOUSE, Marlborough Road and Pall Mall, has been much altered and extended since, mainly by Sir William Chambers in 1771 and Sir James Pennethorne – for the Prince of Wales – in the 1860's. The interior – which contains some lovely eighteenth-century marble fireplaces, early seventeenth-century painted ceilings by Orazio Gentileschi from the Queen's House, Greenwich, and murals of Marlborough's victories by Louis Laguerre – is open to the public when not in use by the Commonwealth delegations for whose use it is now reserved. Conducted tours are given at 12.30, 1.30 and 3.30 from Mondays to Fridays from Easter Tuesday until the end of the last week in October. The house is also open on Saturdays, Sundays and Bank holidays from 2 to 6.

Marlborough House.

4. The third Earl, whose admiration for Palladio did so much to influence English taste in the eighteenth century, would scarcely recognise the present BURLINGTON HOUSE, between Albany Courtyard and Burlington Arcade, Piccadilly. The gateway and the curved colonnades, which once connected it with the street, have

both gone; and the house itself, remodelled inside in 1816 by Samuel Ware for Lord George Cavendish, was altered outside in the 1860s when, having been bought by the government for £140,000, it became the home of the Royal Academy of Arts. Sydney Smirke added an upper storey in 1867 and a few years later new ranges of buildings were built along the Piccadilly frontage and at the back facing Burlington Gardens.

The Victorian additions provide accommodation for various learned societies, including the Royal Society, the Geological Society, the Chemical Society, the Royal Astronomical Society, the Society of Antiquaries of London and the Linnaean Society, and their private rooms are not open to visitors except by invitation.

In Burlington House itself, the Royal Academy's Summer Exhibition is held from May until the middle of August; and various loan exhibitions are also held here in the winter.

5. The handsome YORK WATERGATE, Watergate Walk and Embankment Gardens, is all that remains of the Duke of Buckingham's mansion. Once the gateway leading from his garden to the river steps, it has now been separated from the Thames by the reclaimed land of the Victoria Embankment and Embankment Gardens. Built in 1626 it has been variously attributed to Nicholas Stone, who erected it, Inigo Jones, and Balthasar Gerbier, the Duke's talented agent who purchased for him many of his pictures.

6. Characteristic of the terrace houses built by Nicholas Barbon – although their wooden eaves-cornices have gone and their casement windows have been replaced by sashes – are 36–43 BEDFORD ROW. They may be compared with the houses built a few years later on the west side of QUEEN ANNE'S GATE, Westminster, the best preserved group of early eighteenth-century houses in London. The statue of Queen Anne to the left of No. 15 was placed there in her lifetime.

CHAPTER 8 *(Pages 95–111)*

1. The stones of LONDON BRIDGE begun by John Rennie and finished in 1831, ten years after his death, have been sold to the U.S.A. and are being re-erected in Lake Havasu City, Arizona. It is soon to be replaced. Rennie's WATERLOO BRIDGE

has already been replaced by the modern structure designed by Sir Giles Gilbert Scott (1939) and his SOUTHWARK BRIDGE by Sir Ernest George's which was finished in 1921. Happily surviving, however, is his sons' charming bridge across the Serpentine in Hyde Park (1826) from which there is one of London's most lovely views to Westminster Abbey and the Palace of Westminster.

Three later nineteenth-century bridges also still survive: Thomas Page's cast-iron WESTMINSTER BRIDGE (1854–62), the famous TOWER BRIDGE (1886–94), and BLACKFRIARS BRIDGE (rebuilt, 1865–69). Central London's other three main road bridges are all relatively modern, VAUXHALL BRIDGE (1906), SOUTHWARK BRIDGE (1921) and LAMBETH BRIDGE (1929–32).

2. GWYDYR HOUSE, Whitehall is the only one of these eighteenth-century houses which survives. The design has been attributed to John Marquand.

3. HENRY VIII'S WINE CELLAR may be seen on Saturday afternoons between Easter and the middle of December by application to the Secretary (Dept. A.3/8), Ministry of Public Building and Works, Lambeth Bridge House, S.E.1.

CHAPTER 9 *(Pages 113–23)*

1. Hawksmoor's three masterpieces in the East End, ST GEORGE IN THE EAST, Cannon Street Road (1715–23), CHRIST CHURCH SPITALFIELDS, Commercial Street (1714–29), and ST ANNE LIMEHOUSE (1712–24) were all badly damaged in the War,

Christ Church, Spitalfields.

but it is still possible to appreciate their stupendous grandeur, and to understand how this grandeur would have been emphasised when the surrounding buildings were so much lower. ST ALPHEGE's, Greenwich High Road (1712–14) was also severely damaged in the War but has been carefully restored. It stands on the site where, according to tradition, Alphege, Archbishop of Canterbury, was murdered by the Danes in 1012. After Vanbrugh's death in 1726, the church was finished and the steeple added by John James. ST GEORGE's, Bloomsbury Way (1720–30), now the church of London University, shows Hawksmoor at his grandest and best. The remarkable stepped spire, based on Pliny's description of the tomb of Mausolus at Halicarnassus, bears on top of its obelisk a statue of George I as St George, a rather illogical canonisation which was, in Walpole's opinion, 'a masterstroke of absurdity'. This church, which can be seen in the background of Hogarth's 'Gin Lane', came in for a good deal of contempt in the years following its completion, the *Critical Review of the Buildings in London* (1734) referring to it as 'ridiculous and absurd even to a proverb'. ST MARY WOOLNOTH, Lombard Street (1716–27) has been described by Nikolaus Pevsner as 'the most original church exterior in the City of London'. On Sundays the Swiss Protestant Church holds services here in German. (The Swiss Church's services in French are held in their own church in Endell Street, High Holborn.)

2. ST MARY-LE-STRAND (1714–17) was the first of the 'Fifty New Churches' of Queen Anne's Act, and, with St Martin-in-the-Fields, is generally considered to be James Gibbs's masterpiece.

3. Although St Mary-le-Strand always enjoyed its splendidly open position, ST MARTIN-IN-THE-FIELDS (1722–26) came into its own only on the creation of Trafalgar Square. Architects find fault with the combination of porticoed temple front and tall spire; but the interior, based on Wren's St James's Piccadilly, is a splendid one. A smaller church by Gibbs, ST PETER's VERE STREET (1723–24), designed as the chapel for Cavendish Square, has been described by Sir John Summerson as 'a miniature forecast of St Martin-in-the-Fields, exquisitely carried out'.

4. Thomas Archer solved the problem of tower and portico at ST PAUL's, Deptford

High Street (1712–30) by making his tower circular, giving it a semi-circular projection at the west end, and placing a semi-circular portico of columns beneath the projection. The result, in Pevsner's opinion, is 'one of the most moving eighteenth-century churches in London: large, sombre, and virile'. ST JOHN's, Smith Square, Westminster (1714–28) was known as the footstool church because Queen Anne was said to have shown Archer how she wished it built by kicking a four-legged stool upside down. A fine example of English baroque, it was burned out in the War, but after having remained a ruin for twenty-five years it is being repaired at last through the endeavours of the Friends of St John's.

5. St Olave's was demolished in 1926; but ST GILES-IN-THE-FIELDS, St Giles's High Street (1731–34) still survives amidst the huge new buildings of the area. The inside was extremely well restored in 1953.

6. John James's portico of immense free-standing columns at ST GEORGE's HANOVER SQUARE (1712–25) has always been much admired. In 1734 James Ralph wrote 'that the view down George Street, from the upper side of the Square, is one of the most entertaining in the whole city: the sides of the Square, the area in the middle, the breaks of building that form the entrance of the vista, the vista itself, but, above all, the beautiful projection of the portico of St George's Church are all circumstances that unite in beauty, and make the scene perfect'.

7. Typical of the original houses here is 24 HANOVER SQUARE.

8. The most attractive of the remaining eighteenth-century houses in GROSVENOR SQUARE are numbers 8, 9, 12, and 38.

9. The architect of the GROSVENOR CHAPEL, South Audley Street (c.1730) was probably its builder, Benjamin Timbrell.

10. George Dance's original MANSION HOUSE (1739–53) included a huge two-storeyed superstructure which was removed in 1842. At the top of the building now are the Lord Mayor's private apartments. The magnificent state-rooms beneath, including the 90 foot long Egyptian Hall, the Salon, Conference Room, Ball Room and Drawing Rooms, are shown on Saturday afternoons to visitors who apply in writing to the Lord Mayor's secretary.

The Egyptian Hall, Mansion House.

11. The first BANK OF ENGLAND, Threadneedle Street, was little more than a large town house. Extended by Sir Robert Taylor in 1765 and again between 1782–88, it was rebuilt with great skill and originality by Sir John Soane from 1788–1808; but its subsequent reconstruction in 1921–37 entirely destroyed its original character. Visitors are not permitted beyond the entrance hall.

12. The interior of the HORSE GUARDS Whitehall (1750–58) – in which there are, in fact, few rooms of any interest – is not open to the public. In front of it two mounted troopers of the Household Cavalry are posted each day in their exotic uniforms from 10 to 4. At 11 on weekdays and 10 on Sundays spectators can watch the Changing of the Guard, and a dismounted inspection at 4.

Pedestrians – but not cars – may cross through the arch beneath the clock tower into Horse Guards Parade when in early June (on the Queen's official birthday)

the Brigade of Guards and the Household Cavalry Troop the Colour before the Queen. Applications for tickets may be made to the Brigade Major, H.Q. Household Division, Horse Guards, Whitehall, S.W.1.

13. The façade of SPENCER HOUSE, 27 St James's Place (1756–66) remains much as Vardy left it, although the staircase was remodelled by Sir Robert Taylor (c.1772), and some rooms on the ground floor were altered by Henry Holland (1785). It is now occupied as offices.

14. The lovely façade of James Stuart's LICHFIELD HOUSE, 15 ST JAMES'S SQUARE (1763–66) is also still largely untouched. A former house on the site was the home of the Duchess of Richmond who sat as model for the figure of Britannia on the penny. The interior, remodelled by Samuel Wyatt (c. 1791), is, like that of Spencer House, now occupied as offices. Other good eighteenth-century houses in St James's Square are No. 5 by Matthew Brettingham, (1748–51) though stone faced and given its second floor in 1854; no. 13 probably also by Brettingham (c. 1740); no. 10 by Henry Flitcroft (1734) – this is Chatham House, which has the unusual distinction of having housed three prime ministers, Pitt the elder, Derby, and Gladstone – and no. 20 by Robert Adam (1775–89). No. 4 was built about 1676 and remodelled after a fire in 1725. The remodelling has been attributed to both Hawksmoor and Leoni, but it has now been established by the editors of the *Survey of London* (vol. xxix, pt. 1) and by H. M. Colvin that it is, in fact, by Edward Shepherd who built Shepherd Market in 1735 on the site of the old fairground in Mayfair. No. 16, the East India and Sports Club's palazzo (Charles Lee, 1865) looks as though it has wandered over from Pall Mall.

15. CAMBRIDGE HOUSE, 74 PICCADILLY (1756–60) was designed by Matthew Brettingham for Lord Egremont. The London house of Lord Palmerston from 1855 until 1865 it is now the Naval and Military Club.

16. 44 BERKELEY SQUARE (1742–44), designed for Lady Isabella Finch by William Kent, has claims to being considered the 'finest terrace house in London'. Professor Pevsner has unequivocally termed both its staircase and drawing room as the 'grandest' in any of the capital's eighteenth-century private houses.

17. All of the Middlesex Hospital (James Paine, 1755–75) and most of the FOUNDLING HOSPITAL (Theodore Jacobsen, 1742–52) were demolished in 1928. The offices of the Foundling Hospital have, however, been incorporated into the Hospital's new building in Brunswick Square and contain a scale model of the original building as well as Hogarth's moving and acutely perceptive portrait of the Hospital's great founder, the generous, stout-hearted old sea captain, Thomas Coram. There are several other fine portraits in the Picture Gallery and in the Court Room. The staff will show these rooms to visitors if convenient on Mondays and Fridays between 10 and 12 and 2 and 4.

18. Bessborough House is now MANRESA HOUSE, Roehampton Lane. Designed by Sir William Chambers before 1767 it was one of Roehampton's several fine Georgian country houses.

19. The ROYAL BOTANICAL GARDENS, covering 280 beautiful acres at Kew, were started by George III's grandmother, Queen Caroline. Of the group of royal residences which once stood in or near the Gardens only KEW PALACE, the smallest of the royal palaces, now survives. It was formerly known as the Dutch House, having been rebuilt in the early seventeenth-century by a merchant from the Low Countries in the style favoured by his countrymen. Bought by George III as a home for the older of the fifteen royal children, it was occupied from 1802 until 1818 by their parents, whose taste for a life of quiet domesticity was well-known. It is now shown to the public as far as possible as it was during those years. Sir William Chambers's orangery and pagoda are fine examples of his work. The Gardens are open every day (except Christmas Day) from 10 to 8 in the summer and from 10 to sunset in winter. The Palace is open on weekdays from April to September from 11 to 6; on Sundays from 1 to 6.

20. Melbourne House (1770–74) passed into the hands of the Duke of York and Albany in 1791 and thereafter became known as York House. In 1802 it was sold to Alexander Copland, a young builder, who, with the help of Henry Holland, converted it into the apartments of ALBANY and built two long blocks of chambers on each side of the garden. These blocks were separated – they still are separated – by a paved and covered walk leading from the

Piccadilly entrance into Burlington Gardens. The Burlington Gardens lodges remain, though the new entrance on the Piccadilly front, and the shops which Holland built on either side of it, have disappeared. Albany's residents have always included a number of most distinguished names.

21. SOMERSET HOUSE (1776–86) is, apart from Albany, the only one of Chambers's important London buildings to have survived. The east wing was added by Sir Robert Smirke (1828–34) and the west wing by Sir James Pennethorne (1852–56).

The register of births, marriages and deaths in the north wing, and the wills and testaments in the Probate and Divorce Registry in the south wing may be consulted from Mondays to Fridays from 10 to 4.

22. The simple and graceful ADMIRALTY SCREEN was built to Robert Adam's design between 1759 and 1761. The ADMIRALTY behind it (Thomas Ripley, 1723–26) is a far less successful building.

23. Only remnants of the Adams' ADELPHI (1768–72) now remain. At 8 John Adam Street, however, the ROYAL SOCIETY OF ARTS (1772–74) is a good example of Robert Adam's work. The hall of the

The staircase, Home House.

society may be seen on weekdays (when not in use) by application after 9.30.

24. Adam interiors are not easily to be seen in central London, though there is an exquisite one at Home House, 20 Portman Square, built in the 1770's for the Countess of Home and presented by a subsequent owner, Samuel Courtauld, to the University of London for use as the COURTAULD INSTITUTE OF ART. Its rooms are open to the public in vacation from Monday to Friday from 10 to 5, and in term time on Saturdays from 10 to 1. They are closed in August and for ten days at Easter and Christmas.

Other Adam interiors within easy reach of central London are at SYON HOUSE, Brentford, KENWOOD HOUSE, Hampstead, and OSTERLEY PARK HOUSE on which Robert Adam, beginning in 1767, was to work for nineteen years. All these houses are open to the public. Syon House from 22 March to 30 June (Wednesdays to Saturdays, and Bank Holiday Sundays and Mondays) and 1 July to 1 October (Wednesdays to Sundays and August Bank Holiday Monday) from 1 to 5; Kenwood House (Iveagh Bequest) every weekday (except Good Friday, Christmas Eve, and Christmas Day) from 10 to 7 and every Sunday from 2 to 7, closing at 6 or dusk in winter; and Osterley Park House every day (except Mondays, Good Friday and Christmas Day) from 2 to 6 from April to September and from 12 to 4 from October to March.

25. ALL HALLOWS LONDON WALL (rebuilt 1765–67) has been restored to George Dance's charming design after severe war damage.

26 Some of the stones from Newgate Prison – burned out during the Gordon Riots of 1780 and finally demolished in 1902 – were used for the construction of the Edwardian baroque CENTRAL CRIMINAL COURT, Old Bailey (1902–07). Parties are conducted round the building at 11 on Saturdays, and on other weekdays when the court is not sitting at 11 and 3. When the courts *are* sitting the public is admitted into the public galleries by the Newgate Street entrance at 10.15 and 1.45 except in August. A reminder that a prison once stood here is provided – on the first two days of each session – by the judges carrying posies of flowers and by the floor being strewn with herbs which were necessary once to guard against the foul fumes that caused gaol fever. A few remnants of the interior of the prison are preserved, with many other grisly relics, at Madame Tussaud's waxworks museum in Marylebone Road.

27. BROOKS'S CLUB, 60 St James's Street (1777–78), the leading Whig club in the days of Charles James Fox, is one of several interesting eighteenth-century and early nineteenth-century buildings worth pausing to look at in St James's. Other clubs here are WHITE'S, No. 37 (1787–88, probably by James Wyatt, altered and given bow windows in 1811, and provided with a new façade in 1852); BOODLE'S, No. 28 (1775 by John Crunden); the CARLTON, Nos. 69–70 (1826–27 by Thomas Hopper); the DEVONSHIRE CLUB, No. 50 (the successor to Crockford's, designed by Benjamin Dean Wyatt in 1827). The CONSERVATIVE CLUB No. 74 (by George Basevi and Sydney Smirke) is Palladian in style, early Victorian (1843–45) in date.

Excellent examples of eighteenth- and early nineteenth-century shop fronts and interiors are at No. 3, Berry Bros. and Rudd, wine merchants, and at No. 6, Lock and Son, hatters.

28. In later generations the Duke of Manchester's house became Hertford House, the London residence of the Marquesses of Hertford. It was altered and enlarged by Sir Richard Wallace, illegitimate son and heir of the 4th Marquess, in 1872; and in 1897 Lady Wallace presented the incomparable collection of works of art it contained to the nation.

The WALLACE COLLECTION was started by the first Marquess, an ambassador in Paris and by his son, an ambassador in Berlin and Vienna. But it was the third Marquess, a close friend of George IV – and the original of both Lord Steyne in *Vanity Fair* and of Lord Monmouth in *Coningsby* – who was able to ensure its eventual splendour. For this Marquess married a girl who was claimed as a daughter by the Duke of Queensberry and George Selwyn, both of whom, disregarding the other's claim, left her a fortune. Her son, who lived most of his life in Paris, was accordingly able to indulge his passion for French art of the eighteenth-century. This collection is now the pride of the museum and is here displayed, indeed, in as much profusion as could be found under one roof even in France itself. The armour, for which the Collection is also famous, and the medieval and renaissance works, were assembled by Sir Richard Wallace.

The Collection is open (except on Good Friday, Christmas Eve and Christmas Day) on weekdays from 10 to 5 and on Sundays from 2 to 5.

29. Typical of James Burton's houses are Nos. 18–27 BLOOMSBURY SQUARE (1800–14). They may be compared with those in Bedford Row built by Burton's flamboyant predecessor, Nicholas Barbon, just over a hundred years earlier.

CHAPTER 10 *(Pages 125–40)*

1. Although Carlton House was completely demolished the screen of columns in front of its façade was used for the portico of the National Gallery (see p. 131 and note 4 below). Several of its doors, parquet floors, fireplaces and marble groups were used by Sir Jeffry Wyatville in his reconstruction of Windsor Castle and by Nash at Buckingham Palace.

2. Le Sueur's MONUMENT TO CHARLES I (1633), one of the most spirited of London's monuments, stands on the spot where once stood the original Charing Cross, demolished in 1647. The present CHARING CROSS, outside the courtyard of the railway station, is a Victorian replica of the last of the stone crosses which Edward I set up to mark the resting places of the funeral

The Nelson Column.

cortège which accompanied the body of his Queen, Eleanor, from Lincolnshire to Westminster Abbey in 1291.

3. The NELSON COLUMN was erected between 1839 and 1842. The column itself is by William Railton, the statue by E. H. Baily, the reliefs at the base by John Ternouth and W. F. Woodington, the lions by Sir Edwin Landseer. One reason why it was so very high – 185 feet, including the 17 feet of Lord Nelson – is that its sponsors were anxious that it should rise above Benjamin Dean Wyatt's DUKE OF YORK COLUMN (1831–34).

This column – which has a statue of the Duke (an admirable Commander-in-Chief for all his faults) by Sir Richard Westmacott at the top – towers above the steps in Waterloo Place. It is 124 feet from base to head, of a sufficient height, so it was suggested, to keep the Duke – whose debts amounted to rather more than £2,000,000 at his death – out of the way of his creditors. The cost of the memorial was met largely by stopping one day's pay from every soldier in the Army, in which, hitherto, the Duke had been a popular figure.

4. The NATIONAL GALLERY, Trafalgar Square, houses one of the largest and most catholic collections in the world. Only about 1,500 paintings of its 4,500 are on display; but any picture it possesses which is not to be found on the walls can usually be seen by writing for permission to the Keeper. The rest are on public view (except on Good Friday, Christmas Eve and Christmas Day) from 10 to 6 on weekdays (to 9 on Tuesdays and Thursdays in the summer) and 2 to 6 on Sundays. There are lectures on Tuesdays, Wednesdays and Thursdays at 1, on Tuesdays in summer at 6, and on Saturdays at 2.30. Adjoining the National Gallery, in St Martin's Place, is the NATIONAL PORTRAIT GALLERY (Ewan Christian and Colling, 1890–95, and the Duveen Wing, 1933, by Sir Robert Allison and J. G. West). The National Portrait Gallery has in fact 'to do with history rather than with art,' so a former Director, David Piper has said. 'That it possesses some absolutely stunning pictures is almost incidental to its purposes; it has equally gladly some absolutely appalling ones, as far as artistic quality is concerned. Seek out for example the water-colour of Jane Austen by her sister Cassandra, a daub, but one of the Gallery's dearest treasures. But contrast on the other hand Holbein's

tremendous cartoon of Henry VIII, wherein art and history fuse in inextricable magic.' Here also, as at the National Gallery, those pictures not on display will be shown on request (except on Good Friday, Christmas Eve and Christmas Day) from Monday to Friday from 10 to 5, on Saturdays from 10 to 6, on Sundays and Boxing Day from 2 to 6. On Saturdays from October to March there are lectures at 3.15.

5. The miscellaneous items stored by the early BRITISH MUSEUM, Great Russell Street (1823–52 with Edwardian additions) have eventually expanded into an enormous collection of Egyptian, Greek, Roman, Oriental and British antiquities, of manuscripts and printed books, coins and medals, prints and drawings, postage stamps, primitive art, Benin bronzes and Aztec relics, the Sutton Hoo ship-burial and the Ilbert collection of clocks, together with such a varied assembly of other objects that a lifetime could be spent in their examination. The collections are constantly growing – the number of books added each year, because a copy of every book published in Britain has to be deposited with the Museum, entails alone an extra mile of shelving.

Far more than can be glanced at in a day's visit is open to the public on weekdays (except Good Friday and Christmas Day) from 10 to 5 and from 2.30 to 6 on Sundays. But to use the Reading Room – made in 1854–57 by roofing in, with a huge dome, the central courtyard of Montague House – a ticket is necessary. These are supplied free to those who can give both an acceptable reason for wanting one and a letter of recommendation from a person of recognised position. Tickets are also necessary for admission to the Students' Rooms of the Departments of Manuscripts and of Prints and Drawings. Tickets are not necessary for the latter, however, for those who subscribe (two guineas a year is the minimum subscription) to the National Art Collections Fund. There are lecture tours at 11.30 and 3.

Those depressed or intimidated by the vastness of the British Museum and the size and multiformity of its collections can be recommended to visit the charming, small SIR JOHN SOANE'S MUSEUM at 13 Lincoln's Inn Fields. This is the house which Soane designed for himself in 1812 and where he lived until his death in 1837. As well as his furniture and books and his imposing portrait by Lawrence,

the Museum contains a delightful mixture of antique marbles, bronzes, busts, Greek vases, architectural models, Christopher Wren's watch, Napoleon's pistol, the sarcophagus of Seti I, King of Egypt in about 1370 B.C. (bought by Soane for £2,000 after the British Museum had declined it), as well as some beautiful pictures by Canaletto, Piranesi, Giulio Clovio, Turner and Clérisseau, the four scenes of William Hogarth's 'The Election' and the eight of his 'Rake's Progress'.

The Museum is open from Tuesday to Saturday, from 10 to 5, except in August. There are lecture tours on Saturday at 2.30. Architectural books, drawings and models not on display may be inspected on application to the Curator.

6. Neither the interior of BUCKINGHAM PALACE nor the forty acres of its private garden is open to the public, whether the Queen is in residence or not: her presence is indicated by the Royal Standard flying at the masthead. The former private chapel, however, has been converted into the QUEEN'S GALLERY and here exhibitions are held of paintings, drawings, furniture, works of art and curiosities from the royal collection. The Gallery, which is approached from Buckingham Palace Road, is open from 11 to 5 from Tuesdays to Saturday and from 2 to 5 on Sundays. Further down Buckingham Palace Road are the ROYAL MEWS where the royal horses are stabled and the royal coaches – including George III's coach designed for him by Sir William Chambers and painted by Cipriani – are kept. The Mews are open on Wednesdays and Thursdays except during Ascot week, from 2 to 4.

In the forecourt of the Palace, patrolled by sentries of the Brigade of Guards in full dress uniform, the Changing of the Guard takes place at 11.30 each morning.

7. The MARBLE ARCH (1828) of marble from Seravezza, seems to have been modelled by Nash on the Arch of Constantine at Rome. The reliefs on the south side are by E. H. Baily, who was responsible for the statue of Nelson in Trafalgar Square; and those on the north are by Sir Richard Westmacott, who made the Duke of York statue at the top of the column in Waterloo Place.

Decimus Burton's Corinthian arch at Hyde Park Corner, known as the CONSTITUTION ARCH (1828), or sometimes as the WELLINGTON ARCH, was originally crowned with a statue of the Duke of Wellington. This was replaced in 1912 with the present bronze figure of Peace in a four-horse chariot by Adrian Jones. Burton's Ionic HYDE PARK CORNER SCREEN (1825) is on the pattern of Robert Adam's screen at Syon House.

8. The heavy Edwardian Roman ADMIRALTY ARCH at the eastern end of The Mall was built in 1911 by Sir Aston Webb as part of a memorial to Queen Victoria, more effectively realised by the VICTORIA MEMORIAL, the flamboyant and impressive concoction which Sir Thomas Brock made out of 2,300 tons of white marble and placed in front of the courtyard of Buckingham Palace.

9. Smirke's building was demolished when the present complex of Victorian and Edwardian GENERAL POST OFFICE buildings (1870–1911) made them redundant. The Chief Office, approached from King Edward Street, is open all day and night. The 6½-mile-long underground Post Office Railway (finished in 1908) which carries 40,000 mailbags a day and runs between Whitechapel and Paddington via Liverpool Street Station, is shown to visitors. Applications to see it, the postal museum, and the work of the Post Office and the Central Telegraph Office, should be addressed to the Regional Director, London Postal Region, E.C.1. Three weeks' notice is required. Children are not admitted.

10. The ROYAL MINT, Royal Mint Street (1808–11, enlarged 1882) is shortly to be rebuilt. Visitors may watch the manufacture of coins and see the coin museum by application to the Deputy Master, giving six weeks' notice.

11. The Millbank Penitentiary (1812–21) was demolished in 1890 and the TATE GALLERY (1897) was built on its site. Here are collected not only the main national collection of British painting from 1500, but also modern continental and American paintings, and modern sculpture. It is open on weekdays (except Good Friday, Christmas Eve and Christmas Day) from 10 to 6 and on Sundays and Boxing Day from 2 to 6. There are lecture tours on Tuesdays, Thursdays and Saturdays at 3.

12. James Lewis's Bedlam (1812–15) now houses the IMPERIAL WAR MUSEUM, Lambeth Road. Its portico and dome

were added by Sydney Smirke in 1846, and its wings later demolished. The Museum contains a unique collection of material and equipment, relics, models, paintings, books, maps, photographs and films relating to all three armed services of the British Commonwealth since 1914. It is open (except on Good Friday and Christmas Day) on weekdays from 10 to 6 and on Sundays from 2 to 6. Films from the Museum's archives are shown from Mondays to Fridays at 12 and on Saturdays and Sundays at 2.45.

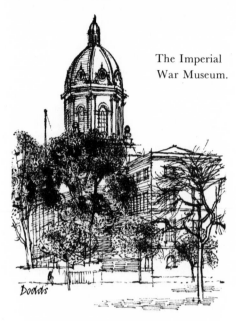

The Imperial War Museum.

13. The enormous CUSTOM HOUSE, Lower Thames Street (designed by David Laing, 1813–17), occupies a site used for its present purpose since the fourteenth century. The central part of the riverside front of the building, which can be seen from London Bridge, was remodelled by Sir Robert Smirke between 1825 and 1826.

14. The Brethren of the Corporation of Trinity House, an association of English mariners, received their first charter from Henry VIII in 1514. Entrusted by Henry with the direction of the naval dockyard at Deptford, they soon acquired authority to erect beacons and later to build and maintain lighthouses, lightships and buoys, to act as nautical assessors and to supervise the work of pilots. Originally based in Deptford, their headquarters were transferred

to London in the eighteenth century and the charming, elegant small TRINITY HOUSE, Trinity Square, was built for them between 1793 and 1795 from designs by Samuel Wyatt. Severely damaged in the War it has been well restored. Dwarfed by the massive Edwardian building of the Port of London Authority (Sir Edwin Cooper, 1912–22), Trinity House is shown on Saturday afternoons at 2.30 to parties of visitors who make previous application to the Secretary.

15. The most distinguished and interesting of the early nineteenth-century churches that survive are ST PANCRAS PARISH CHURCH, Woburn Place, built at a cost of £70,000

St Peter's, Regent Square.

between 1819 and 1822 and designed by William Inwood, a surveyor, and his son Henry who had studied architecture in Greece; the Inwoods' three other churches in the same parish – ALL SAINTS, Camden Street, Camden Town (1822–24), ST PETER'S, Regent Square (1824–26) and the Gothic ST MARY'S, Eversholt Street, Somers Town (1824–27); three churches by Sir John Soane – ST PETER'S, Liverpool Grove, Walworth (1823–25), HOLY TRINITY, Marylebone (1824–28), and ST JOHN'S, Cambridge Heath Road, Bethnal Green (1824–28); Sir Robert Smirke's ST MARY'S, Wyndham Place, Marylebone (1823–24); James Savage's ST LUKE'S, Sydney Street, Chelsea (1820–24), the earliest stone-vaulted church of the Gothic Revival, and the same architect's ST JAMES'S, Thurland Road, Bermondsey (1827–29); three Gothic

churches by Charles Barry in Islington: ST JOHN THE EVANGELIST, Holloway Road, ST PAUL, Ball's Pond, Essex Road, and HOLY TRINITY, Cloudesley Square, all dating from 1827–28; and four churches with Greek porticoes built between 1822 and 1824 in the by now extensive parish of Lambeth – ST MATTHEW'S, Brixton, ST MARK'S, Kennington, ST LUKE'S, West Norwood, and ST JOHN'S, Waterloo Road. Better known than any of these, however, because of its fashionable associations is HOLY TRINITY, Brompton Road (1826–29, by T. L. Donaldson, with a new chancel by Sir Arthur Blomfield). Numerous nonconformist chapels were also built at this time, and, although most have disappeared the QUAKER MEETING-HOUSES in Highshore Street, Peckham (1826) and in Yoakley Road, Stoke Newington (1828) are good examples of the simplicity advocated by John Wesley for the Methodist Chapel builder.

16. Smirke's Covent Garden Theatre was the second to have been built on the site. The first, built in 1732, was burned down in 1808, as Smirke's building was to be in 1856. The present massive ROYAL OPERA HOUSE (1856–58) is by Edward M. Barry who in 1859 was also to design the Floral Hall nearby.

17. Benjamin Dean Wyatt's Drury Lane Theatre (1811–12) still survives. It is the fourth to have been built here and is

The Royal Opera House.

considered by Professor Pevsner to be still the finest theatre building in London. The Ionic colonnade in Russell Street was added in 1832 and the auditorium reconstructed in 1922. The vestibule, rotunda and staircases are the only remaining interior parts of a Georgian theatre surviving in London. The first theatre, where Nell Gwyn is supposed to have been an orange-seller, was built in 1663 and rebuilt, probably by Wren, after a fire, in 1674. Restored in 1775, it was rebuilt by Henry Holland for Sheridan in 1791–94. It was while watching this building being destroyed by flames in 1809 that Sheridan was heard to observe, 'Surely a gentleman may warm his hands at his own fireside.'

18. Nash's portico on the THEATRE ROYAL, Haymarket still closes the vista down Charles II Street from St James's Square, but the interior of the theatre was rebuilt in 1905.

19. Smirke's United Service Club was replaced in the 1850s by Nelson and Innes's Junior United Service Club, and in the 1950s this gave way in its turn to the offices of the United Kingdom Atomic Energy Authority. Wilkins's University Club was replaced by Sir Reginald Blomfield's building in 1906. But Nash's UNITED SERVICE CLUB, 116–19 Pall Mall, still survives. It was remodelled in 1858 by Decimus Burton. All the other Pall Mall clubs, except those demolished since the Second World War, remain much as their architects left them, though the top storey of the ATHENAEUM (1828–30) was added in 1899.

20. LANCASTER HOUSE, Stable Yard, (formerly known as York House, then as Stafford House), was given its present name by the first Viscount Leverhulme who presented the Crown lease to the nation. Until 1941 it housed the exhibits of the London Museum, but it is now used for international conferences, receptions and banquets. When not needed for such purposes its exotic interior is open to the public from 2 to 6, on Saturdays, Sundays and Bank Holidays, from Easter to mid-December.

21. Apsley House, 149 Piccadilly (Hyde Park Corner) was originally built in the 1770s for Henry Bathurst, Lord Apsley, by the Adam Brothers. It was reconstructed

and enlarged in 1829 for the Duke of Wellington by Benjamin Dean Wyatt who added the big portico and covered the brick walls with Bath stone. The seventh Duke, whose family retains private apartments in the house, gave it to the nation in 1947, and five years later it was opened as the WELLINGTON MUSEUM. It contains a marvellous collection of Wellingtoniana, and of works of art that came his way in his long career, including numerous fine paintings, breathtaking services of silver and porcelain, foreign orders and a gigantic statue of the naked Napoleon by Antonio Canova (1810) and a more modest bust of the Duke himself by Joseph Nollekens (1813).

Napoleon by Canova.

The Museum is open (except on Good Friday and Christmas Day) on weekdays from 10 to 6 and on Sundays from 2.30 to 6.

22. CLARENCE HOUSE, Stable Yard Gate, as the home of the Queen Mother, is not open to the public. It derives its name from George IV's brother, the Duke of Clarence, for whom it was built in 1825 by Nash.

23. MARBLE HILL HOUSE, Richmond Road, Twickenham, was built for Henrietta Howard, mistress of George II, by Roger Morris under the general direction of Lord Islay and Lord Herbert between 1728 and 1729. It was later the home of another royal favourite, Mrs Fitzherbert, the secret wife of George IV. Recently – and very sympathetically – restored, it is a particularly fine example of the English Palladian School. It is open on weekdays, except Mondays, from 10 to 6 from April to September, from 10 to 5 from March to October, and from 10 to 4 from November to February; on Sundays from 2.

Marble Hill House.

24. Horace Walpole's 'little Gothic castle', STRAWBERRY HILL (1748–76), Waldegrave Road, Twickenham, is now St Mary's College. It stands close to the road so that its 'plaything' exterior can be enjoyed without disturbing the students. To see the interior, however, visitors must apply to the Principal's secretary in writing.

25. Only the gateway and one or two other fragments remain of the sumptuous palace at Richmond which Henry VII built and in which his granddaughter, Queen Elizabeth, died. But the great expanse of its Tudor chase, still stocked with herds of the fallow and red deer originally introduced into it by Charles

I, survives as RICHMOND PARK. Around the Park and on Richmond Hill are many beautiful houses dating from the time when the Prince and Princess of Wales held court at Richmond Lodge in the later years of the reign of George I.

26. HAM HOUSE, Petersham, built in 1610 for Sir Thomas Vavasour was much altered at later periods of the seventeenth-century, in particular by Charles II's minister, the Duke of Lauderdale, and his formidable Duchess of whom two marvellous portraits by Sir Peter Lely hang in the Round Gallery. The house, whose interior is perhaps the most evocative of the Lauderdale's time of any in the country, contains a fine collection of Stuart furniture. It is open every day (except Mondays, Good Friday and Christmas Day) from April to September from 2 to 6, and from October to March from 12 to 4.

27. Sir Hans Sloane's house, Beaufort House, has now disappeared – Beaufort Street, Chelsea, crosses the site – but a gateway built there by Inigo Jones in 1621 was removed in 1736 to the gardens, which were created by William Kent around Lord Burlington's exquisite country villa at Chiswick, CHISWICK HOUSE (1725–29). It is open in April from 10.30 to 5, from May to September from 10.30 to 7, and from October to March (except on Mondays and Tuesdays) from 10.30 to 4.

CHAPTER II *(Pages 143–79)*

1. At the top of THE MONUMENT, Monument Street and Fish Street Hill, designed by Wren and his friend, Robert Hooke, there is an urn in which stands a gilt ball surrounded by flames. Wren would have preferred a statue of Charles II, but Hooke had his way. The King, however, is represented on the west side of the pedestal in a relief by C. G. Cibber which depicts him, in Roman dress, encouraging his people to rebuild their capital city. The energetic visitor may climb to the platform at the top on weekdays from 9 to 6 (from 9 to 4 in the winter) and on Sundays in the summer from 2 to 6.

2. After George II's death at KENSINGTON PALACE in 1760, it ceased to be a main royal residence, though William III and Mary II and Queen Anne all died here and Queen Victoria, born here in 1819, lived in the Palace until that well-remembered

morning in 1837 when she was roused from her bed to receive the news of her accession. The furniture, toys and oddments in her bedroom have been assembled to provide a moving evocation of her childhood.

The apartments on the first floor of the Palace are open (except on Good Friday, Christmas Eve and Christmas Day) on weekdays in the summer from 10 to 6, and in winter from 10 to 4; on Sundays from 2.

The Orangery, Kensington Palace.

The ground floor and basement are at present the home of the LONDON MUSEUM which illustrates the history of London and its social life from Roman times. Until the collection is moved, together with the Guildhall Museum, to its larger permanent home in the City only part of it can be displayed; but objects not on view may be seen on application to the Director. Times of admission are the same as those for the State Apartments.

3. Prime Ministers have lived at No. 10 DOWNING STREET since the house was offered to Sir Robert Walpole by George II in 1732. Rebuilt in 1764–66, it has been redesigned internally several times since,

and is, in fact, a far larger and grander house than its modest front suggests. The street owes its name to Sir George Downing, a Secretary to the Treasury, who built the first houses in it.

4. The modest late seventeenth-century house – DR JOHNSON'S HOUSE – on the west side of Gough Square, Fleet Street, contains various relics of the great man who lived here from 1748 to 1759. In the attic he compiled his famous dictionary helped by six amanuenses – 'and let it be remembered by the natives of North Britain, to whom he is supposed to have been hostile,' the Scottish James Boswell recorded triumphantly, 'that five of [these amanuenses] were of that country'. The house is open on weekdays (except Bank Holidays) from 10.30 to 5 in summer and from 10.30 to 4 in winter.

Houses of other London writers and artists which are also open to visitors are:

HOGARTH'S HOUSE, Great West Road, Chiswick (next door to the Hogarth Laundry). In Hogarth's time a 'little country box by the Thames' it is now surrounded by factories, flats and the lorry-filled arterial road. It contains very little furniture – none of Hogarth's – but numerous prints. It is open on weekdays from 11 to 4 in winter, and from 11 to 6 in summer.

THE DICKENS HOUSE, 48 Doughty Street. This is the house where Dickens lived from 1837 to 1839 during the early years of his fame, where the end of *Pickwick Papers, Oliver Twist,* and *Nicholas Nickleby* were written, and where his adored sister-in-law Mary Hogarth died in his arms. Dickens rented it for £80 a year at a time when Doughty Street was 'a broad, airy, wholesome street; none of your common thoroughfares, to be rattled through by vulgar cabs and earth-shaking Pickford vans, but a self-included property, with a gate at each end, and a lodge with a porter in a gold-laced hat, and the Doughty Arms on the buttons of his mulberry-coloured coat'. The house was not bought by the Dickens Fellowship until 1924 after many other owners had lived in it, so it does not convey any impression of Dickens's presence. It does, however, contain an interesting collection of Dickensiana. It is open on weekdays, except Bank Holidays, from 10 to 12.30 and from 2 to 5.

CARLYLE'S HOUSE, 24 Cheyne Row, Chelsea. Carlyle lived here for forty-seven years until his death in 1881 and it is very much like it was when he and Jane Welsh entertained their friends and ate their strange meals, worried about their health and got angry with their maid.

Thomas Carlyle's kitchen stove.

Their furniture is here, their books and photographs, his wide-brimmed hat on its peg by the garden door, his writing-table in the sound-proofed room in the attic – too hot for him in summer, too cold in winter – all sorts of articles which suddenly bring them both, most movingly, to life: Carlyle's clay pipes, tobacco-box and smoking-cap, Jane's beech-wood sofa (bought second-hand in 1835) her sewing-case and beadwork footstool. It is open on weekdays, except Tuesdays, from 10 to 1 and in the afternoons (also Sunday afternoons) from 2 to 6, or dusk.

KEATS HOUSE, Wentworth Place, Keats Grove, Hampstead. This house, built in 1815, was John Keats's home from 1818 until 1820, the year of his death in Rome. It contains several of his annotated books, letters and other relics. It can be seen on weekdays from 10 to 6.

Two other interesting London houses open to the public are:

LEIGHTON HOUSE, 12 Holland Park Road, the exotic Victorian home built in 1866 by Lord Leighton, the immensely successful painter and sculptor who was elected President of the Royal Academy in 1878; and WESLEY'S HOUSE, 47 City Road, the far more modest home (c. 1770) of the founder of Methodism who died in the bedroom here in 1791. Leighton House is open on weekdays

except Bank Holidays from 11 to 5, and Wesley's House on weekdays from 10 to 1 and from 2 to 4.

5. The watermen raced for Doggett's Coat and Badge, a livery coat of orange cloth and a silver badge of the House of Hanover. Thomas Doggett, manager of Drury Lane Theatre, provided a sum in his will for the continuation of this annual race for all time in celebration of the coming of the Hanoverians to the English throne. The race is still held each year along a course of $4\frac{1}{2}$ miles from London Bridge to Chelsea.

6. Very badly damaged in the War what remains of HOLLAND HOUSE may be seen in Holland Park. Formerly a large and handsome Jacobean mansion, all that is now left is the east wing of about 1640, the arcaded ground floor of the south court and the orangery. The two gate piers in the grounds to the east of the house were designed by Inigo Jones and executed by Nicholas Stone. When owned by the third Lord Holland and his formidable wife Holland House was the centre of early Victorian intellectual society.

7. Although never occupied by a reigning monarch after the death of George II in 1760, the State Rooms of HAMPTON COURT PALACE and their magnificent paintings were not opened to the public until the reign of Queen Victoria.

Wolsey's palace was enlarged and enriched by Henry VIII, repaired by Charles II and rebuilt by William and Mary, for whom Wren demolished part of it to form a new east front in a classic renaissance style and for whom the beautiful gardens were replanned in the well-ordered manner favoured in contemporary France.

It is open every weekday (except Good Friday, Christmas Day and Boxing Day) at 9.30, and closes at 6 from May to September, at 4 from November to February, and at 5 in March, April and October. On Sundays it is open from May to September from 11 to 6, from November to February from 2 to 4, and in March, April and October from 2 to 5.

8. The LORD'S CRICKET MUSEUM is open on weekdays during the season from 10.30 to close of play. In the winter the hours are from 10 to 4.

9. The GEORGE INN, Borough High Street, Southwark was rebuilt in 1677 after a fire. It has the last remaining

seventeenth-century gallery in London. It is mentioned in Dickens's *Little Dorrit*. The White Hart Inn, in whose courtyard Sam Weller meets Mr Pickwick, has, however, disappeared. White Hart Yard occupies its site, as Talbot Yard does the site of the Tabard Inn from which Chaucer's characters set out on their pilgrimage.

CHAPTER 12 *(Pages 181–98)*

1. Although parts of all of them have been rebuilt, these stations retain much of their original character. Philip Hardwick's Doric Triumphal Arch at Euston was demolished, however, in 1963, and ST PANCRAS STATION lies threatened by a similar fate. For the moment St Pancras remains a wonderful evocation of its period. 'It stands without rival,' a Victorian critic wrote, 'for palatial beauty, comfort and convenience. The style of architecture is a combination of various medieval features the inspection of which calls to mind the Lombardic and Venetian . . . while the critical eye of the student will observe touches of Milan and other Italian terra-cotta buildings, interlaced with good reproductions of details from Winchester and Salisbury Cathedrals, Westminster Abbey, etc.'

2. BROMPTON ORATORY, the London Oratory of St Philip Neri, was designed by Herbert Gribble and is a splendidly exultant memorial in Italian baroque to the Catholic Revival of mid-Victorian England. The Roman Catholic WESTMINSTER CATHEDRAL, Ashley Place, Victoria Street, (John Francis Bentley, 1895–1903), with its alternating bands of red brick and Port-land stone is a contrasting exercise in early Christian Byzantine. The nave, which has room for a congregation of 2,000 is the widest in England, and the campanile – from the galleries of which a fine view can be obtained of western London – is nearly fifty feet higher than the west towers of Westminster Abbey. There are services on Sundays every half hour from 6 to 9, at 10.10 and at 10.30 (Capitular High Mass), 12, 3.15 and 7; on weekdays every half hour from 6.30 to 9 (at 6 on the first Friday in the month), 10.10, 10.30 (High Mass), 3.30, 6, and 8.

3. The STOCK EXCHANGE, Throgmorton Street, had first been built in 1802. It was reconstructed by Thomas Allason in 1853–54, enlarged thirty years later by J. J. Cole,

and is soon to be demolished. Visitors are admitted to the Public Gallery from Monday to Friday, from 10.30 to 3.

4. An elaborately Gothic counterpart to St Pancras Station, though in stone not brick, the LAW COURTS are open to the public who are admitted to the galleries during the legal terms from Monday to Friday, 10 to 4.15.

5. George Gilbert Scott would have preferred a picturesque Gothic structure for the FOREIGN OFFICE, something on the lines of his St Pancras Station. But Palmerston insisted on an Italian classical style. Scott tried to compromise with an Italian design overlaid with Byzantine motifs which Palmerston condemned as a 'regular mongrel-affair'. Scott then bought some expensive books on Italian architecture and settled down with a will 'to rub up' his knowledge. The worthy result is shortly to be demolished.

Next door to the Foreign Office across King Charles Street, with long frontages to Parliament Street and Great George Street, is the TREASURY, covering remains of Henry VIII's Whitehall Palace. The original, much smaller building, was designed by William Kent in 1734–36. Extended by John Soane in 1827 it was remodelled and refaced by Charles Barry in 1847.

6. On Saturdays, on Easter Monday and Tuesday, Whit Monday and Tuesday, and each Monday, Tuesday and Thursday in August and each Thursday in September the Houses of Parliament are open from 10 to 4.30. The entrance is beside the Victoria Tower. Most Members of Parliament find time to conduct their constituents round if given sufficient notice.

The Houses of Parliament.

When the HOUSE OF COMMONS is in session visitors are allowed into the gallery, by St Stephen's Porch, on Mondays to Thursdays between 11 and 11.30 and on Fridays between 2.30 and 3 if they can obtain an order from their Member, or apply at the Admission Order office in St Stephen's Hall after 4.15 on Mondays to Thursdays and after 11.30 on Fridays.

The Stranger's Gallery of the HOUSE OF LORDS is also open to the public when the House meets, which it does usually on Tuesdays, Wednesdays and Thursdays (sometimes on Mondays) at 2.30. The entrance is by St Stephen's Porch. The doors are opened at 2.40 on Tuesdays and Wednesdays and at 4.10 on Thursdays.

7. The present Renaissance façade of the VICTORIA AND ALBERT MUSEUM, Exhibition Road and Thurloe Place, is by Aston Webb

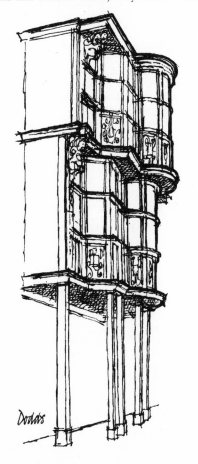

Sir Paul Pindar's house.

and was finished in 1909. Although there are works which it might be expected to possess in the British Museum, the Victoria and Albert Museum contains the national collection of fine and applied art, water colours and miniatures, and sculpture other than classical (which is in the British Museum) and modern (which is in the Tate Gallery). It also houses the national library of art.

As well as treasures of infinite beauty like the Raphael cartoons, as well as Elizabethan miniatures, Constable landscapes, Chelsea and Derby porcelain figures, wax models by Michelangelo, Bernini's *Neptune and Triton,* the Museum has a wonderful collection of bits and pieces illustrative of London's past – shopfronts, doorways, ironwork balconies, windows. Nearly the whole façade of Sir Paul Pindar's house (c.1600) in Bishopsgate is here, as well as part of Garrick's drawing-room in the Adelphi as decorated by Robert Adam.

The Museum is open on weekdays (except Good Friday and Christmas Day) from 10 to 6 and on Sundays from 2.30 to 6. There are lecture tours on Tuesdays, Wednesdays, Thursdays and Fridays at 1.15, and on Saturdays at 3. The Library is also open on weekdays (except Bank Holidays) from 10 to 5.45 to readers who may obtain tickets as for the British Museum (see note 5, p. 259).

Opposite the Victoria and Albert Museum is the NATURAL HISTORY MUSEUM, Cromwell Road, a huge Byzantine building designed by Alfred Waterhouse and built between 1873 and 1880. Times of opening are the same as for the Victoria and Albert. There are lecture tours on weekdays at 3.

In Exhibition Road are the GEOLOGICAL MUSEUM (designed by J. H. Markham, 1933–35) and the SCIENCE MUSEUM (Sir Robert Allison, 1913). Both these are open on weekdays (except Good Friday and Christmas Day) from 10 to 6 and on Sundays from 2.30 to 6. There are lectures in the Science Museum on Tuesdays, Thursdays and Saturdays at 3 and in the Geological Museum on Tuesdays, Wednesdays, Thursdays and Saturdays at 3.

In addition to these South Kensington Museums, and those others previously mentioned, there are seven other London Museums which are of unusual interest:
The GEFFRYE MUSEUM, Kingsland Road, Shoreditch, was converted before the first World War from a row of delightful

almshouses built in 1715 under a bequest of Sir Robert Geffrye, Lord Mayor in 1685–86. It contains a unique collection of furniture and woodwork. It is open on weekdays (except Mondays and Christmas Day) from 10 to 5; and on Sundays from 2 to 5.

The JEWISH MUSEUM, Woburn House, Upper Woburn Place is open from Monday to Thursday from 2.30 to 5; on Friday and Sunday from 10.30 to 12.45. It is closed on Jewish holy days.

The PUBLIC RECORD OFFICE MUSEUM, Chancery Lane (the Chancery Lane addition is by Sir John Taylor, 1891–96; the Fetter Lane end by Sir James Pennethorne, 1851–56) is open (except on Bank Holidays) from 1 to 4 from Monday to Friday. Occupying the site of the chapel of a house founded in 1232 by Henry III for converted Jews, this museum contains selections from the Public Record Office's collection of national archives and legal records, including the Domesday Book, Wellington's Waterloo despatch and a document bearing Shakespeare's signature.

The ROYAL GEOGRAPHICAL SOCIETY MUSEUM, Kensington Gore, has had to be closed to the general public through lack of staff. The Map Room, containing over half a million maps and atlases, is still open from Monday to Friday from 9.30 to 5.30 and on Saturdays from 9.30 to 1.

At FENTON HOUSE, The Grove, Hampstead, a lovely late seventeenth-century house in a walled garden (open on weekdays, except Tuesdays, from 10 to 1 and from 2 to 5, or dusk; on Sundays from 2 to 5 or dusk) there is a fine collection of furniture, porcelain and keyboard instruments.

Two interesting medical museums are the HUNTERIAN MUSEUM, the Royal College of Surgeons, Lincoln's Inn Fields, formed around the collection of John Hunter, the founder of scientific surgery; and the WELLCOME HISTORICAL MEDICAL MUSEUM, Wellcome Building, Euston Road. The Wellcome Museum is open (except on Bank Holidays) from Monday to Friday, 10 to 5; the Hunterian Museum by application to the secretary of the R.C.S.

Finally, there are three art collections which should not be missed, but are far less frequented than the collections already mentioned:

The COURTAULD INSTITUTE GALLERIES, Woburn Square, is especially rich in Impressionist and early Post-Impressionist paintings. It is open on weekdays from 10 to 5 and on Sundays from 2 to 5.

The DULWICH PICTURE GALLERY is housed (at College Road, Dulwich) in one of Sir John Soane's architectural masterpieces. Designed in 1811–12, it was badly damaged in the War but has now been restored. Its remarkable collection of Old Masters – built around the nucleus left by the Shakespearean actor, Edward Alleyn, founder of Dulwich College – is to be seen from Tuesday to Saturday from 10 to 4 and on Sundays from April to September from 2 to 5.

The PERCIVAL DAVID FOUNDATION OF CHINESE ART, 53 Gordon Square, comprising 1,500 works of art of the Sung, Yuan, Ming and Ch'ing dynasties, is open on Mondays from 2 to 5; from Tuesday to Friday 10.30 to 5, on Saturdays 10.30 to 1, except on Bank Holidays, for the first two weeks in September and on 24 – 31 December.

8. Described a decade after its completion as 'a pile worthy of Rome in its palmiest days' and rejected but a few years later as being 'on the familiar curves of the common bandstand', the simple and practical design of the ALBERT HALL, Kensington Gore, is now widely admired. Its cavernous yet congenial interior, which can seat 8,000 people, is open to the public when not in use. London's other main concert hall, the ROYAL FESTIVAL HALL (Sir Robert H. Mathew and Sir Leslie Martin, 1951) is acoustically more satisfactory but lacks the Albert Hall's charm.

9. The Regent's Park zoo – officially the Gardens of the Zoological Society of London – contains in its thirty-five acres the most representative collection of animals in the world. A few of Decimus Burton's original buildings survive, but the rest are a delightful hotch-potch and have recently included Sir Hugh Casson's concrete elephant house and Lord Snowdon's aviary. The Zoo which is approached from Outer Circle, Prince Albert Road, or the Broad Walk, is open every day (except Christmas Day) from 9 to 7, or sunset, in the summer, and from 10 in the winter.

CHAPTER 13 *(Pages 201–29)*

1. The time to see the main LONDON MARKETS is early in the morning. At six o'clock Covent Garden Market, Billingsgate and Smithfield are all at their liveliest,

with porters jostling, lorries roaring, dealers dealing – the streets of Covent Garden littered with straw, husks, leaves and stalks and wrapped in the smell, faint but unmistakable, of fruit and vegetables, the pavements at Billingsgate wet and smelling of fish, the expanse of Smithfield's Central Meat Market crammed with the grotesque carcasses of slaughtered animals heavy on their hooks, and with beefy porters in blood-stained coats of blue and white.

The London street markets – there are still over a hundred of them – can be enjoyed at less uninviting hours. The most worthy of a visit are those held in Berwick Street, Soho, Leather Lane, Holborn, Mile End Waste, Whitechapel, and Lambeth Walk. The Farringdon Road market is good for books. On Saturdays Camden Passage, Islington and Portobello Road, Notting Hill, are the places for antiques, oddments, curiosities and junk. On Sundays pets are offered for sale in Club Row, Shoreditch, potted plants in Columbia Road, Bethnal Green, and almost anything in Middlesex Street off Whitechapel Road, the celebrated Petticoat Lane.

2. NEW SCOTLAND YARD, Victoria Embankment, an inevitably rather forbidding – or perhaps to some reassuring – building in brick and stone was begun by the prolific Norman Shaw in 1871. The Police have now moved their headquarters from here to Broadway.

CHAPTER 14 *(Pages 231–7)*

1. Scott's Restaurant (now removed to Mount Street) and Alfred Gilbert's statue in PICCADILLY CIRCUS are of the same date, 1892. The statue is of the Angel of Christian Charity and was placed there in honour of that most charitable and Christian of men, the 7th Earl of Shaftesbury. But it is always known as Eros and as Eros it has become London's mascot.

Sources

In the London Library alone there are well over two hundred feet of shelves devoted to books on the history and topography of London. These books listed here are merely those which I believe to be the most useful and interesting. There is not – nor could there ever be – a comprehensive bibliography of London.

ALLEN, THOMAS
    The History and Antiquities of London
    (1827–29)

ASHLEY, MAURICE
    Life in Stuart England (Batsford, 1964)

BANKS, F. R.
    The Penguin Guide to London (Penguin, 4th Edn 1968)

BARBON, DR NICHOLAS
    An Apology for the Builder (1685)

BARKER, THEODORE and R. M. ROBBINS
    A History of London Transport (Allen & Unwin, 1963)

BARTON, N. J.
    The Lost Rivers of London (Phoenix House, 1962)

BEDFORD, JOHN
    London's Burning (Abelard-Schuman, 1966)

BELL, WALTER G.
    The Great Fire of London (1920)
    The Great Plague in London (Bodley Head, Reprinted, 1951)

BESANT, SIR WALTER
    Early London: Prehistoric, Roman, Saxon and Norman (1908)
    London in the Time of the Stuarts (1903)
    London in the Time of the Tudors (1904)
    London in the Eighteenth Century (1902)
    London in the Nineteenth Century (1909)

    London North of the Thames (1911)
    London South of the Thames (1912)
    London City (1910)
    Mediaeval London (1906)

BINNELL, ROBERT
    A Description of the River Thames (1758)

BIRD, RUTH
    The Turbulent London of Richard II (Longmans, 1949)

BIRKENHEAD, SHEILA
    Peace in Piccadilly: The Story of Albany (Hamish Hamilton, 1958)

BONE, JAMES
    The London Perambulator (1926)

BOOTH, CHARLES
    (Ed.) *Life and Labour of the People in London* (1902–03)

BOSWELL, JAMES
    Boswell's London Journal, 1762–1763 (Ed. Frederick A. Pottle, Heinemann, 1950)
    The Life of Samuel Johnson (1791)

BOULTON, W. B.
    The Amusements of Old London (1901)

BRAYBROOKE, NEVILLE
    London Green: The Story of Kensington Gardens, Hyde Park, Green Park and St James's Park (Gollancz, 1957)

BRAYLEY, E. W.
    Londiniana (1829)

BRETT-JAMES, NORMAN G.
The Growth of Stuart London (1935)

BRIGGS, ASA
Victorian Cities (Odhams, 1967)

BRIGGS, MARTIN S.
Wren the Incomparable (Allen & Unwin, 1953)

BROOKBANK, SIR J. G.
History of the Port of London (1921)

BROWN, IVOR
London (Studio Vista, 1965)
Winter in London (Collins, 1951)

BRYANT, SIR ARTHUR
The Medieval Foundation (Collins, 1963)
Protestant Island (Collins, 1967)

BURTON, ELIZABETH
The Elizabethans at Home (Secker & Warburg, 1958)
The Georgians at Home (Longmans, 1967)
The Jacobeans at Home (Secker & Warburg, 1962)

CALTHROP, SIR HENRY
Liberties, Usages and Customs of the City of London (1642)

CAMPBELL, R.
The London Tradesmen (1747)

CARPENTER, EDWARD
(Ed.) *A House of Kings: The History of Westminster Abbey* (John Baker, 1966)

CHAMBERLAIN, H.
New History of London (1770)

CHAMBERS, R. W. AND M. DAUNT
A Book of London English, 1384–1425 (1931)

CHANCELLOR, E. B.
History of the Squares of London (1907)
London Recalled (1937)
Lost London (1926)
Pleasure Haunts of London during Four Centuries (1925)
Private Palaces of London (1908)
The Eighteenth Century in London (1920)
The West End of Yesterday and Today (1926)

CHURCH, RICHARD
London Flower of Cities All (with drawings and paintings by Imre Hofbauer, Heinemann, 1966)
Over the Bridge (Heinemann, 1955)
The Royal Parks of London (H.M.S.O., 1956)
City of London: A Record of Destruction and Survival, (The Architectural Press, 1951)

CLARKE, BASIL F. L.
Parish Churches of London (Batsford, 1966)

CLODE, C. M.
London during the Great Rebellion (1892)

CLUNN, HAROLD P.
The Face of London (1932)

Coach and Sedan pleasantly disputing for Place and Precedence, the Brewer's cart being Moderator (1631)

COLQUHOUN, PATRICK
Treatise on the Commerce and Police of the River Thames (1800)

COLVIN, H. M.
Biographical Dictionary of English Architects 1660–1840 (John Murray, 1954)

COOK, G. H.
Old St Paul's (Phoenix House, 1955)

CRACE, FREDERICK
A Catalogue of Maps, Plans and Views of London (1878)

CRAIG, SIR JOHN
The Mint: A History of the London Mint from A.D. 287 to 1948 (Cambridge University Press, 1953)

CUNNINGHAM, PETER
A Handbook for London (1849)

DAVIS, DOROTHY
A History of Shopping (Routledge & Kegan Paul, 1966)

DELAUNE, THOMAS
Angliae Metropolis (1690)
The Present State of London (1681)

DE MARÉ, ERIC
London's Riverside: Past, Present and Future (1958)

DESANT, A. T.
Grosvenor Square (1937)
Piccadilly in three centuries (1914)
The History of St James's Square (1895)

Diary of John Evelyn, The (Ed. William Bray, Dent, 1907)

Diary of Samuel Pepys, The (with notes by Lord Braybrooke, Dent, 1906)

DITCHFIELD, P. H.
(Ed.) *Memorials of Old London* (1908)

DODWELL, C. R.
Lambeth Palace (Country Life, 1958)

DOUTHWAITE, W. R.
Gray's Inn (1876)

DUGDALE, G. S.
  Whitehall through the Centuries (Phoenix House, 1950)

DYOS, H. J.
  Victorian Suburb: A Study of the Growth of Camberwell (Leicester University Press, 1961)

EADES, GEO. E.
  Historic London (The Queen Anne Press and The City of London Society, 1966)

Early Victorian England (Oxford University Press, 1934)

ELLIS, AYTOUN
  Three Hundred Years of London River (Bodley Head, 1952)

EMERSON, G. R.
  London: How the City Grew (1862)

EVELYN, JOHN
  Fumifugium, or the Inconvenience of the Aer and Smoak of London Dissipated (1661)

FLETCHER, GEOFFREY
  The London Nobody Knows (Hutchinson, 1962)

FOORD, A. S.
  Springs, Streams and Spas of London (1910)

GAY, JOHN
  Trivia, or the Art of Walking the Streets of London (1716)

GASPERY, W.
  Tallis's Illustrated London (1851)

GAUNT, WILLIAM
  Chelsea (Batsford, 1954)
  Kensington (Batsford, 1958)
  London (Batsford, 1961)

GEORGE, M. DOROTHY
  London Life in the Eighteenth Century (Reprinted by the London School of Economics, 1951)

GODFREY, W. H.
  (Ed.) *François Colsoni's Guide de Londres, 1693* (Cambridge University Press, 1951)

GOMME, SIR LAURENCE
  The Making of London (1912)
  London (1914)
  The Governance of London (1907)

GOUGH, J. W.
  Sir Hugh Myddelton, Entrepreneur and Engineer (Clarendon Press, Oxford, 1964)

GREEN, A. S.
  Town Life in the Fifteenth Century (1894)

GRIFFITHS, ROGER
  A Description of the River Thames (1746)

GRIMES, W. F.
  The Excavation of Roman and Mediaeval London (Routledge & Kegan Paul, 1968)

GWYNN, J.
  London and Westminster Improved (1766)

HARBEN, H. A.
  Dictionary of London (1918)

HARRISON, MICHAEL
  London Beneath the Pavement (Peter Davies, 1961)
  London by Gaslight 1861–1911 (Peter Davies, 1963)
  London Growing (Hutchinson, 1965)

HATTON, EDWARD
  A New View of London (1708)

HAYWARD, ARTHUR L.
  (Ed.) *The London Spy by Ned Ward* (Cassell, 1927)

HEADLAND, C.
  The Inns of Court (1909)

HEAL, SIR AMBROSE
  The London Furniture Makers (1953)

HEARSEY, JOHN E. N.
  Bridge, Church and Palace in Old London (Murray, 1961)
  London and the Great Fire (Murray, 1965)

HIBBERT, H. G.
  Fifty Years of a Londoner's Life (1916)

HILL, WILLIAM THOMSON
  Buried London (Phoenix House, 1955)

HIND, A. M.
  Wenceslaus Hollar and His Views of London (1922)

HOME, GORDON
  Mediaeval London (1927)
  Roman London A.D. 43–457 (Eyre & Spottiswoode, 1948)

HOWELL, J.
  Londonopolis (1657)

HUGHSON, DAVID
  Walks through London (1817)

HUNT, J. H. LEIGH
  The Town (1848)

INDERWICK, F. C.
  The Inner Temple (1896)

JENKINSON, W.
Royal and Bishops' Palaces in Old London
(1921)

JESSE, J. H.
Literary and Historical Memorials of
London (Collected works, 1847)
London and its Celebrities (Collected
works, 1847)

JOHNSON, B. H.
Berkeley Square to Bond Street
(John Murray, 1952)

Johnson's England (Ed. A. S. Turberville,
Clarendon Press, Oxford, 1933)

JONES, G. P.
The London Mason in the Seventeenth
Century (Manchester, 1935)

KENT, WILLIAM
(Ed.) An Encyclopaedia of London (Dent,
Revised Edn, 1951)
The Lost Treasures of London (Phoenix
House, 1947)

KINGSFORD, CHARLES LETHBRIDGE
(Ed.) A Survey of London by John Stow
(Oxford, 1908)
Chronicles of London (1905)
The Early History of Piccadilly, Leicester
Square, Soho and their Neighbourhood
(1925)

KNIGHT, CHARLES
(Ed.) London (1841–1844)

LANG, JANE
Rebuilding St Paul's after the Great Fire
(O.U.P., 1956)

LARWOOD, JACOB
The Story of the London Parks (1872)

LEMON, MARK
Up and Down the London Streets (1867)

LETHABY, W. R.
London before the Conquest (1902)

LETTS, M.
As the Foreigner Saw Us (1935)

LEWIS, R. A.
Edwin Chadwick and the London Health
Movement (1952)

Lichtenberg's Commentaries on Hogarth's
Engravings (Tr. Innes and Gustav
Herdan, Cresset Press, 1966)

LILLYWHITE, BRYANT
London Coffee-houses (Allen & Unwin,
1963)

LITHGOW, WILLIAM
Surveigh of London (1643)

LOCKS, W. A.
East London Antiquities (1902)

'London in 1689–1690. The Manuscript
Diary of Mr Robert Kirke' in London
& Middlesex Archaeological Society
Transactions. New Series. Vols. vi
and vii.

London in 1710 from the Travels of Z.C. von
Uffenbach (Tr. W. H. Quarrell and
M. Mare, 1934)

London in Miniature (1755)

London Topographical Record

LYSONS, DANIEL
The Environs of London (1792–1800)

MACMICHAEL, J. H.
The Story of Charing Cross (1906)

MAGALOTTI, LORENZO
Travels of Cosimo, Grand Duke of
Tuscany through England (1821)

MANCHÉE, W. H.
The Westminster City Fathers 1585–1901
(Bodley Head, 1934)

MAITLAND, WILLIAM
The History of London (1759)

MALCOLM, JAMES PELLER
Anecdotes of the Manners and Customs
of London in the Eighteenth Century (1808)
Londinium Redivivum (1802–07)

MARSHALL, J.
Topographical and Statistical Details of
the Metropolis (1832)

MARTIN, WILLIAM
The Early Maps of London (1916)

MATTHEWS, W. R. AND W. M. ATKINS
A History of St Paul's Cathedral (1957)

MERRIFIELD, RALPH
The Roman City of London (Ernest Benn,
1965)

MISSON, H.
Memoirs and Observations in his Travels
Over England (1719)

MITCHELL, R. J. AND M. D. R. LEYS
A History of London Life (Longmans,
1958)

MORITZ, C. P.
Travels in England in 1782 (Tr. P. E.
Matheson, 1924)

MORRIS, CORBYN
Observations on the Past Growth and
Present State of London (1751)

MUMFORD, LEWIS
   The City in History (Secker & Warburg,
      1961)

NAIRN, IAN
   Nairn's London (Penguin, 1966)

NOPPEN, J. G.
   Royal Westminster (1937)

NORTHOUCK, J.
   New History of London (1773)

OGILBY, JOHN
   London Surveyed (1677)

ORDISH, T. F.
   Shakespeare's London (1897)

ORMSBY, H.
   London on the Thames (1924)

PAGE, WILLIAM
   *London: Its Origin and Early
      Development* (1923)
   (Ed.) *The Victoria History of London*

PARREAUX, ANDRÉ
   Smollett's London (A. G. Nizet, Paris,
      1968)

PARTINGTON, C. F.
   (Ed.) *National History and Views of
      London* (1834)

PASSINGHAM, W. J.
   London's Markets (1935)

PENDRILL, CHARLES
   Old Parish Life in London (O.U.P., 1937)

PENNANT, THOMAS
   Some Account of London (1813)

PETRIE, SIR CHARLES
   Scenes of Edwardian Life (Eyre and
      Spottiswoode, 1965)

PEVSNER, NIKOLAUS
   *London: The Cities of London and
      Westminster* (Penguin, Revised Edn,
      1962)
   *London Except the Cities of London and
      Westminster* (1952)

PHILLIPS, HUGH
   The Thames about 1750 (Collins, 1951)

PIPER, DAVID
   The Companion Guide to London (Collins,
      1964)

POPE-HENNESSY, JAMES
   London Fabric (Batsford, 1940)

PRIESTLEY, HAROLD
   London: The Years of Change (Muller,
      1966)

PRITCHETT, V. S.
   London Perceived (Chatto & Windus and
      Heinemann, 1962)
   A Cab at the Door (Chatto & Windus,
      1968)

QUENNELL, PETER
   Hogarth's Progress (Collins, 1955)
   (Ed.) *London's Underworld* (William
      Kimber, 1950)
   (Ed.) *Mayhew's Characters* (William
      Kimber, 1951)
   (Ed.) *Mayhew's London* (Spring Books,
      n.d.)

RALPH, JAMES
   *A Critical Review of the Public Buildings
      in and about London* (1734)

RASMUSSEN, STEEN EILER
   London: The Unique City (Pelican, 1961)

READER, W. J.
   Life in Victorian England (Batsford, 1964)

REDDAWAY, T. F.
   *The Rebuilding of London after the
      Great Fire* (Cape, 1940)

RICHARDSON, A. E. AND C. LOVETT GILL
   London Houses from 1660 to 1820 (1911)

RILEY, HENRY THOMAS
   Memorials of London and London Life
      (1868)
   (Tr.) *Liber Albus: The White Book of the
      City of London* (1861)

ROBINSON, E. F.
   *The Early History of the Coffee-House in
      England* (1893)

ROUND, J. H.
   The Commune of London (1899)

*Royal Commission on Historical Monuments
   (England): An Inventory of the Historical
   Monuments in London* (1924–30)

RUBINSTEIN, STANLEY
   Historians of London (Peter Owen, 1968)

RYE, W. B.
   *England as seen by Foreigners in the days of
      Elizabeth and James I* (1865)

SALMON, J.
   *Ten Years growth of the City of London
      1881–1891* (1891)

SANDS, MOLLIE
Invitation to Ranelagh 1742–1803
(John Westhouse, 1946)

SAUNDERS, HILARY ST GEORGE
Westminster Hall (Michael Joseph, 1951)

SCOTT, J. M.
The Book of Pall Mall (Heinemann, 1965)

SEKON, G. A.
Locomotion in Victorian London (1938)

SEYMOUR, ROBERT
Survey of London (1735)

Shakespeare's England (Clarendon Press, Oxford, 1926)

SHARPE, R. R.
London and the Kingdom (1894–95)

SHEPPARD, EDGAR
Memorials of St James's Palace (1894)
The Old Royal Palace of Westminster (1902)

SMITH, CHARLES ROACH
Illustrations of Roman London (1859)

SMITH, H. CLIFFORD
Buckingham Palace: Its Furniture, Decoration and History (1931)

SMITH, SIR HUBERT LLEWELLYN
The History of East London (1939)

SMITH, J. T.
Antiquities of Westminster (1807–09)

Sophie in London in 1786 (Trans. and Ed. Clare Williams, 1933)

SOUTHWORTH, JAMES GRANVILLE
Vauxhall Gardens (Columbia University Press, 1941)

SPENCER, HERBERT
London's Canal (Putnam, 1961)

STANLEY, A. P.
Historical Memorials of Westminster Abbey (1868)

STENTON, F. M.
Norman London (with a translation of William Fitz Stephen's Description by Professor H. E. Butler and A Map of London under Henry II by Marjorie B. Honeybourne, S. Bell & Sons, 1934)

STEPHENSON, HENRY THEW
Shakespeare's London (1905)

STOW, W.
Remarks on London and Westminster (1722)

SUMMERSON, JOHN
Sir Christopher Wren (Collins, 1953)
Georgian London (Pelican, 1962)

SUMMERSON, JOHN *(continued)*
John Nash (Allen & Unwin, 1935)
Inigo Jones (Penguin, 1966)

SUNDERLAND, S.
Old London Spas, Baths & Wells (1915)

SUTHERLAND, L. S.
A London Merchant, 1695–1774 (Oxford, 1933)

Survey of London, The
(Later volumes edited by F. H. W. Sheppard, Athlone Press)

SYDNEY, WILLIAM CONNOR
England and the English in the Eighteenth Century (1892)

TANNER, L. E.
History and Treasures of Westminster Abbey (1953)

THOMPSON, RICHARD
Chronicles of Old London Bridge (1839)

THOMPSON, G. SCOTT
Life in a Noble Household (1937)
The Russells in Bloomsbury (1940)

THORNBURY, WALTER
London Old and New (1897)

THRUPP, SYLVIA L.
A Short History of the . . . Bakers of London (1933)
The Merchant Class of Medieval London (University of Chicago Press, 1948)

TIMBS, J.
Clubs and Club Life in London (1872)

Transactions of the London and Middlesex Archaeological Society

TRENT, CHRISTOPHER
Greater London: Its Growth and Development (Phoenix House, 1965)

UNWIN, G. H.
The Guilds and Companies of London (1908)

WALCOTT, M.
Memorials of Westminster (1851)

WALFORD, EDWARD
Greater London (1882–85)

WEALE, JOHN
(Ed.) *London Exhibited* (1851)

WESTLAKE, H. F.
The Abbey of Westminster (1920)

WHEATLEY, H. B.
London Past and Present (1891)
Round About Piccadilly (1870)
Short History of Bond Street (1911)

WHEELER, R. E. M.
  London in Roman Times (London Museum
    Catalogues, No. 3, 1930)

WHITE, R. J.
  Life in Regency England (Batsford, 1963)

WILLIAMS, GWYN A.
  *Medieval London from Commune to
    Capital* (Athlone Press, 1963)

WILLIAMSON, J. BRUCE
  The History of the Temple (1924)

WILSON, F. P.
  The Plague in Shakespeare's London (1927)

WROTH, WARWICK
  *London Pleasure Gardens of the
    Eighteenth Century* (1896)

YOUNG, ELIZABETH AND WAYLAND
  Old London Churches (Faber, 1956)

Index

Morris, Roger, Marble Hill House, 262
Music halls, the Oxford, *196*; the Old Bedford, **219**; Evans's, 231
Muswell Hill, water for City from, 48
Myddleton, Hugh, *49*; and the New River venture, 48–51, *50*
Myddleton Square, 139
Mylne, Robert, 248

Nash, John, his history, 128; and Regent's Park, *127*, 128, 139; and Regent's Street, 128–9; and All Souls', Langham Place, *129*, and Buckingham Palace, 131–3, *133*, 134, 258; Theatre Royal, Haymarket, 135, 262; United Service Club, 135, 262; T. Lawrence portrait, **138**; Royal Lodge Windsor, 139; designs Royal Opera Arcade, 148; opinions on his architecture, 177–8; Marble Arch, 259; Clarence House, 262
National Gallery, houses national picture collection, 131; in Mr Angerstein's house, **139**; its portico, 258; times of opening and lectures, 258
National Maritime Museum, times of admission, 250
National Portrait Gallery, times of opening and lectures, 258–9
Natural History Museum, times of opening and lectures, 267
New Bond Street, 116, 150
New Burlington Street, 115
Neale, Thomas, and Seven Dials district, 88
Nelson, Horatio, Admiral Viscount, his tomb in St. Paul's, 252; the Nelson Column, *132*, 258, 259
Newcourt, Richard, 70
New Cross, 186
New Exchange, Strand, 57; built, 95; fashionable shopping centre, 95–6; assignations in, 104
New Oxford Street, 189
Newgate, gap in Roman wall at, 12; mansion and hovels inside, 18; building around, 31; Great Fire spreads to, 67; Market, 147, 218
Newgate Prison, sightseers visit, 100; Dance the younger restores, 121; in Gordon Riots, 163; Boswell visits, 165; work in, 229; stones used for Central Criminal Court, 257
Newgate Street, 18, 36, 257
Newington, New River passes, 50
New River, Colthurst conceives, 48; Myddleton takes over, 48–50; James I interested in, 49–50; New River Head built, *50*; difficulties over water pollution in, 50–1; achieves popularity, 51
New Road, bypass for Oxford Road, 139
New Scotland Yard, 269
Newton, William, 56
Nine Elms, 186, 197
Norman architecture, in 12th cent. London, 12
North, Sir Edward (later Lord North), builds Charterhouse, 38, 249
North, Roger, on Barbon, 90; Middle Temple Gateway, 249
North Street, Red Lion Square, Barbon's houses in, 92
Northumberland, John Dudley, Duke of, 249
Northumberland Avenue, route of, 189
Northumberland House, 44, 189; R. Adam's design for drawing-room, **123**; Boswell at, 166
Norwood, gipsies at, 104; suburb develops at, 184
Nottingham House, 140
Notting Hill, drainage problems at, 47; built up, 190–1; Portobello Road market, 268
Nuffield House, Piccadilly, 239

Oates, Titus, in the pillory, **99**
Of Alley, 91
Ogilby and Morgan, mapmakers, 72, *79*, *82*
Old Bailey, 167; times of admission, 257
Old Burlington Street, architecture of, 115
Old Jewry, 16; waxworks in Green Court, 171
Old Royal Mews, Trafalgar Square built on site of, 130
Old Swan Stairs, and rapid water under London Bridge, 41

Omnibuses, fare of horse-drawn, 184; drivers and conductors, 214–15, *214*, *233*; motor, 233
Osterley Park House, Barbon buys, 90; times of admission, 257
Oxenden Street, brothels in, 223; prostitution in, 224
Oxford, Edward Harley, Earl of, develops the Harley Estate, 118
Oxford Street, 197; Stratford Place, 48; Grosvenor Estate and, 116; Pantheon, 121, **122**, 170; German visitors' opinion of, 150; tiger-baiting in, 172–3; Punch and Judy in, 220; stores built in, 233

Paddington, 139; effect of railway on development of, 182; Great Western Railway terminal, 183, **211**; Yorkshire Stingo, 184; Disraeli on uniformity of, 186; Post Office Railway terminal, 260
Paine, James, and Palladianism, 119; Middlesex Hospital, 255
Palladio, Andrea, 118; influences Inigo Jones, 57; inspires Burlington House, 86; St Martin-in-the-Fields in style of, 114; *I quatro libri dell' architettura*, 116; and Bank of England, 118
Pall Mall, 87, 130, 148; original of name, 81; Schomberg House, 84, 252; Ozinda's Coffee House, 101; Carlton House, 125; Angerstein's house in, 131, **139**; club-land, 135; bookshops in 147; Wedgwood considers it too far East, 150; gas lighting in, *158*; Star and Garter, 165; prostitutes in, 223; United Service Club, 262
Pantheon, Oxford Street, **122**
Panton, Colonel, buys Shaver's Hall, 88
Panton Street, prostitution in, 224
Paris Garden, 46; bear baiting in, 47
Park Crescent, 128
Park Lane, Grosvenor Estate east of, 116; Chesterfield House, 119; Marble Arch moved to top of, 134; robbery in, 157; hotels in, 239, 241
Park Lane Hotel, 239
Park Square, 128
Parliament (*see also* House of Commons, House of Lords), attempted arrest of five members, 62; and Buckingham Palace, 130, 133; votes money for British Museum, 131; Moritz on, 144; road conditions debated, 144–5; how to visit, 266
Parliament Square, 192
Pastimes and Pleasures, 14–5, 36; hawking, *11*; at Court of Henry VIII, 43; theatrical performances, 46–7, 221–2; bear-, bull- and cock-fighting 47, 166, 172; skating, 109, *151*, **171**; sightseeing, 143; gambling, 168–9; cricket, **171**; in 19th cent. 197–8; costermongers, 204; street entertainers, **218**, **218–19**, 220–1; rat-matches, 221, *222*; 'penny gaffs', 222
Paternoster Row, 77; bookshops in, 96, 147
Paxton, Sir Joseph, designs Crystal Palace, 193
Peabody, George, 186
Pearson, Charles, suggests underground railway, 184–5
Peasants' Revolt (1381), 21
Peckham, 139; Quaker Meeting House, 261
Peel, Sir Robert, and Metropolitan Police Act, 224, 226; Home Secretary, 226
Pelham Crescent, 140
Pelham Place, 138
Pembroke, Earl of, and Westminster Bridge, 118
Pennethorne, Sir James, alterations to Marlborough House, 252; Public Record Office, 267
Pentonville, 139; Prison, 228, 229
Pepys, Samuel, *94*, 111; the accident in Newgate Street market, 36; unalarmed by Fire, 67; in the Tower, 99; on dangerous journey under London Bridge, 108; watches Great Fire, 246
Percival David Foundation of Chinese Art, times of admission, 268
Peter of Colechurch, 12
Petersham, Ham House, 140
Petticoat Lane, 218, 268
Petty, Sir William, and rebuilding after Great Fire, 69–70; and population statistics, 95